MW01002611

HIDING YOUR MONEY

HIDING YOUR MONEY

Everything You Need to Know
About Keeping Your Money
and Valuables Safe from
Predators and Greedy Creditors

JEROME SCHNEIDER

ALLISON HOPE WEINER

PRIMA MONEY
An Imprint of Prima Publishing

3000 Lava Ridge Court • Roseville, California 95661
(800) 632-8676 • www.primalifestyles.com

Interior photographs by Stephen Nyran, nyrotic.com

Materials for photographs on pages 121 and 155 supplied by Spy City. Materials for photograph on page 203 supplied by Carousel Casino Resources, Ltd.

Library of Congress Cataloging-in-Publication Data on file

ISBN 0-7615-2340-5

00 01 02 03 04 05 HH 10 9 8 7 6 5 4 3 2 1
Printed in the United States of America

How to Order

Single copies may be ordered from Prima Publishing, 3000 Lava Ridge Court, Roseville, CA 95661; telephone (800) 632-8676 ext. 4444. Quantity discounts are also available. On your letterhead, include information concerning the intended use of the books and the number of books you wish to purchase.

Visit us online at www.primalifestyles.com

Visit the author's Web site at www.offshorewealth.com

CONTENTS

Before You Read This Book vii

Introduction xv

1 A Time to Hide: Why Do You Need
   to Hide Your Money?   1

2 Isn't Hiding Your Money Illegal?   19

3 Men Behaving Badly   43

4 The Undercover Tourist:
   Cash and the Careful Traveler   67

5 Life in the Red Lane: Staying One
   Step Ahead of Creditors   91

6 Hiding and the Single Gal   111

7 Victoria's Secrets   127

8 Please Give Me My Space: Finding
   the Ultimate Personal Hiding Place   147

9 Take the Money and Run: Keeping
   the IRS Out of Your Business   167

10 Extreme Hiding: Playing
   the Hiding Game for All It's Worth   189

11 Turning the Tables: How the Experts
   Find the Hidden Money   215
12 The Dirty Dozen: A Twelve-Step Hiding Program   233

   Index   257

BEFORE YOU READ THIS BOOK

When I began work on this book, some people started asking me questions about hiding. My best friend's wife wondered where the safest place was to hide her jewelry. My neighbor wanted tips on where to hide his rare coin collection.

More often than not, though, people would hear about my book's topic and announce that they didn't need to worry about hiding assets because they really didn't own anything worth hiding.

I would smile and reply, "If you've got a name, you've got something worth hiding. Your identity is worth millions on the open market. And it's one of the easiest things to steal. All an identity thief needs to become you is your social security number, a simple home computer, and a dream."

And then I'd tell them the same story that I'm about to tell you.

A friend of mine went to Saks Fifth Avenue to do a little birthday shopping. Once she had all her perfumes and make-up selected, she went over to the salesclerk to have everything rung up. The clerk took her credit card and then, after scanning the card several times, asked her to step aside while the credit department was contacted. The credit department representative informed the salesclerk that she needed to speak with my friend immediately.

When my friend picked up the phone, she learned that not only was she $20,000 over her credit limit, but apparently, her last $5,000 check to the store had bounced. The credit department was on the verge of turning the matter over to collections unless, of course, my friend immediately made out a check for half the amount owed. The important part of the story is that my friend had never charged more than $2,000 on her Saks card in any given year. In fact, when she had applied to join the exclusive Saks Insider's Club, her application had been rejected because she didn't spend enough money at the store.

Now she was being told that she was a member of the Insider's Club who had obviously abused the privilege. My friend angrily insisted that her card had been stolen, but the credit department representative remained skeptical, repeatedly asking her why she still had her card if it had been stolen. My friend suggested that perhaps just the number had been stolen, which prompted the credit personnel to again verify the name and address on the account—revealing for the first time that the address on the account had recently been changed to a post office box. Finally, the credit representative began to concede that something strange was going on.

While my friend unsuccessfully tried to convince any-one who would listen that someone had somehow stolen her credit card number, a small crowd gathered, drawn by the loud voices and obvious commotion. As a group of well-dressed women with disapproving glances listened to my friend insist that she'd never bounced a check in her life, the assistant manager arrived. She listened patiently to my friend's version of events, acknowledged that the card number had obviously been stolen, and then suggested that they both go upstairs to discuss the situation.

For the next hour, the assistant manager and my friend went through the purchases charged to her card, slowly trying to decipher which items had been purchased by the credit card thief. The items ran the gamut from size 16 ladies' clothes to men's Ferragamo belts. My friend pointed to the charges for more than $5,000 worth of large-sized ladies' clothes, arguing that since she wore a size 8, it was unlikely that she'd have made those particular pur-chases. The assistant manager spent only a few more min-utes reviewing the charges before suggesting that the matter be turned over to the fraud department.

According to Saks Fifth Avenue's fraud division, my friend had been the victim of a sophisticated scam in which a customer's credit card is maxed out long before the customer ever becomes aware of the theft. The scam usually involves stealing the credit card bill out of a cus-tomer's mail box and then applying for a change of address. Once the address is successfully changed, the criminal can charge large amounts of merchandise, with the bill being sent to a post office box. While the bill sits unread at the fake address, the thief can continue using the card without the customer's knowledge. In the sce-nario involving my friend, the thief even sent a rubber check to Saks Fifth Avenue. (This kept the store from closing the credit card account for a few extra weeks, buy-ing the thief more time to continue making fraudulent purchases.)

It took my friend almost six months to complete all of the necessary paperwork in connection with the theft of her credit card number. She had to carefully review all the purchases made on her card, distinguishing her purchases from those made by the crook. She also spent hours notarizing her paperwork, talking on the phone with the credit bureau, and repairing her credit history.

But even after all the paperwork had been filled out and her new card number had been issued, my friend continued to have problems with her credit. Every time she applied for a new card, the Saks incident would make an appearance. And every time she went shopping at Saks, her credit card would be declined. For some reason, the computer continued to have problems separating her fraudulent Saks account from her new account. Whenever she complained about the problem, the salesclerk would inevitably suggest that she contact the credit department to discuss the matter. It seemed that as far as Saks Fifth Avenue was concerned, my friend would forever be an overweight woman with a passion for blue size 16 dresses and men's Ferragamo belts.

While I sympathized greatly with my friend's frustration over the Saks Fifth Avenue credit card incident, I also let her know that things could have been a lot worse. As technology has become more sophisticated, so have crimes involving identity theft. Using a driver's license, social security number, and a credit card and/or bank account, identity thieves can fictionalize another life. He can set up false accounts in department stores. He can write bad checks for merchandise all over the country and even the world. He can use personal financial information to qualify for credit cards and even a home mortgage. He can even buy cell phones or rent property.

Identity theft is one of the fastest growing crimes in America and around the world. Actual losses associated with identity fraud totaled $442 million in 1995, $450 million in 1996, and $745 million in 1997.[1] Moreover, an official with Trans Union Corporation, one of the national credit bureaus, reports that two-thirds of all consumer inquiries to the company's Fraud Victim Assistance Department involved identity fraud.[2] According to this official, the total number of inquiries increased from 35,235 in 1992 to 522,922 in 1997.[3] (The official attributed this trend to both increased cases of identity theft and company growth.)

Identity thieves get information using a wide variety of techniques. They can gain access to a credit report or simply shoulder surf at ATM machines and phone booths to get pin numbers. They can steal mail from mailboxes to get newly issued credit cards or rustle through trash to get credit card and loan applications (or credit statements and bank statements). They can snatch purses, steal wallets (or find lost ones), or get hold of mortgage or loan applications. I even know of a scenario in which a waiter would take a customer's credit card, scan the card, and then return the card without the customer ever knowing that the number had been stolen—until the legitimate cardholder was notified that his or her card had been maxed out.

Identity thieves work fast once they have acquired someone's personal information. Generally, by the time the victim discovers the theft, it's far too late to do anything. For example, many identity thieves operate out of hotels. They take credit cards out of hotel room safes, scan the cards with an easily purchased scanner, and then return the cards to the safe. The card owners never know their card number has been stolen until they go to use it and find out that they're far over their credit limit.

And once an identity thief has stolen your identity, it takes years to repair the damage. Think about the troubles my friend continues to have at Saks Fifth Avenue . . . and her problems are minuscule compared to those of other identity theft victims.

In January 1999, Betty Lake's purse was stolen out of her car. The thieves used her driver's license, social security number, and credit cards to effectively become her. She got all new documents, credit cards, and bank accounts but still has to police her credit reports monthly to protect her financial identity because she continues to find new accounts set up in her name.

In July 1995 Burt and Maggie Hanks were informed that they'd been the victim of identity theft. A thief, using their social security numbers, had managed to successfully obtain a credit card in their name with a $6,000 advance. Four years after first discovering that their identities had been stolen, the Hanks are still trying to clean up their credit reports. They've logged hundreds of hours talking to authorities and writing letters to credit bureaus.

At a seminar on the Illinois Financial Identity Theft Act, Michael Carroll, a postal inspector with the U.S. Postal Inspection Service, noted that there are several things you can do to try and protect yourself against identity theft.[4] You should promptly remove mail from your mailboxes; always deposit mail in the post office mailboxes and not in personal mailboxes that are accessible to others; never give your social security number or birth date over the phone unless you've made the call; shred all pre-approved credit card applications, bills, or receipts before throwing them away; keep only the credit cards you plan to use in your wallet; and memorize your PIN and social security numbers just in case your wallet or purse is stolen.[5]

While a lot of these techniques might help prevent identity theft, you should also consider taking another important step to protect yourself—learn how to best hide your personal documents. The best way to protect your identity is to keep all of your sensitive documents effectively hidden from potential thieves. This means learning where to hide your bank statements, credit card statements, stock certificates, loan documents, and other revealing financial information. Remember, anyone can become a victim of identity theft. All it takes is for you to leave one revealing document in the wrong place to enable someone to ruin your good name—and your life.

This is why the time you spend reading this book could save you a lot of aggravation and misery. All you need to know are some simple hiding places to keep your most revealing financial documents and your most valuable assets. For example, all an identity thief needs to empty out your savings account is your bankbook and maybe one piece of identification. If you keep such documents sitting on the kitchen counter, it will only take a professional thief seconds to clean you out. But if you've taken the time to hide these items inside an air duct, you've saved yourself a lot of aggravation—and money.

This book provides people who are concerned about privacy and asset protection with the information they need to effectively hide their most personal and valued possessions. If you have tangible assets and/or documents that you want to hide, this book will give you concrete suggestions on how to best protect those items. If you want to have immediate access to those items, the book delineates a number of home hiding locales. And if you're a bit more adventurous, you can explore hiding these valuable items in some more exotic and sunny locales—maybe somewhere like the Caribbean.

We all have something that we need to protect—whether it be cash, stocks, bonds, and jewelry or only our good name. And the more precious the asset, the more important it is that we pick the right hiding spot.

The concept is a simple one—but the execution is a bit more complicated. That's where I come in. I'm here to give you the information that you need to protect yourself and those things you hold dear from predators and greedy creditors.

REFERENCES

1. "Identity Fraud—Information on Prevalence, Cost, and Internet Impact Is Limited," Government Accounting Office Report, May 26, 1998.
2. Ibid.
3. El-Faizy, Monique, "Identity Theft Is on Rise: High Tech Criminals Are Costing Americans Millions," *Daily News,* November 1, 1999.
4. Wilson, Terry, "With Just Few Basic Facts, Thieves Are Stealing Identity, Experts Say," *Chicago Tribune,* December 3, 1999.
5. Ibid.

INTRODUCTION

Even though a recent 1998 Harris Poll indicated that many Americans believe they've lost control over their personal financial data, most people remain resigned to this extreme invasion of privacy. They figure that, no matter what they do, their income disclosures, tax return data, bank account numbers, employment history, and other confidential information will most likely end up in the hands of some information broker.

They're wrong.

You can take effective steps to keep control over your personal financial data, as well as your money. In fact, the process of protecting your financial privacy is easier than you think. All you need to do is read this book to discover how you can keep your private financial information truly private and how you can hang on to those assets that you've worked so hard to acquire.

First of all, you should know that unlike other books that deal with protecting your assets, this book isn't only for the extremely wealthy. As much as I'd like to think they need my help, the fact is that truly wealthy people have a head start on the rest of us when it comes to hiding their money and keeping their financial information private. After all, they've been doing it for years . . . that's probably why they're still wealthy.

However, the secrets the super-rich use to become financially invisible can be enjoyed by people with more modest assets. That's why I wrote this book: It's for those of you who probably don't have years of experience in hiding your money from greedy relatives, freeloading friends, and the ever-present IRS.

So while you may not be able to afford the best financial planner in the country to advise you on how to keep your money safe from prying governmental eyes or to tell you how to safeguard your assets from frivolous lawsuits, you do have me. I'm a lot less expensive, which means that one of the best parts about taking my advice on hiding your money is that when you've finished reading, you'll still have some money left to hide.

All types of people—besides the ultra wealthy—at some time in their lives need to hide their money. In fact, they may have an even greater need to hide their assets than their wealthier counterparts. That's because if someone steals the cash or valuables of a middle-class individual, chances are the victim won't be able to replace his or her nest egg.

The biggest problem for people of modest wealth who want to safeguard their cash is that, unlike their wealthier counterparts, they have no idea where the best hiding places are. They don't know the first thing about floor safes, safe deposit boxes, or offshore accounts. They don't know that their home, office, and car are filled with excellent hiding places for all sorts of items.

All they know is that they're going out of town for a few days, and they want to conceal their jewelry and their emergency cash supply just in case someone breaks into their house. They go it alone and end up hiding their cash and most treasured items in all of the worst places. Sometimes, the jewelry and cash are still there when they get home. Often, however, their poor hiding places are quickly discovered, and their treasured items are gone forever.

Bob Thompson never thought he'd need to hide any cash until one fateful December day when his life changed forever. Prior to then, Bob Thompson was just a regular guy who, despite his $40,000/year construction job and the part-time income of his wife, Susan, still never seemed to have enough money.

Between his kids, the cars, and a lack of construction jobs, Bob had been forced to take out a second mortgage on his house. And to make matters worse, a few months ago he'd accidentally hit a parked car while pulling into a gas station. Although the motorist was in the bathroom at the time of the accident, the man was currently suing Bob for emotional distress and loss of consortium. Amazingly enough, the motorist claimed that his dented car fender had caused him to be unable to have sex with his wife. Although Bob joked about the length some guys will go to in order to avoid having sex with their wives, it was hard for him to find anything funny about his mounting legal bills.

Finally, one day in early December, Bob decided that he had to get away. He didn't care anymore if he ended up having to file for bankruptcy. He and Susan needed a few days to themselves—a few days away from the hassles of demanding kids, condescending bosses, and endless stacks of bills. So, he made arrangements for the kids to stay with his mother and told Susan to pack a few frilly things. Soon they were on a plane to Las Vegas with $500 and the hope of striking it rich.

In Vegas, they took just a few minutes to settle into their hotel room before heading to the blackjack tables. Bob waited for the dealer to shuffle and then slowly placed a fifty-dollar chip on the table. He glanced over his shoulder at Susan and smiled nervously. They'd agreed that he would only play with $500 and if he lost that money, he'd stop. The dealer surveyed the table and then began deftly tossing cards to the players.

Seconds after a card landed in front of him, Bob flipped it up. An Ace. His heart began to beat a little faster. The dealer tossed another card his way. Its colors vibrated under the bright casino lights—a King. Twenty-one, he silently rejoiced. The dealer finished with the other players and then finished his own hand. Eight, ten, dealer sticks at eighteen. He looked over at Bob. Twenty-one. Blackjack. He placed seventy-five dollars in chips in front of Bob. And so it began.

The $50 bets turned to $100 bets and then to $500 bets, and Bob's luck just kept holding. By midnight, Bob and Susan were $50,000 richer. And by the next morning, they were jumping up and down on the bed in their room, wondering aloud about how they'd spend their newfound fortune.

"Let's buy a living room set," Susan proposed between sips of champagne.

"Not a chance. This money is going for something a lot more frivolous," Bob replied excitedly. "We'll take a trip to Maui. Just you, me, and a nice island breeze blowing through our luxury suite."

"You know what I really want?" Susan said longingly. "I want a new engagement ring. A two-carat, pear-shaped diamond. . . . "

The spending suggestions flowed as freely as the champagne. It wasn't until later that evening, after they'd taken a long, much deserved nap, that Bob suddenly realized that once his creditors learned about his new fortune, it would be gone in a matter of seconds.

"Forget about the creditors," Susan chimed in nervously. "What about your sister? Once she hears that we have money, she'll be hounding us night and day."

He nodded as he stared at the stack of cash on the dresser. "We've got to hide it," he said suddenly. "We've got to find a place to keep it that no one will ever find. Otherwise, we can kiss it all good-bye."

"You're right. Why don't we just put it in the bank and not tell anyone about it. That way, we can withdraw it slowly, without anyone ever finding out about it."

"Or, we could use it to buy a new car. God knows, I need one. That old Volvo station wagon is a wreck. I've always wanted to drive a BMW."

Susan thought a minute and then suggested, "We should probably just buy a safe and keep it all in the house. That way, it'll be close by."

And there you have it, suggestions from the book of bad ideas. Bob and Susan ultimately put all of their suggestions into play. First, they bought a new car, arousing the jealousy and suspicions of their neighbors, co-workers, friends, and relatives. Second, they deposited around $15,000 in their bank account, which caused their bank manager to file a Currency Transaction Report with the IRS because the transaction was over $10,000. This triggered an IRS audit and also alerted the plaintiff in the fender-bender lawsuit that Bob had not disclosed the true amount of his assets. Third, since they'd broadcast their newfound wealth by buying splashy cars, furniture, and jewelry, the safe was stolen within months of its purchase. And so, only five months after striking it rich in Vegas, poor Bill and Susan were forced to declare bankruptcy.

Bob and Susan shouldn't feel stupid about the choices they made. Like most people who suddenly come into money, they weren't prepared. And like most people, they ended up losing most of their assets. Although their choices turned out to be disastrous, we really shouldn't judge them too harshly. They didn't have a staff of trained professionals to advise them on the best places to hide their money.

Now let's discuss the case of Anna Lee, a forty-five-year-old attorney at one of New York City's largest law firms. Although it's been a tough ten years, Anna is at the top of her profession and basically has the world by the tail. She owns a beautiful loft in Tribecca and spends her summer weekends in the Hamptons. Her clothes are Armani, her purses from Gucci, and her shoes, Manolo Blanick. Anna Lee has the best taste in everything— except men. And that's what's worrying her these days. She's got a new man in her life, and, based on her past history, she's a little nervous about letting him know too much about her finances. His name is Ames Plantaine. He's handsome, charming, educated, but, alas, currently unemployed. He knows that she's rich, but he doesn't know how rich. So far, she's been careful not to tell him about her substantial inheritance from her father. And, she's also not filled him in on the beautiful and enormously expensive jewelry collection her Aunt Mimi left her. It's not that she doesn't trust Ames. Shall we just say that she has reservations?

The last time that Anna had reservations about someone, she woke up one morning to find most of her cash, some jewelry, her keys, and her credit cards gone. Eduardo "I've never felt like this" Cedeno had managed to purloin both her virtue and her credit in one evening. Ever since that unfortunate night, Anna had vowed to be more careful with her choice of lovers. But knowing her own limitations, she'd also vowed to be more careful with her money. It's not that she doesn't love Ames. In fact, she has such strong feelings for him that she agreed to marry him just last week. They're planning a beautiful wedding at her house in the Hamptons and then a long honeymoon in Florence. But before they start setting up a joint checking account, Anna wants to make sure that a good portion of her assets remain safe—just in case things don't work out.

Unlike Bob and Susan, Anna does a little research on how to hide her money before the big wedding day. She calls me, and we discuss how she can best safeguard her assets in the "unlikely" event that things don't work out between her and Ames. The first thing I recommend is that she set up a non–interest bearing checking account in her maiden name in another state. This will protect a small portion of her assets if Ames decides to check out her actual net worth by calling most of the banks that are in close proximity to her New York apartment. He most likely will not think to check whether she has an account in New Jersey. In order to further protect her privacy, I suggested that she have all her New Jersey bank account statements mailed to a post office box that can be rented at a New Jersey branch of Mail Boxes, Etc. Because Anna does a lot of investing with her New York broker, I suggest that she establish a checking/savings account in another state—somewhere far away, like Texas. (She can use the Internet to set up the Texas account and avoid having to take an obvious trip there.) I then tell her that when she decides to sell some of her stock, to have the New York broker wire the proceeds to the Texas bank account. Now, if she and Ames decide to get a divorce and Ames does an assets search, the only assets he'll find are those on hand with the New York broker.

Anna is also concerned that Ames will find out about the large inheritance she received from her father a few years ago. Currently, the bulk of that inheritance is sitting in the bank. I suggest that she consider investing it offshore. Once she decides to do that, I also suggest that she place all paperwork related to her offshore investments (as well as her significant property holdings) in her New Jersey mailbox. While she's thrilled that most of her assets are now safely hidden, she is still concerned about the safety of her valuable jewelry collection. I tell her to remove the grill from the air duct at her Hamptons house and place several of her most valuable pieces of jewelry in the duct, taking great care to keep all the jewelry boxes far away from the grill in case someone thinks to shine a flashlight up there. She decides not to hide all of her jewelry in the Hamptons because she wants to keep some of it available to wear in the city. So, at my suggestion, she purchases an empty utility box. She fills the box with several of her more valuable necklaces and rings and then attaches the box to the wall just outside her bedroom. Finally, just to make sure that Ames doesn't stumble onto the secret of her New Jersey mailbox, she goes out to her Hamptons home to find a suitable hiding place for the mailbox key. She surveys the slate sidewalk leading to her garden. She puts the key to her New Jersey mailbox in a Ziplock bag and then places it under the slate stone.

And so, with a little help, Anna can go forward with her wedding, secure in the knowledge that a large portion of her fortune is safely hidden. Anna is just one of many who have come to me over the years seeking advice on how to hide money. In fact, I've talked to hundreds of people about the best ways to hide their assets.

Unfortunately, I've often met with them when it was too late to help. And that brings me back, dear reader, to the reason I wrote this book.

If you are serious about hiding your money, assets, and wealth, you need to be proactive. You can't sit around waiting until someone files a lawsuit against you and then try to hide the bulk of your assets. You've got to have your strategy already in place—just in case someone tries to get his or her hands on what you've worked so hard to acquire.

In my twenty-five years of advising clients on how to protect their assets, I've read just about every book that exists on this subject. I've researched a wide variety of innovative techniques for hiding assets, and I've interviewed those professionals who specialize in identifying money-hiding schemes, such as bank compliance officers and forensic accountants.

Now I'm ready to pass on what I've learned to you.

I will teach you the best places to hide your money, assets, and wealth without getting caught. And I will teach you how to behave before, during, and after you've hidden that money. In a few simple chapters, I've provided you with all the information you will need to make sure that your assets will be there when you need them.

Want to hold on to your money? Then hold on to this book.

CHAPTER 1

A TIME TO HIDE: WHY DO YOU NEED TO HIDE YOUR MONEY?

When Jennifer and her husband, Joe, went to the bank to refinance their home, they expected that everything would go smoothly. Jennifer was a successful accountant with a mid-size firm in downtown Seattle, and Joe ran one of the city's most profitable insurance companies. The husband and wife, who'd never bounced a check or made a late payment on their mortgage, prided themselves on their stellar credit history. That's why they were shocked when their bank officer turned down their refinancing request, noting that their credit report showed at least five different accounts in arrears.

It took them quite a while to sort out all the facts, but they finally discovered that a woman named Gene Blake had successfully stolen Jennifer's identity. She'd used Jennifer's name and social security number to obtain five different credit cards and made purchases totaling over $100,000. She'd also managed to obtain a $20,000 loan for

1

> **Generally, identity fraud is defined by authorities as "stealing" another person's personal identifying information, such as their social security number (SSN), date of birth, and mother's maiden name.**

a mobile home, three car loans, a motorcycle, and a Rolex watch. And it had all been relatively easy.

After a lengthy investigation, the police determined that this same woman who'd masterminded the theft of Jennifer's identity had also stolen the identities of twenty other people, for a profit of over $2 million. As far as the police could determine, the crook's methods were simple but effective. She'd take a job baby-sitting and, while the parents were out for the evening, copy their credit card, social security, and bank account numbers. The thief explained to the police that because most people usually leave this kind of information lying about in their homes, it was generally quite easy for her to copy the information without arousing suspicion. She'd be long gone before the parents ever figured out that anything of value had been stolen.

Generally, identity fraud is defined by authorities as "stealing" another person's personal identifying information, such as their social security number (SSN), date of birth, and mother's maiden name. Criminals like Blake use such information to establish credit, run up debt, or to take over existing financial accounts. The scope of identity fraud ranges from the one-time unauthorized use of a credit card to the total takeover of a person's identity. Because most law enforcement agencies do not track identity fraud cases, it's difficult to gather statistics regarding the prosecution of these crimes. However, officials at the Social Security Administration's Office of the Inspector General note that SSN misuse in connection with program fraud increased from 305 in the fiscal year 1996 to 1,153 in 1997.[1]

Arrests involving credit card applications by another federal law enforcement agency, the Postal Inspection Service, have remained steady during fiscal years 1995 to 1997. Arrests involving change-of-address fraud (which involves the surreptitious diversion of a person's mail to addresses controlled by the criminals) have more than doubled, from 53 in fiscal year 1996 to 115 in fiscal year 1997.[2] Moreover, the Postal Inspection Service investigations show that identity fraud is perpetrated by organized criminal enterprises or groups and has a nationwide scope.[3]

According to David Medine, associate director for credit practices at the Bureau of Consumer Protection of the Federal Trade Commission, the issue of identity theft is really more one of personal privacy than fraud.[4] Because identity theft revolves around someone illegally appropriating another person's name, address, social security number, and professional licenses in order to commit fraud, it's a privacy invasion of the most complete and devastating sort. And the worst part about it is how easily it can be accomplished. Someone's entire personal financial profile can be accessed with only the barest of personal facts.

Medine notes that once the perpetrators identify their victims, they often need only that person's social security number to facilitate identity fraud. The social security number "opens the door to an individual's financial life—providing access to checking accounts, savings accounts, brokerage accounts, etc. . . . Social security numbers and other unique identifiers can be gleaned from a wide variety of sources, including public records (like certain Department of Motor Vehicles records), student transcripts, medical insurance records, survey response forms, and even warranty cards."[5]

The accessibility of this information has been made even easier by the growth of the Internet, which obviously creates greater opportunities for criminal activity, including identity fraud. Federal law enforcement officials have no specific trend data regarding the link between the Internet and identity fraud, but they recognize that numerous instances of identity fraud have been perpetrated online. At a congressional hearing in 1997, an FBI official testified that "Technological advances have also facilitated . . . the availability and misuse of electronic account and personal information. Identity theft poses significant risks to financial institutions and individuals alike."[6]

Computerized database services—frequently referred to as "individual reference services" or "look up services"—are used widely by the public and private sector to locate or verify the identity of individuals. These services exist to collect and disseminate identity information. They can also easily be used by the public or private sector as a database of names for those wishing to commit identity fraud. The Federal Trade Commission has tried to work with industry representatives to encourage self-regulation. And while the reference services have agreed not to distribute non-public information such as social security numbers and dates of birth on request, they continue to sell this information.

Keeping your personal financial data private in the face of increasingly sophisticated technology is especially difficult due to a phenomenon known as *pretexting*. Pretexting means obtaining personal financial information under false pretenses—for example, an investigator who obtains a bank account balance by posing as the account holder.

As a result of pretexting, financial privacy is rapidly becoming an endangered species. In his July 28, 1999, remarks to the Congressional Committee on Banking and Finance, Mozelle W. Thompson, commissioner of the Federal Trade Commission, warned that pretexting ". . . appears to be gaining in popularity—especially in the burgeoning Internet marketplace—because of the booming market for comprehensive personal information.

"Now, increasing numbers of high-tech private eyes, also known as 'information brokers,' are touting their ability to obtain surprisingly sensitive information without the subject ever knowing. Pretexting is a troubling, and apparently growing, problem facing consumers."[7]

In fact, it's such a growing problem that consumers are beginning to revolt and demand that the financial services industry take steps to protect their privacy. Recently, Minnesota's attorney general filed suit against U.S. Bankcorp over its information-sharing practices,[8] and Congress is currently considering limiting the ability of banks to sell customer data to telemarketing firms. In addition, in May 1999 President Clinton proposed legislation that would put limits on information-sharing.

Although Washington politicians seem intent on passing some legislation to limit information-sharing, don't be surprised if the millennium is a distant memory before anything is on the books. So, while you're sitting around waiting for Washington to act, you might want to take some concrete steps of your own to protect your financial privacy, and that's where this book comes in handy.

It shows you how to avoid turning over your private financial data to pretexters, as well as to legitimate information brokers like your local neighborhood bank. By the time you've finished reading this book, you'll have a better understanding of how simple, everyday activities can result in an unwilling disclosure of your most private financial information. For example, the next time you fill

Pretexting means obtaining personal financial information under false pretenses—for example, an investigator who obtains a bank account balance by posing as the account holder.

out a warranty card for a new toaster, stop and consider the amount of information that you're being asked to disclose about yourself. More important, the next time you fill out an application for a mortgage loan, take a close look at the incredibly detailed personal information you're being asked to divulge, and consider who might have access to that information.

As you're probably aware, few things are more intrusive or intimate than a mortgage application. It generally requires information such as how much you've made in the past few years, where you work, how frequently you've changed jobs, how much you've paid in taxes, your credit card and banking account numbers and balances, and, in some cases, details about your major assets, including stocks, real estate, and partnerships.[9] While we might understand why the broker needs this information to access our loan request, what is more difficult to understand is why the broker is allowed to store this information and sell it to anyone who wants it. In fact, no federal statutes currently prevent mortgage brokers or independent mortgage companies from storing this information electronically and then selling it. So, if you're intent on keeping such personal data as, say, your medical records from falling into the hands of your mortgage broker, you'd better learn how to keep your personal financial information out of the hands of telemarketers and database compilers.

A Secret Service official noted that losses to the victimized individuals and institutions associated with the agency's investigation of financial crimes involving identity fraud totaled $442 million in 1995, $450 million in 1996, and $745 million in 1997.[10] Moreover, the "human" costs of identity fraud are also quite substantial. These include emotional costs, as well as various financial and/or opportunity costs—for example, victims of identity theft often remain unable to refinance their homes or, in some cases, obtain jobs, purchase cars, or qualify for mortgages.

Because a social security number can give a criminal almost complete access to a person's entire financial history, learning how to safeguard one's personal financial documents has become more important than ever. Even if you've got no money in the bank and owe thousands in student loans, if you've got a name, you've got something worth stealing. All it takes for your identity to be stolen is for you to be careless with one important financial document. By tossing one bank statement into the trash or letting one credit card number be copied, you could condemn yourself to losing your identity and spending the next five years trying to reclaim it.[11]

There are a number of ways to keep yourself from becoming a victim of identity theft.[12] The experts advise you never to carry your social security card, birth certificate, or passport in your wallet. They also advise you to carry only those credit cards that you regularly use. All other important documentation should be carefully hidden. You might opt to keep everything in a bank safe deposit box, but that generally limits your access. Therefore, if you're serious about protecting your identity, you need to start looking around your home, yard, and office for good and effective hiding places. Even when you think you've got nothing to hide, you probably do! And I'm here to help you find the perfect hiding spots.

But before you even begin to consider where to hide your assets, you have to understand one simple concept: Even the best hiding place is useless if someone is completely determined to find or steal your assets. So, the best way to keep your assets safe is not to let others know that they even exist. This means that if you've just come into money, you don't go out and buy yourself a new mansion, a new car, or a new wife. Just ask any government investigator how government officials figured out that one of their own was a Russian spy and he'll invariably answer, "Well, he bought himself a million-dollar mansion on a government salary. You do the math!"

My point here is a simple one: The key to hiding your assets is *discretion*. As I always say, "Stealth is wealth." *Stealth is wealth.* If you've got it, don't flaunt it. If you can resist showing everyone how rich you are, you'll probably be rich longer.

The concept of "stealth is wealth" is something that many "old money" Americans have adhered to for decades. They believe that ostentatious displays of money are garish, and they subscribe to the notion that it's easier to hold on to your money when no one knows you have it. And while I don't particularly care about whether someone deems my new home a garish display of new money, I do care if the IRS deems my new home a garish display of new, unreported money.

The "stealth is wealth" lesson is one I learned from my father when I was only seven years old. After years of driving to his shoe store in a dilapidated, ten-year-old Buick station wagon, my father finally decided to purchase a Lincoln Continental—the dream car for every successful immigrant. I still remember the day he brought the glimmering black Lincoln home and parked it in the driveway for the entire neighborhood to admire.

Within minutes, a large crowd of neighbors had gathered to ooh and aah, and for over an hour, my father fielded questions about his glorious new purchase. It wasn't until my father prepared to pull the Lincoln into the garage for the evening that the tone of the gathered crowd began to change.

Computerized database services are used widely by the public and private sector to locate or verify the identity of individuals. They can also easily be used by the public or private sector as a database of names for those wishing to commit identity fraud.

"Guess the shoe business is doing pretty well," his close friend from next door muttered, his voice tinged with jealousy. And before my father could respond, another neighbor asked excitedly, "Now that you're in the money, maybe you would consider investing in my son's new business. From the looks of things, you've got more than enough to spare."

For the next few weeks, our phone rang off the hook with business proposals, loan requests, and, in one case, an arranged marriage for me with a neighbor's less-than-attractive daughter. It seemed that with one high-profile purchase, my father had in the eyes of the neighborhood transformed himself from the owner of a small, moderately successful shoe store into a titan of high finance.

Every night after he arrived home from work, neighbors would drop by to tell their tales of financial woe. Before my mother had finished bringing out the coffee cups and cake, they'd ask for a loan. "You can afford it," they'd say with a glance toward the garage.

When my father would decline their requests and politely explain that he was just a small businessman trying to support a family, the atmosphere in the room would turn chilly. Behind his back, the neighbors called my father stingy, greedy, and rotten. And to his face, they were cold and disapproving. The general perception in the neighborhood was that Mr. Schneider had made good, but he wouldn't share. And soon, my father's joy in his Lincoln turned to discomfort as he drove down our street past jealous and resentful neighbors.

While the hostility and insults upset my father, they didn't hurt half as much as what occurred next. Only one month after he drove his beautiful new Lincoln home from the show room, it was stolen, never to be seen again. Although my father mourned the theft of his prized automobile, it wasn't long before he realized that its disappearance was really a blessing in disguise. Once he was back behind the wheel of his trusty old station wagon, life returned to normal: no more loan requests, no more envious stares, and no more marriage proposals for me.

In only one short month, my Dad learned a lesson that some Americans never grasp—that even small displays of wealth make people targets. At the very least, a display of one's wealth invites envy, and, more often than not, an open display of assets invites theft.

While you clearly want to take steps to hide your assets from potential thieves, pretexters, and greedy government agencies, it's possible that the greatest threat to your financial security is sleeping in the bed right next to you. Let's assume you're married, and over the last few years, things haven't gone so well between you and your husband. So you decide to divorce him. Although you're worried about being alone, you're not particularly worried about your financial future because years ago, you had the foresight to open a bank account in only your name.

The next day, you skip off to your lawyer's office to get the divorce ball rolling, and that's when you learn the awful truth—half of everything you own, including your separate bank account, belongs to him. As your lawyer explains to you, it doesn't matter that the money in the account came out of your paycheck. You throw up your hands and yell hysterically, "Why, oh why, didn't I think to hide that money?"[13]

Don't be too hard on yourself. You didn't know that there were ways to hide your assets just in case you eventually decided to kick the jerk out.[14]

For those of you who are just now considering marriage (or are already married and are interested in protecting your finances), read, learn, and implement. With a little careful planning, you might be able to avoid having to turn over half of everything to your ex–special someone. That's why I've included some suggestions as to how you might maintain a separate bank account that your spouse knows nothing about. I've also included some other places, besides banks, where you might want to

A Secret Service official noted that losses to
the victimized individuals and institutions
associated with the agency's investigation of
financial crimes involving identity fraud
totaled $442 million in 1995, $450 million in
1996, and $745 million in 1997.[10]

hide assets to protect them from an angry ex-spouse bent
on destroying you.

Even if you're a single woman who has managed to
avoid the legal entanglements associated with marriage,
learning how to hide your assets can still be advanta-
geous if you plan on having any romantic life at all. As
most single women know, you don't have to be married to
have a man try to get his hands on your money. Single
women are often targeted by predatory men who make a
habit of living off, or stealing from, successful women.
These men don't need a marriage license to use the courts
to go after a woman's assets. That's why I've included
advice for single women on how to protect their finances
from these unsavory operators.

As I later discuss in more detail, women (and men)
who are dating need to think twice about providing potential suitors with highly personal information, such as their
home address, phone number, e-mail address, or, in some
cases, work address. Providing a potential suitor (who is
often a complete stranger) with intimate personal information can put not only one's wealth, but also one's security, at risk. A single woman who is about to get involved
with a stranger needs to consider where in her home,
office, yard, or other locale she should hide things, ranging
from her jewelry to her bank account numbers. With a little thought (and my chapter on financial privacy and the
single woman), she'll learn that she can take specific steps

to protect her wealth. As I always insist, the key to ensuring financial privacy is to be proactive, not reactive.

Now, if you're neither married nor bent on getting involved with a beautiful, litigious blond, don't assume that you're safe from a lawsuit. Marriage, cohabitation, or a brief fling aren't the only "encounters" that can lead to litigation. Anyone can become the target of a nasty lawsuit. And once that happens, you'd better hope that you not only read this book, but that you memorized it—chapter and verse.

Once a lawsuit has been filed against you, a process known as discovery begins. Discovery generally allows the person (or company) that sues you to request all documentation related to the allegations in his lawsuit. What that means in plain English is that if some guy sues you for breaching a contract with him, he can ask to see every document in your possession related to any and all transactions that you ever undertook with him. And, since he's asking for you to pay significant damages, he can ask to see all of your company's books and any and all financial documents relating to the running of your business. (This is only a small sample of the types of things that can be requested during a lawsuit. Just keep in mind that discovery requests often run as long as twenty to thirty pages and they tend to ask for all of your private financial information, including your tax returns.)

If you have any interest in protecting yourself from frivolous (or even meritorious) lawsuits, you'd better be

> The key to hiding your assets is *discretion*. As I always say, "Stealth is wealth." If you've got it, don't flaunt it. If you can resist showing everyone how rich you are, you'll probably be rich longer.

proactive about hiding your assets. As we all know, even if a lawsuit is ultimately unsuccessful, the cost of defending yourself in one can completely bankrupt your once-thriving company. And, as I just mentioned, the mere filing of a lawsuit can force you and/or your company to reveal so much sensitive financial information that it becomes virtually impossible to continue to operate your business. Fortunately, this book can help you prepare for the worst, even as you continue to hope for the best.

Finally, there is one other extremely important reason to learn how to hide your assets: the United States government. As anyone who has ever been audited knows, nothing makes government officials angrier than people who make more money than they do. And unfortunately, when government officials get angry and jealous, they tend to equalize the playing field by making sure that at the end of the day, others are as poor and bitter as they are. The thing to always remember about government officials is that they believe in justice equalization. If they can prove you got your assets illegally, you don't get to keep them . . . if you bought your house or your car with "bad" money, you can kiss them both good-bye.

So if parting from your assets brings you sweet sorrow, then you'd better take some steps now to hide them. Because no one will enjoy dismantling your empire as much as some poorly paid government worker who rents a one-bedroom apartment next to the freeway and who drives to work in an '87 Chevy with bad brakes and no air-conditioning.

You can try to hide your money from the government yourself, but before you go off on your own and start stashing cash in your mattress, you might want to ask yourself, "Do I feel lucky?" In order for you to successfully prevail against the United States government, you will need a hell of a lot of luck.

The government currently has a million and one ways to keep track of every penny that goes into your pocket. Not only do a plethora of government agencies monitor your financial activities,[15] but the government also enlists the "help" of private institutions in tracking your net worth. Even worse, Congress is currently considering legislation that would force banks and savings and loans to tell federal law enforcement agencies if any customer made the slightest deviation in deposits to a checking or savings account and to determine the source of those funds. That will turn your friendly neighborhood banker into a spy for the United States government, and it means that if you should receive a large inheritance, a bonus, or some other windfall, you'll end up in some federal computer with the term "suspicious" right between your first and last name.

Even if the "Know Your Customer" legislation doesn't pass, your local bank still must follow some specific governmental reporting requirements that enable the government to better keep track of your banking transactions. Every time a bank, savings and loan, or credit union disburses or receives more than $10,000 from a customer on any given day, that bank must file a Currency Transaction Report (CTR) with the U.S. Treasury Department. This reporting requirement has been in effect since the passage of the Currency and Foreign Transactions Reporting Act of 1970. What it means is that the United States government has monitored transactions of $10,000 and over for around thirty years. It has the names, the addresses, and the account numbers stored in its computers, and once our government gets information, it's not likely to part with it. Therefore, if you're truly committed to keeping some of your assets private and out of the hands of an increasingly intrusive federal government, you need a plan. In fact, you need a lot of plans. And that's where this book comes in.

Before you explore a plan to hide your assets, you need to know what's legal and what's not. Currently, the government has a number of rules and regulations in place that help it track your assets. That's why I've taken some time and effort to set out most of the critical government reporting requirements, including specifications that direct banks to look out for transactions and transaction patterns that fall outside the norm.

Once you're clear on what types of transactions are reported and monitored by the government, you can work on a good, legal plan to hide your assets that won't set off government alarm bells. For example, let's say that you just inherited $10,000, and you decide to take the money and deposit it at your local bank—the same bank where you keep a checking account with a usual balance of $500. As soon as you give the deposit slip to your teller, she is required to fill out a CTR—the document used to report transactions of $10,000 and over to the IRS.

As you drive away from the bank, you assume that all paperwork in connection with your deposit has been completed. Think again. While you're busy planning how you will spend your inheritance, your bank could be busy filling out yet another form. Although your deposit was perfectly legal, let's say the bank manager decides that there's something suspicious about it and reports it pursuant to the Suspicious Activity Report.[16] Now your name (and all other personal financial information in the possession of your bank) is on its way to Washington.

The fact is, if you were concerned about protecting your financial privacy and avoiding a possible government investigation of your account activities, you should have considered depositing your inheritance check somewhere

> **Single women are often targeted by predatory men who make a habit of living off, or stealing from, successful women. These men don't need a marriage license to use the courts to go after a woman's assets.**

else besides your local bank. After reading this book, you'll have a much better idea of how to make sure your windfall ends up in a place where an overly intrusive bank manager doesn't feel obliged to tell the federal government (and God knows who else) about it. You'll also learn how to avoid conducting transactions that bank compliance officers deem to be suspicious.[17]

Take typical electronic fund transfers, for instance. A friend of mine who is a compliance officer for a bank down South told me that the key to avoiding detection is consistency. He explained that if you send money by bank wires consistently, they generally won't be detected. You won't stand out because your pattern of activity is consistent. Bank compliance officers tend to look for the unusual.

That means you *will* arouse suspicion if you go into a bank where you usually make a weekly deposit of $2,000 and ask your teller to wire $10,000 to a bank in Fiji. But if over the years you've established a pattern of always wiring money to your broker in New York, and you come in one day and ask your teller to wire a large check to that broker, it probably won't raise any eyebrows. And then you can have your brokerage house wire that check (and maybe some other funds) to a lovely, offshore bank in Fiji.

Always remember, while you read this book, that an awful lot of people out there want to get their hands on your money and on your personal financial information. Left to your own devices, you'd probably figure out one or two ways to hide your valuables and your personal information from those who would do you harm. If you put yourself in my hands, however, you'll learn a multitude of ways to keep your financial information safe from prying eyes and even, in some instances, the tax man. And you'll discover that with careful planning and quiet living, you can hide your money in places where not even your own mother could find it. The choice is yours.

REFERENCES

1. General Accounting Office Report, *Identity Fraud—Information on Prevalence, Cost, and Internet Impact Is Limited,* May 26, 1998.
2. Ibid.
3. Ibid.
4. Prepared Statement for the Federal Trade Commission on "Identity Theft," Before the Subcommittee on Technology, Terrorism and Government Information of the Committee on the Judiciary United States Senate, by David Medine, associate director for credit practices, Bureau of Consumer Protection, Federal Trade Commission, May 20, 1998.
5. Ibid.
6. Government Accounting Office Report, *Identity Fraud—Information on Prevalence, Cost, and Internet Impact Is Limited,* May 26, 1998.
7. Financial Information Privacy Act: Mozelle W. Thompson. Congressional Testimony, July 28, 1998.
8. This lawsuit was still on-going when this book went to press.
9. Harney, Kenneth R., "What You Disclose About Your Finances Might Spread: Issue Under Debate," *Daily Press, Inc.,* June 21, 1999.
10. "Technology, Terrorism and Government Information of the Committee on the Judiciary United States Senate," by David Medine, associate director for credit practices, Bureau of Consumer Protection, Federal Trade Commission, May 20, 1998.
11. If you become a victim of identity theft, you can contact the Privacy Rights Clearinghouse and the California Public Interest Research Group (CALPIRG) for a fact sheet on "Identity Theft: What to Do If It Happens to You." Send a stamped, self-addressed envelope to Privacy Rights Clearinghouse, 1717 Kettner Avenue, Suite 105, San Diego, CA 92101. You might also want to pick up a copy of attorney Mari Frank's book, *From Victim to Victor: A Step-by-Step Guide for Ending the Nightmare of Identity Theft.* Laguna Niguel, CA: Porpoise Press, 1998.
12. The experts advise you to get off of mailing lists and to cease giving your social security number out routinely. You must provide it to the IRS, your employer, and for financial transactions. But don't use it when not

necessary. You should also check your credit report regularly to see if there has been any illegal use of your name.

13. Also keep in mind that in most situations where a husband and a wife divorce, the wife's standard of living generally goes down while the husband's generally stays the same.

14. And for those men out there who wake up each night in a cold sweat for fear that they'll be completely wiped out by an angry ex-wife, don't despair. I'm an equal-opportunity adviser when it comes to hiding assets. Be you male or female, my methods for hiding assets are available for your perusal.

15. Within the United States federal government the following agencies were created to regulate and control the flow of money: the Internal Revenue Service for taxes (income, excise, inheritance, etc.); the Federal Bureau of Investigation (FBI) for bank fraud, racketeering, etc.; the Securities and Exchange Commission (SEC) for securities fraud, stock market manipulation, etc.; U.S. Customs for import and export duties; and the Treasury Department's Financial Crimes Enforcement Network (FinCEN).

16. The Suspicious Activity Report was created by a joint effort of the banking regulators and the Treasury Department's Financial Crimes Enforcement Network. Its effective date was April 1, 1996. The reporting requirements include instances when there is a suspected violation of the Bank Secrecy Act or of the laws of money laundering, and/or the transaction has no apparent business or lawful purpose or is not the sort in which the particular customer would be expected to engage and the bank knows of no reasonable explanation for the transaction.

17. Bank compliance officers are hired by the bank to help it comply with governmental reporting rules and regulations. The bank compliance officer's job is to report any suspected violations of the United States' banking regulatory laws and to monitor and report any unusual transactions that may or may not violate IRS and Treasury laws.

CHAPTER 2

ISN'T HIDING
YOUR MONEY ILLEGAL?

When I first discussed writing this book with my friends, most responded with one simple question: "Is it really legal to hide your assets?" And I always responded with one simple answer: It depends on two major factors. First, are the assets that you plan to hide legally obtained? Second, whom do you plan to hide the assets from?

For example, if you cash your paycheck and then hide half the money in a space behind your bathroom medicine cabinet, that would probably be legal if the paycheck was legally obtained, and you're not hiding the cash for any illegal purpose. But if you're married and you neglect to tell your wife where you've hidden most of your paycheck, then you are illegally withholding money from the community (*community,* in the sense of the marriage's "community property"). And that does not constitute legal hiding.

When I think about illegal hiding, I'm always struck by how intensely vulnerable it can make you, even when you think that you've covered all of your bases and that you've been enormously clever with your hiding scheme. Invariably, you've left one tiny, loose thread that can—and will—unravel with just a simple tug. That loose thread could be a trusted friend or family member. It happens more often than you'd think. I remember trying to explain this principle to one potential client named Clark but he never listened. Clark thought he had come up with the perfect illegal hiding scheme, until his wife convinced him otherwise.

Clark, who called me shortly after his wife of almost twenty years filed for divorce, was interested in hiding money offshore so that his wife wouldn't be able to get it in the divorce settlement. Fortunately for all involved, Clark and his wife, Melinda, settled out of court. The story of how Melinda brought a speedy end to her divorce proceedings is an illustrative one.

When Melinda and Clark first met, he was a hardware store clerk and she was a recent college graduate. With a little start-up capital from Melinda's dad, he and Melinda opened their own store—called, appropriately enough, Clark's Office Supply Empire. The first store was an instant success, and together Clark and Melinda built a chain of businesses.

But while their financial status continued to improve, their marriage steadily deteriorated. Clark began to play around, spending large amounts of money on his mistress *du jour*. At first, Melinda looked the other way, but inevitably Clark's numerous affairs took their toll, until she was tired of Clark's sleeping with every twenty-something blonde who crossed his path.

Melinda filed for divorce, citing irreconcilable differences. She sought alimony and 50 percent of the Clark's Office Supply Empire business.

As soon as Clark was served with divorce papers, he began illegally hiding assets—without my help, of course. By the time his attorney filed a list of his assets, the net income from the chain of the stores was seriously down from the year before. In fact, according to Clark, the stores were barely making a profit. Realizing that Clark's financial statement grossly undervalued not only their business empire but also their personal worth, Melinda decided that drastic measures were necessary.

It turned out that for years, Melinda and Clark had skimmed large amounts of cash from the business by not ringing up a percentage of their sales. They'd put this money into bonds, gold bars, cars, gold coins, and real estate. Clark didn't happen to mention these investments on his asset list, most of which were purchased through an anonymous trust.

Melinda threatened to spill the beans about the money skimming if Clark didn't offer her a fair divorce settlement. And that is how Melinda got Clark to settle out of court in only four months.

I must admit that when Clark first called asking for my help in moving some of his investment profits offshore, I was tempted. I knew that Clark had a lot of money and could potentially become a good client. So, before I politely ended our telephone conversation, I took a moment to explain to Clark why I couldn't help him.

First, we discussed how I knew that most of the money he wanted to send offshore was unreported income obtained through illegal means. He assured me that the IRS was too dense to ever figure out that he'd been skimming. I told him that while the IRS may have missed his little scheme in the past, it was a safe bet that if he didn't give his wife her "fair share" of the business profits, the

> I will always assist a client who wants to use an offshore haven for tax avoidance, but I will not assist him with tax evasion. There's a big difference between the two.

IRS would take a closer look at him this year. And I let him know that as much as I valued his friendship, I wasn't interested in attending his audit.

After I had explained that it's wrong and illegal to hide money from the IRS when you're going through a bitter divorce, I told him why investing his money offshore wouldn't help him keep assets out of his wife's hands. Because Clark lived in California, he would be required to file a financial disclosure statement wherein he would have to list all of his assets. The only way he could effectively keep his wife from getting a part of the business was to lie. And not only would he have to lie about the business's profits, he'd also have to lie about the fact that a large portion of those profits was located in an offshore account. His entire financial disclosure would have to be a lie—and while that might work temporarily, it could eventually get Clark into a lot of trouble.

We discussed two very different scenarios relating to Clark's submitting a false financial disclosure statement with the court. The first scenario had Clark's wife accepting the false figures in the statement and riding off into the sunset. We both agreed that this scenario was extremely unlikely. The second scenario involved Clark submitting the phony, meager net worth statement to the court, and his wife responding by hiring a skilled forensic accountant to audit everything in sight. In this far more likely scenario, the skimming action would come to light and Clark would face not only the wrath of the court but also a full and complete IRS investigation. (Even if Clark got away with hiding the money from his wife, she could, under a recent California Court of Appeals ruling, potentially sue him in civil court for fraud.[1])

As you can imagine, due to my expertise in offshore investment opportunities, potential clients like Clark who seek to hide money from someone or something frequently approach me. Before I agree to work with the client, we always discuss whether the source of his funds is legal and why he's interested in moving his money off-shore. Both of these "discussion areas" help me to determine whether my client can legally invest his funds offshore.

It's not a perfect system, but it has generally worked well for me. The bottom line when it comes to hiding money is that unless you're interested in spending a long time in prison, you need to know the rules and how to apply them. With the proper guidance, it's possible to legally and successfully hide money without interference. A lot of people don't understand this simple fact. And so it's often my job to help set them straight.

I'm tested almost weekly. Last year, we had an individual come up to Vancouver with a million dollars in a suitcase. He explained that the cash came from his very profitable "coffee business" in northern California, and in order to minimize taxes, he needed my help in getting the cash offshore. As I eyed the overflowing suitcase, I muttered something about how it had apparently been a very good year to be in the coffee business. I then politely showed him to the door.

I suppose it is the rather sordid reputation of offshore havens that leads many potential clients to me with the assumption that I will assist them in hiding their illegal assets with no questions asked. Potential clients seem surprised to learn that while I believe in using offshore investment havens to the best possible legal advantage, I'm not interested in using them to evade the law.

For instance, I will always assist a client who wants to use an offshore haven for tax and estate planning, but I will not assist him with tax evasion. There's a big difference between the two. When you avoid a tax, you decide to use all legal means available to reduce your tax burden—including "hiding" your assets in an offshore bank or other offshore investment vehicle. On the other hand, when you intentionally fail to report, or "hide," a part of your income so as to reduce taxes, you're breaking the law.

Think of the difference this way: It's illegal to hide
any percentage of your money—no matter how small—
from the U.S. government. It is not, however, illegal to
move your money outside the government's sphere of tax
authority. That's where the beauty of offshore banking
comes into focus. A wide variety of legitimate offshore
investment opportunities can provide you with an opportunity to legally hide money from the U.S. government.
That's why, out of the world's top fifty banks, forty-seven of
them engage in offshore investment—including CitiBank,
Chase Manhattan, and Bank of America.

As many U.S. individuals and corporations have
indeed discovered, offshore investment can be both legal
and profitable. Even Peter Djinis, associate director for
FinCEN (Financial Crimes Enforcement Network),
agrees that "there are all sorts of legitimate reasons why
both individuals and companies may want to set up overseas financial operations. They include having lower tax
rates, insulating themselves from liability, having the
flexibility to deal with financial institutions on sight, and
providing services for international customers. These are
all legitimate."[2]

But while Djinis acknowledges that not everyone
who invests offshore is doing so illegally, he also points
out that "offshore havens have historically been used as a
vehicle for laundering funds so as to virtually evaporate
the paper trail and make investigation of criminal activity difficult or impossible."[3] As a result, FinCEN and
other government agencies tend to look upon every offshore investment with a suspicious eye.

As Djinis explains it, even though many people use
offshore havens for legitimate investments, "the problem
is that for every legitimate purpose, there could be someone hiding behind the guise of legitimacy who is interested in taking illegal assets and transferring them
abroad to make it impossible for investigators to trace the
illegal funds."[4]

In Djinis's view, therefore, the good guys often get mixed in with the bad guys. This means that being a good guy doesn't protect you from government scrutiny of your investments, accounts, and purchases.

OFFSHORE HAVENS: WHEN DOES OFFSHORE HIDING BECOME ILLEGAL?

Contrary to its depiction in the movies, offshore investment doesn't always involve money laundering, drugs, and the Mafia. More often than not, offshore investment merely involves a successful U.S. businessperson who is looking to catch a break on his tax exposure. But the illicit silver screen image of offshore havens is based on some degree of reality: Offshore investment has been—and always will be—used to evade creditors and launder money.

Many of the people who choose to go offshore simply don't follow the law. They don't report the income that

Be sure to follow the rules so you never end up here.

they earn offshore; they don't report the offshore accounts; and in some situations, they use the offshore haven as a means to launder money. Therefore, many law enforcement officials immediately look at offshore investors with a jaundiced and suspicious eye.

So, to a certain extent, those individuals and corporations who've used offshore havens as a means to illegally hide money have ruined it for the rest of us. This is particularly true of Raul Salinas, the former brother of the president of Mexico, who managed to hide over $100 million in illegal funds offshore before he was caught by the Mexican government. The method by which Salinas managed to funnel millions out of Mexico was so complex that even after he was indicted by the Mexican government on illegal enrichment charges, prosecutors were unable to trace Salinas's ill-gotten gains.

This was because, like many others who have used offshore havens to launder and hide illegal money, Raul Salinas had help. In fact, he had a lot of help.

According to a congressional report released by the U.S. General Accounting Office (GAO) in 1998, Salinas was able to illegally transfer between $90 million and $100 million by using a private banking relationship formed with Citibank New York. The funds were transferred through Citibank Mexico and Citibank New York to private banking investment accounts in Citibank London and Citibank Switzerland.[5] After a lengthy investigation, the General Accounting Office concluded that with the assistance of his private banker, Amy Elliot, Salinas was able to move his fortune from accounts in Mexico to untraceable shell companies in the Cayman Islands. The report specifically states that Citibank through Elliot:

1. Set up an offshore private investment company— a shell company—named Trocca, to hold Mr. Salinas's assets, through Cititrust (Cayman), and investment accounts in Citibank London and

Citibank Switzerland. (London and Zurich Citibank's "Confidas" affiliate in Zurich invested Trocca's money in stocks and bonds. It, too, was shrouded in Swiss secrecy laws.)

2. Waived bank references for Mr. Salinas and did not prepare a financial profile on him or request a waiver for the profile, as required by Citibank's existing "know your customer" policy

3. Facilitated Mrs. Salinas's use of another name to initiate fund transfers from Mexico. (At the time of her introduction to Citibank Mexico officials to begin the transfers, Mrs. Salinas had not yet married Mr. Salinas.)

4. Had funds wired from Citibank Mexico to a Citibank New York concentration account that commingles funds from various sources—before forwarding them to Trocca's offshore Citibank investment accounts.[6]

According to the GAO report, Citibank officials not only helped Salinas wire millions out of Mexico into various offshore accounts, they also helped him set up a shell company—Trocca—that completely masked his ownership of those foreign accounts.

Because the company was set up in the Cayman Islands, all documentation connecting Mr. Salinas to Trocca was considered confidential under the islands' strict banking privacy laws. And to further insulate Mr. Salinas's connection to Trocca, Cititrust (Cayman) used three additional shell companies to function as Trocca's board of directors, and Trocca's executive officer and chief shareholder was yet another shell company.

For at least two years, Citibank officials facilitated the Salinas fund transfers out of Mexico. It wasn't until his arrest in 1995 on murder conspiracy and illicit enrichment that Citibank's vice president for legal affairs put a watch on the Salinas Citibank New York accounts and

> The bottom line when it comes to hiding money is that unless you're interested in spending a long time in prison, you need to know the rules and how to apply them. With the proper guidance, it's possible to legally and successfully hide money without interference.

Trocca's Citibank London and Citibank Switzerland accounts. Under the watch, the vice president would have been notified by bank officials if Mr. Salinas attempted to move funds in those accounts, and he had the discretion to stop him from doing so. However, according to the Citibank representative, the Mexican Division VP personally contacted Mrs. Salinas in Mexico in the summer of 1995, without the representative's knowledge or consent, and advised her to move all funds associated with Trocca out of Citibank. Mrs. Salinas was arrested in Switzerland in November 1995 for money laundering and drug trafficking while attempting to withdraw funds from a Swiss bank account.[7]

According to Citibank's representative, Citibank earned $1.1 million in fees associated with the Salinas/Trocca accounts. The Salinas/Trocca accounts have been frozen but remain in Citibank's control. The GAO report found that one aspect of Citibank's "know your customer" policy was violated—preparation of a financial profile—which could have assisted in verifying the source of Mr. Salinas's wealth and transferred funds.[8] First, Elliot did not ask Salinas for two bank references, as Citibank guidelines dictate. Second, as the brother of Mexico's then-president, Salinas could have been turned down altogether because of what one former Citibank executive says is another bank rule—that private bankers should be wary of accepting heads of state and their families as customers.[9] (It seems that Salinas was not the only relative of a head of state to benefit from Citibank's private bank. Citibank allowed Asif Ali Zardari, husband of the then–Pakistani prime minister, Benazir Bhutto, to open a Swiss bank account. According to Swiss and Pakistani authorities, the accounts were used to launder ill-gotten gains.[10])

The GAO finally noted that it could not determine whether Citibank's actions regarding Mr. Salinas's private banking relationship had violated the then-applicable laws and regulations.[11] Along with the GAO, the Department of Justice and the Federal Reserve failed to compile sufficient evidence to charge Citibank with any wrongdoing in the Salinas affair. Prosecutors were apparently unable to make the money laundering charge stick, in that they had to prove not only that Salinas was a criminal but that Citibank knew he was a criminal when it provided services. So, Citibank was never charged in connection with the Salinas matter, despite the fact that Citibank helped Salinas disguise "the origin, destination, and beneficial owner" of roughly $100 million.[12]

Salinas, on the other hand, was found guilty of plotting the murder of a high-ranking official in his brother's political party and is currently in prison.

THE RISKS THAT COME WITH HIDING YOUR CASH OFFSHORE

The Salinas affair (and other money-laundering scandals) served to focus international attention on the rapidly growing international private banking industry and its role in helping drug dealers launder enormous amounts of money. Following the Salinas scandal, several senators called for a full-scale investigation into whether U.S. banks are helping criminals move funds to offshore havens around the world. Others criticized the boom in private banking, arguing that private banks exist either to assist their clients in money laundering and/or tax evasion.

Of course, there is no denying that while offshore havens provide a wide variety of perfectly legal services, they can, and do, also provide the U.S. citizen with an avenue to either cheat on his taxes and/or to launder ill-gotten gains. According to one money-laundering expert, while around 140,000 foreign-bank accounts are reported to the IRS each year, there are as many as 1.5 million anonymous offshore accounts around the world—and about 40 percent of those accounts are held by Americans.[13]

So, although a lot of legitimate "hiding" is going on in offshore havens, quite a bit of illegitimate hiding is also occurring. Many offshore havens have become targets of opportunity in America's war against drugs, precisely because they've helped drug smugglers launder drug profits into legitimate money-market deposits and investments in resort hotels and car dealerships. Drug lords now use the same international financial services available to Fortune 500 companies to achieve great success in laundering drug profits. According to police, ". . . the basic fee for recycling money of dubious origin is 4 percent, while the rate for drug cash and other hot money is 7 percent to 10 percent. Drug lords and other lawbreakers are believed to be buying valuable chunks of the American economy, but clever Dutch sandwiches [The Netherlands Antilles] and other subterfuges make it almost impossible for the U.S. authorities to track foreign investors."[14]

Money laundering basically involves transforming the monetary proceeds from criminal activity into funds with an apparently legitimate source. The three traditional stages of money laundering are: the initial placement of illegal funds into the banking system; the layering of funds through a series of mechanisms, such as wire transfers, designed to complicate the paper trail;

and finally, the integrating of the laundered funds back into the legitimate economy through the purchase of properties, businesses, and other investments.

FinCEN (the Financial Crimes Enforcement Network) has developed a model of the money-laundering cycle that includes the three phases: placement, layering, and integration.[15] In the placement stage, the currency is converted into some other form, or it is physically moved. The placement of illegal money relies on businesses that deal heavily in cash, as well as traditional and nontraditional financial institutions. The upside of placing illegal money in a bank is that the large amount of cash will no longer attract a great deal of unwanted attention. On the downside, once the cash is in the bank, a paper trail automatically begins that leads in two directions from the initial deposit.[16]

In the second stage of money laundering, the criminal attempts to layer this paper trail so as to make it more difficult for law enforcement to follow. In the Salinas matter, Citibank took the concept of layering to dizzying new heights. It first allowed Salinas's wife to use an alias when depositing cashier's checks into Citibank Mexico. Citibank then wired the dirty money to its New York City office, where the money was dumped into an anonymous "concentration account." From there, the funds were wired into accounts of a shell company in the Cayman Islands, where any documents connecting Salinas to the account would be protected by the islands' strict banking secrecy laws. But just in case someone managed to follow the layering scheme, Citibank took things one step further by having the shell company invest in accounts at Citibank Zurich and London that were managed by a Citibank affiliate in Zurich called "Confidas." These accounts held stocks and bonds.

Finally, in the third stage of money laundering, the criminal attempts to integrate the illegal funds back into the American economy. This stage requires that the criminal figure out a way to spend his ill-gotten gains while somehow making the money seem as if it came from a legitimate source. Integrating illegal funds back into the economy is often achieved by investing in real estate, buying cars, or using other retail outlets.

Placement and layering are used by criminals to break the money trail and keep investigators from being able to follow the illegal cash. Prior to 1970, two of the criminal's most popular methods for breaking the money trail were cash transactions and the use of offshore banks and businesses that didn't have stringent record-keeping or reporting requirements. Criminals would take their illegal cash offshore without informing the U.S. government. They would then deposit the cash in offshore banks where their anonymity would be protected. And of course, in keeping with the placement and layering scenario, they would never report the existence of these offshore accounts to the IRS.

In 1970, Congress passed the Bank Secrecy Act (BSA) to address these two popular methods of money laundering. The BSA requires that certain cash transactions, including deposits, withdrawals, cashier's check purchases, currency exchanges, and any transaction above a certain amount ($10,000) be reported to the Treasury Department and the IRS. The BSA also requires that individuals who are citizens or resident aliens and who maintain an interest in, or hold significant authority over, a foreign bank account report this fact to the IRS on an annual basis. This applies if an account has a balance during the year of over $10,000. The act also mandates that individuals who transport cash or certain monetary instruments into or outside of the United States must file a report with the Customs Service if the amount exceeds $10,000. The purpose of the BSA is to create a paper trail for cash transactions and to have a direct impact on the placement and layering stages of the money-laundering cycle.

While the BSA provided criminal penalties for the improper movement of funds offshore, concealing the placement of the funds in financial institutions, and the unreported holding of a foreign bank account, it did not specifically criminalize money laundering.[17] However, the Money Laundering Control Act of 1986, codified in Title 18 U.S.C. Sections 1956 and 1957, did provide severe criminal penalties for money laundering and also imposed stiff financial penalties for the conduct of financial transactions designed to launder dirty money. (Under the statute, certain crimes identified as Specified Unlawful Activities, or SUAs, and transactions involving the proceeds of SUAs, were deemed to be criminal offenses in and of themselves.) Under 18 U.S.C. 1956(a)(1) or (2), violators are liable for a civil penalty of not more than the greater of the value of the property, funds, or monetary instruments involved in the transaction or $10,000. The criminal penalty under 18 U.S.C. 1956(a)(1) is a fine of up to $500,000 or twice the value of the monetary instruments involved, whichever is greater, or up to twenty years' imprisonment, or both. The punishment for violation of 1956(a)(3) is an undetermined fine, or imprisonment of up to twenty years, or both. Since 1986, Congress has passed additional legislation that has further defined the crime of money laundering.[18]

Congress has also sought to crack down on money laundering by passing the money laundering forfeiture statutes. Title 18 U.S.C. Section 981 set out what can and cannot be forfeited pursuant to civil law, and Title 18 U.S.C. Section 982 covers the same ground under criminal law. Under civil forfeiture statutes, the government may seize property based upon probable cause that it was allegedly purchased with illegal funds. Under criminal law, the government may also seize property owned by the defendant that facilitated the crime, as well as all property that constitutes the proceeds of the crime. Under the civil section of the forfeiture statutes, all property involved in a money laundering offense and/or violations of the Bank Secrecy Act involving reporting requirements would be forfeitable.[19] This could include both real and personal property. Moreover, the legal procedures are such that the government is allowed to seize your assets before proving you guilty of any crime.

The forfeiture statutes mean the government has the power to confiscate your real and personal property, based on that property's alleged use or involvement in criminal activities. Civil asset forfeiture is a risk for anyone who becomes involved in criminal activities. Before you make any investments with illegally obtained funds or ignore government reporting laws, remember that under the current forfeiture laws, the government has the power to seize your business, home, bank account, and personal property, all without prior indictment, hearing, or trial.

THE RULES TO FOLLOW WHEN GOING OFFSHORE

As I've discussed, the use of offshore havens can be a perfectly legal proposition, provided the investor (and/or investment institution) files the appropriate reports with the government. If a bank, savings and loan, and/or credit union receives from a customer more than $10,000 in currency on any given day, that institution is required to file an IRS Form 4789a Currency Transaction Report (CTR). This must be done within fifteen days of the transaction. This particular rule affects the institution and not the customer, as it is the financial institution that is held responsible if the form isn't properly prepared and submitted. But, as the customer, you should still be aware that all of your currency transactions involving $10,000 or over will be submitted to the IRS. You should also be aware that at least twelve million CTRs are filed each year, making it difficult, but not impossible, for the IRS to track each and every one of them.

Of course, there is no denying that while offshore havens provide a wide variety of perfectly legal services, they can, and do, also provide the U.S. citizen with an avenue to either cheat on his taxes and/or to launder ill-gotten gains.

Many people attempt to get around the CTR problem by always depositing less than $10,000 in the bank on any given business day. They make their deposits at several different banks and always keep the amount below $10,000 to avoid having their bank inform the IRS.

While this may be a clever way to get around having your bank file a CTR, it's also a crime called "structuring" under the Banking Secrecy Act. (Structuring was inserted into the BSA in 1977; the definitions were promulgated by the Money Laundering Control Act of 1986.) The statute specifically prohibits structuring, which occurs when a person or an entity attempts to make multiple deposits at one or more institutions for under $10,000 for the specific purpose of evading the reporting requirements under Section 103.11 of the BSA. Under Section 103.11, structuring includes ". . . the breaking down of a single sum of currency exceeding $10,000 into smaller sums, including sums at or below $10,000. The transaction or transactions need not exceed the $10,000 reporting threshold at any single financial institution on any single day in order to constitute structuring within the meaning of this definition."

Since April 1996, a reporting requirement has been imposed on all financial institutions: the Suspicious Activity Report (SAR). When it appears that a transaction has no apparent business or lawful purpose or is not the sort in which the particular customer would normally be expected to engage, and the bank knows of no reasonable explanation for the transaction after examining the available facts, including the background and possible purpose of the transaction, the bank is required to report said transaction.[20] (Casinos and investment firms have similar reporting requirements.)

In order to make sure the CTRs are completed on time and that all suspicious activities are reported to the government, many banks have hired compliance officers who, in effect, police their own customers. The compliance officer has become necessary in the last fifteen years because of increasing criticism that the banking industry is now a willing participant in flagrant money-laundering schemes. Richard Schreiber, a regional compliance officer for Republic Bank of New York, oversees Republic's south Florida banking activities by making sure that the bank complies with all federal banking regulations.

Schreiber states that because of the increased use of financial institutions for money laundering and other illegal activities, compliance officers need to be more watchful than ever. "You have to be careful because the bank's reputation is at risk. Once any company gets a public black eye, it's hard to erase."[21]

Republic, like many banks, has both an international and a private unit that deal with affluent clientele who want to safeguard their wealth. Sometimes these customers come from unstable political climates and are truly looking for a safe investment opportunity. Sometimes, however, Republic deals with capital flight situations, in which it must be cautious about people and institutions that it does business with.

"When a new customer opens up an account, we ask for valid identification," Schreiber explains. "This usually includes some type of letter of reference from an existing customer or another office of Republic, or, at the very least, from someone who is well known to our bank. We make sure that to the best of our knowledge, the information provided does have some veracity. We then get a qualitative and quantitative idea about what kinds of transactions the new customer wants to engage in—what to expect from that person."[22]

Schreiber also notes that even after the customer has been accepted, the bank monitors that customer's transactions to see what types of account activity are being conducted and how often. For example, if the customer claims to be a textile maker and then begins conducting transactions that seem inconsistent with his stated business, the bank will usually take a closer look. "If the transactions turn out to be different from what the customer originally told us," notes Schreiber, "we have to act. We get more involved when they [the customers] do something that is materially different from what we expected."[23]

Commenting on the Salinas case, for instance, Schreiber explains that it appears as if the amount of money coming into Citibank could not be justified by Salinas's declared business interests. (According to the Citibank New York's Mexican division, the bank believed that all of Mr. Salinas's funds had been obtained legally, with a large portion resulting from the sale of a construction company that he owned.[24])

"There is no way that activity like that, or such a huge volume of money, could have escaped detection," argues Schreiber. "Salinas filtered as much as $100 million through personal investment companies. The money flowed from Mexico to New York and then on to Citicorp affiliates in Switzerland. Most every bank has reports for this kind of activity."[25]

If you legitimately deposit money in a U.S. financial institution, you have nothing to fear from the compliance officer. He is looking to report people who violate tax laws or currency laws. But if you are engaged in illegally hiding assets, it is the compliance officer's duty to report your "suspicious activity" to the government. Most of the time, the government follows through.

> By placing your assets offshore, you can construct a series of obstacles that make it difficult and extremely expensive for your creditors to seize your assets. Not only must your creditors fight their way through the strict banking secrecy laws of many offshore havens, but they must then make their way through the maze of offshore banks, trust companies, and management firms that specialize in helping you protect your assets.

If you want to send money to an offshore haven other than by bank wire, you will have to fill out a form to make everything legal. It's called a Currency and Monetary Instruments Form (CMIR). Title 31 CFR 103.23 requires that each person (or organization) who physically transports, mails, or ships currency or any other monetary instruments in an aggregate amount of over $10,000 at one time from the United States to any place outside of the United States, or into the United States from any place outside the United States, must file a CMIR with the Customs Service. Monetary instruments commonly include traveler's checks, money orders, or bearer bonds.[26] CMIR forms are kept by Customs and can be obtained by contacting your local Customs office.

Clearly, the CMIR form can put a damper on anyone who tries to take more than $10,000 in currency or monetary instruments out of the country. Therefore, if you intend to do so, I recommend consulting with an attorney and/or accountant regarding your obligation to file a CMIR.

If you follow the previously referenced reporting requirements, you can legitimately use offshore havens to protect your assets from potential claimants. By placing your assets offshore, you can construct a series of obstacles that make it difficult and extremely expensive for your creditors to seize your assets. Not only must your creditors fight their way through the strict banking secrecy laws of many offshore havens, but they must then make their way through the maze of offshore banks, trust companies, and management firms that specialize in helping you protect your assets. Moreover, if you are a party to a hostile divorce or partnership dissolution, you can legally open an offshore account using tax-neutral money with a second passport in a second name (an "also known as") so long as it's not for fraudulent intent.[27]

But before you go transferring all of your assets offshore, you need to do some investigation. For instance, the Uniform Fraudulent Conveyances Act and the Uniform Fraudulent Transfers Act can void U.S. property transfers that are intentionally designed to hinder, delay, or defraud creditors. In other words, if you know you're being sued and suddenly transfer your assets into your wife's name, U.S. law can be used to void that transfer. So, if you transfer your assets to a trust at an offshore center, you need to be sure that the local laws do not recognize the Uniform Fraudulent Conveyances Act and the Uniform Fraudulent Transfers Act.[28]

WHEN CAN I LEGALLY USE WIRE TRANSFERS TO HIDE MY MONEY?

Using wire transfers to move money from one account to the next is extremely convenient and efficient, and it can also be perfectly legal. But like offshore investment, the transmission of funds by wire has traditionally been a tactic often employed by money launderers. As such, it is often viewed suspiciously by law enforcement.

Congress has attempted to regulate the use of wire transmitting agencies via Title 18 U.S.C. Section 1960(a), which states in pertinent part that "Whoever conducts, controls, manages, supervises, directs, or owns all or part of a business, knowing the business is an illegal money transmitting business, shall be fined in accordance with this title or imprisoned not more than five years, or both."

The statute connects to the Bank Secrecy Act, which also requires that businesses engaged in the transmission of funds be registered with the Secretary of the Treasury and subject to regulatory control by the states or the IRS.[29]

All wire communication businesses are also required to abide by Title 26 and Title 31 cash reporting requirements and regulations pertaining to record keeping and the identification of their customers.[30] Moreover, you should be aware that in May 1997, the Clinton administration announced that all street-corner check-cashing services, as well as large money-transmittal services such as Western Union and American Express, are required to file reports with the Treasury Department for all wire transfers of more than $750. So, if you're wiring more than $750 and less than $10,000, you should use a full-service bank. (Remember, however, that if you wire $10,000 or more, a full-service bank will have to report that transaction.)

Clearly, the regulations governing wire transfers were meant to deter money launderers from being able to "clean" their dirty funds through repeated wire transfers. If you are a bank customer seeking to use wire transfers for legitimate business purposes, it is unlikely that your transactions will be noticed by either the federal government or your bank's compliance officer.

Bank compliance officer Richard Schreiber notes that if a bank customer ". . . transfers money by wire constantly, it won't stand out. That's because your pattern of activity is consistent with what we've seen over time and probably with what you told us to expect. We look out for the unusual."[31]

Therefore, if you plan on using wire transfers to hide your money, you should also plan on being consistent.

REFERENCES

1. Kristof, Kathy, "Suspect Your Ex-Spouse of Hiding Assets? Now You Can Sue," *LA Times,* September 26, 1999.
2. December 15, 1998, interview with Peter Djinis, associate director for Financial Crimes Enforcement Network— Division of the Treasury Department.
3. December 15, 1998, interview with Peter Djinis.
4. Ibid.
5. After an extensive investigation of the Salinas matter, the report was issued on December 4, 1998, by Congress's investigative arm, the General Accounting Office ("GAO").
6. General Accounting Office Report, December 4, 1998.
7. Ibid.
8. Ibid.
9. Dwyer, Paula, and Steven Solomon, "Finance Investigations: The Citi That Slept?" *Business Week,* vol. 3602 (November 2, 1998).
10. Gwynne, S. C., and Adam Zagorin, "Business: Just Hide Me the Money, a Government Report Criticizes Citibank's Services to Accused Mexican Murderer Raul Salinas— And Illuminates a Quiet Global Boom in 'Private Banking,'" *Time* (December 14, 1998).
11. At the time of this printing, no charges had been filed against Citibank for its role in the Salinas money laundering scheme.
12. United States General Accounting Office Report, December 4, 1998.
13. Gwynne, S. C., and Adam Zagorin, "Business: Just Hide Me the Money, a Government Report Criticizes Citibank's Services to Accused Mexican Murderer Raul Salinas— And Illuminates a Quiet Global Boom in 'Private Banking,' *Time* (December 14, 1998).
14. Beatty, Jonathan, and Richard Hornik, "A Torrent of Dirty Dollars—Money Laundering Is a Runaway Global Industry That Serves Customers Ranging from Cocaine Cartels to Tax-Dodging Corporations," *Time* (December 18, 1989).

15. Madinger, John, and Sydney A. Zalopany, *Money Launder-ing: A Guide for Criminal Investigators,* Boca Raton, FL: CRC Press, 1999, pp. 16–17.
16. Ibid., p. 15.
17. Madinger, John, and Sydney A. Zalopany, *Money Launder-ing: A Guide for Criminal Investigators,* pp. 16–27.
18. Anti-Drug Abuse Act of 1988, Annunzio-Wylie Anti-Money Laundering Act of 1992, Money Laundering Suppression Act of 1994, and the Terrorism Prevention Act of 1996. For more information about anti-money laundering legisla-tion, see also Madinger, John, and Sydney A. Zalopany, *Money Laundering: A Guide for Criminal Investigators,* p. 43.
19. Madinger, John, and Sydney A. Zalopany, *Money Launder-ing: A Guide for Criminal Investigators,* p. 62.
20. The New Suspicious Activity Report, effective April 1, 1996.
21. July 19, 1999, interview with Richard Schreiber.
22. Ibid.
23. Ibid.
24. General Accounting Office Report, December 4, 1998, p. 8.
25. July 19, 1999, interview with Richard Schreiber.
26. For more information on what constitutes currency or other monetary instrument, see chapter 4, "The Under-cover Tourist: Cash and the Careful Traveler."
27. Cornez, Arnold, *The Offshore Money Book,* Chicago: Con-temporary Books, 1998, p. 130.
28. Schneider, Jerome, *The Complete Guide to Offshore Money Havens,* Roseville, CA: Prima Publishing, 2000, p. 152.
29. Madinger, John, and Sydney A. Zalopany, *Money Launder-ing: A Guide for Criminal Investigators,* p. 91.
30. Ibid.
31. July 19, 1999, interview with Richard Schreiber.

CHAPTER 3

MEN BEHAVING BADLY

For almost ten years, I acted as a financial consultant to Eileen and Robert Fulworth. Although Robert was an attorney with a sophisticated practice, Eileen handled most of the family's investments. They'd only been married about three years when she first sought my advice regarding offshore investment opportunities. The investments did well and so, the following year, she booked another consultation with me and we again managed to make several profitable investments. After a few years of doing business together, we became friends and our conversations tended to encompass both personal and professional subjects.

I believed that Robert and Eileen were a happily married couple, coping with the usual stresses of modern living. In fact, it wasn't until I received a call from Eileen one cold December evening that I realized that my impressions of life in the Fulworth home were far from accurate.

> I've found there are usually only two reasons why someone having an affair would leave such an obvious trail of evidence: Either he wants his wife to find out about the affair, or he's just plain stupid. Actually, there is really a third and more plausible explanation: The person cheating tried to be discreet and failed miserably.

As soon as I heard Eileen's voice, I knew there was a problem. Her manner was cool and detached, almost as if she were in shock. Robert had gone to Phoenix to take a deposition, Eileen told me. Last night, after putting the kids to bed and while waiting for Robert to call, she'd sat down to pay the bills.

"I'd just entered the amount of the gas bill in the check register," she explained. "That's when I noticed that the previous entry in the register had been made out to a J. Mercer in the amount of $200. I realized that I didn't know anyone named J. Mercer. I kept thinking and thinking, and then I decided that maybe J. Mercer wasn't a person, it was a business. I started looking through the check register to see if I could find out anything else about this J. Mercer. That's when I noticed something kind of strange. Last month Robert made out another check to J. Mercer for the same amount. And the month before that, there's another entry for $200 made out to guess who?"

"J. Mercer?" I asked, already knowing the answer to my question and, frankly, dreading what would come next.

"Right. Three checks to some business or some person that I can't place for the life of me." Eileen paused. "Something is off here, don't you think?"

"It's worth looking into."

"So, what would you suggest? How do I find out who this J. Mercer is?"

"Call information and ask for J. Mercer. And then, give J. Mercer a call."

"Good idea. Thanks for the advice. I'm sure it's nothing, but I'd just like to know."

With that, she hung up. Twenty minutes later the phone rang again.

"Jerome, it's Eileen," her voice broke. "Robert's having an affair."

"I gather you've spoken with J. Mercer."

"Yes, and she's definitely having an affair with Robert."

I could hear the anguish in Eileen's voice. "Did she just come out and admit it?"

"Almost." She took a deep breath, struggling to maintain her composure. "At first, she just kept saying that she didn't know me and she didn't know him. For a few minutes there, she actually had me convinced that I'd called the wrong J. Mercer. But then, when I was just about to hang up, she told me that maybe Robert can sort this all out when he comes back from his business trip. But the thing is, I never told her my husband was away. Robert must have told her himself."

"I don't know what to say. I'm just so sorry."

"The worst part of this is that it's all such a horrible cliché. I didn't suspect a thing. If I hadn't seen that stupid entry in the check register, I never would have found out. Well, I can tell you this much," Eileen vowed. "I'm going to make him pay for humiliating me this way. By the time I get through with him, he isn't going to have enough money left to take J. Mercer out for a pizza."

"I understand how upset you are," I said forcefully, "but you've got to pull yourself together. The important thing is for you to be smart and not angry."

I hesitated, realizing that the time had come for me to take sides. Both Robert and Eileen were my clients, but my heart went out to Eileen, a good wife, a mother, and the more vulnerable of the two.

"Eileen, listen to me carefully," I said. "Think of your children. You've got important decisions to make and you need to have a clear head to decide what you're going to do next."

WAYS TO SECRETLY FUND YOUR BAD BEHAVIOR

When Robert Fulworth finally called home that cold December night, Eileen didn't answer the phone. As per my advice, she was too busy making copies of the credit card statements and check registers to pick up. By the time Robert stepped off the plane from Phoenix, all his bank accounts were empty, the locks on his home were changed, and the phone number to his house was unlisted. With just three small entries in a check register, Robert had changed the landscape of his life forever.

Even though I ended up advising Eileen in this situation, I am not here to discuss whether Robert should have cheated on his wife. I'll leave moral judgments to others.

I am here, however, to comment on the techniques Robert used. I am here to inquire into why he felt the need to write checks to his mistress and then enter her name in the family check register. And why, during his four-month "courtship" of the apparently irresistible J. Mercer, he used his joint credit card to buy jewelry, rent hotel rooms, and finance a romantic trip to Maui.

Finally, I have to wonder what he was thinking when he took out a lease in his own name on a two-bedroom, ocean-view apartment in Santa Monica. Why didn't he use another name?

I've found there are usually only two reasons why someone having an affair would leave such an obvious trail of evidence: Either he wants his wife to find out about the affair, or he's just plain stupid. Actually, there is really a third and more plausible explanation: The person cheating tried to be discreet and failed miserably.

Robert Fulworth clearly falls into the third and most common category. He never wanted Eileen to find out about the affair; he just didn't know what steps to take to prevent detection. Although at first glance it appears as if Robert did everything but draw his wife a map to J. Mercer's house, the fact is that Robert did try to conceal his affair. He wrote off his lunches with Mercer as business expenses. He made sure they were never seen in public together, and initially, at least, he paid for the Best Western motel room in cash. It wasn't until they moved their trysts to the Beverly Hills Hotel that he got sloppy and used a credit card.

And don't think Robert was unusual in his carelessness. Like most men, Robert tried to conceal his affair from his wife. It's just that, like most men, he failed.

Robert Fulworth, law school graduate and partner in one of L.A.'s biggest law firms, left behind a paper trail that a two-year-old could have followed. And the sad thing is that Robert's sloppy behavior is the rule, rather than the exception, when it comes to men stepping out on their wives.

Men want to be able to have a discreet affair and then return to their wives. Yet they're usually their own worst enemies. They buy their girlfriends presents and leave the receipts on their nightstands. They rent their girlfriends condos and pay for them with checks or sign their own names on the lease. Some (like our friend Robert) actually enter their girlfriends' names in their checkbooks.

The reality is that men don't just behave badly, they behave stupidly. Their libido, instead of their brains, operates their pocketbook and credit cards.

While I'm not in a position to stop anyone from cheating on his wife, I am in a position to help that person

> **Robert Fulworth, law school graduate and partner in one of L.A.'s biggest law firms, left behind a paper trail that a two-year-old could have followed. And the sad thing is that Robert's sloppy behavior is the rule, rather than the exception, when it comes to men stepping out on their wives.**

avoid being caught. I am firmly committed to the principle that with careful planning and thought, a clever man can engage in a wide variety of *bad behavior* without his wife ever knowing. I wrote this chapter for just such a man.

GIFTS FOR YOUR SWEETIE

If you're a man who's thinking about stepping out on his wife, you need to know one thing up front—it's going to cost you. This is particularly true if you plan on behaving badly with someone who is considerably younger than you.

Although the occasional young woman is attracted to an older man because he reminds her of her father, this is the exception, not the rule. Even if you look better than you have in years, it usually takes some serious spending to turn a young lady's head. Remember, green looks good on everybody. For starters, be prepared to accumulate lots of cash, particularly $100 bills.

If you're considering having an affair, you need to also consider how you will afford this bad behavior.

While at first you'll probably just be required to pick up an occasional dinner or a flower bouquet, things will most likely change with the passage of time. Before long, the situation will invariably call for more meaningful gifts, like jewelry, perfume, a car, or, in some cases, an apartment. Before you know it, you'll be facing the age-old dilemma of how to give your girlfriend a few meaningful gifts without your wife finding out.

The best approach to total anonymity when making payments is to establish a bank account in a pseudonym. Many states and counties have a procedure entitled registration of a legal alias or a fictitious business name statement. Both are legal methods of filing a notice with the appropriate public authority, letting the world know that you are operating under a different name. For example, John Paul Jones could have a pseudonym calling him Jack Jones, which is his legal alias. Many men use their middle name as their first name, so in this case, it could be Paul Jones.

In addition to the pseudonym, the account should be set up out-of-state and make certain that the account does not pay interest, and as such, you will not be required to provide your social security number. Often you may be able to obtain a secured credit card and/or an ATM card in the pseudonym.

The fictitious business name concept entitles the registrant to use a business name for the account. For example, John Paul Jones could set up the business as Lucky Construction. Lucky Construction, therefore, is a fictitious business name for John Paul Jones. Once filed with the county clerk, you will receive a certificate that you can take to a bank and open up a non-interest bearing checking account. Therefore, when Lucky Construction needs to make a payment to your sweetie, there should be no problem.

It is not impossible to keep relationships incognito for long periods of time. Take the story of famed newsman Charles Kuralt:

For 29 years, Charles kept a secret mistress and maintained a separate family, and he provided for them as a father and a husband.

While his legal wife resided in New York, his mistress, Patricia Elizabeth Shannon, lived in Montana. Patricia was a divorced 34-year-old mother of three when they met in 1968. He was covering her efforts to have a park built in a black community. He asked her to dinner and showed up with roses. They spent the evening talking in the hotel lounge.

Charles was able to visit her for two or three days every few weeks. He was able to attend her family functions, her children's graduations, and holidays. He would often send her gifts and money.

It is estimated that she received $600,000 in the first ten years of their relationship. Charles financed homes for her family in San Francisco, spent $400,000 to help her start a small business, and paid for her to go to school in London. He sent her son to college, paid for her daughter to attend law school, and bought her a cottage in Ireland during the course of their relationship. He also purchased 20 acres of land in Montana. On this land he built a cabin, and Patricia moved into it. He orchestrated a mock sale of 20 twenty acres to her three months before he died and then sent her $80,000 to buy the property.

Kuralt also purchased an additional 90 acres, which abutted the original 20 acres, and moved an old schoolhouse onto the land, which he converted at a cost of $180,000. In September of 1999, after Kurault's death, Patricia sued his estate, seeking the 90 acres and the schoolhouse, valued at around $600,000.

Patricia's claim was based upon a letter Kuralt had written her two weeks before his death. In the letter,

Kuralt wrote, "I'll have the lawyer visit the hospital to make sure you inherit the rest of the place in Montana, if it comes to that."[1]

In March 2000, a judge awarded Kuralt's Montana fishing retreat to Patricia. The judge agreed with her that Kuralt's "last minute" letter was a valid will giving her the 90 acres along the Big Hole River.

Most of Kurault's spending involved cash. This seems to be the best way to finance an affair. But the man who wants to take some cash out of his business without being caught still needs to be clever about it.

For example, let's take the case of a client of mine, Peter Miller, a restaurant and bar owner. Peter, who has been married around six years, recently got involved with Jenny, a waitress who worked at his restaurant. At first, Peter and Jenny met at a Motel 6 for their afternoon trysts. After a few weeks, Jenny suggested that they move the party to the Four Seasons. Peter agreed to the change of location without a second thought. It wasn't until later that day that he realized he had a problem: How would he pay for the expensive room without his wife finding out? He knew he couldn't use a credit card because his wife would spot the extra $400 hotel charge in a minute. And taking cash out of the joint account on a tri-weekly basis would also generate suspicion. So, he came up with another plan. He would take the cash from some of the restaurant's unrecorded sales (mostly bar charges paid in cash), use the extra cash to buy merchandise for the restaurant, and pocket the difference for his extracurricular activities.[2]

If Peter's plan sounds too difficult for you, don't worry. There are less complicated ways to let your business work for you. Let's say you're a contractor, and you're hired by Mr. Rice to build him a second bathroom. After you finish the job, you tell Mr. Rice to make out a check directly to you for $20,000. You then cash the check and give your girlfriend $10,000 and tell her to buy, say, a car. She has the dealer put the car in her name and it's as if the $10,000 never existed. You put the remaining $10,000 in the business account and no one is the wiser. One experienced forensic accountant tells the tale of a businessman who on his frequent business trips to Vegas fell in love with a hooker. When the wife learned of the affair, she commenced divorce proceedings. She then hired a forensic accountant to go over her husband's corporate ledger. The forensic accountant recalls that while he was looking at the businessman's corporate ledger, he noticed that the man's lunches were routinely around $55 and that his airfare to Vegas was usually around $300; then he spotted a check for $5,000. After further investigation, the accountant discovered that the romantic businessman was buying the prostitute nicer jewelry than he bought his wife.

The lesson here is, if you're going to give your mistress money from your business, remember to make the payments look consistent with the rest of your business expenses. Don't make the same mistake as our Las Vegas lover who never spent $5,000 on anything and then one day decided to use the corporate account to buy the hooker a diamond necklace.

If you're truly concerned that certain entries on your corporate ledger might look suspicious to the trained eye, you might want to consider putting your mistress on the business payroll. That way, you can make her an employee and give her a "check" every week to cover her expenses. You could even make up the name of an "employee" and write out checks to that person every week. This gives you the extra cash you need without forcing you to put your mistress's name on any business document where it could easily be discovered.

If you're going through a particularly messy divorce, you can also use your girlfriend to "safeguard" some of your assets. After Mark Thompson's divorce, he had difficulty making his alimony payments and the payments on

> **If you're a man who runs a cash-based business, congratulations. You're probably in a better position than most to buy your girlfriend things without tipping your wife off to the affair.**

his house. So, he told the court that he had severe financial problems and could no longer afford his home. He then quitclaimed it to his girlfriend, Cassandra. Months later, the court reduced the amount of his alimony payments in light of his recent financial setbacks. Two years later, Mark had Cassandra quitclaim the house back to him. Fortunately for him, they were still together.

A HOME FOR YOUR SWEETIE

Want to put a roof over your girlfriend's head? It's simple to do when you know how.

You go to the landlord of a beautiful beach-front apartment building and tell him that you'd like to rent a lovely one-bedroom. You're the president of Smith Enterprises, a company that manufactures a variety of office supplies. The landlord draws up the lease and you sign it, "Bob Smith, President of Smith Enterprises." The landlord doesn't request your wife's signature because you're renting the apartment in the name of your business. You make out a check to the landlord for the first and last month's rent from your corporate account and sign the check "Bob Smith, President and Treasurer of Smith Enterprises." And you've got yourself an apartment that your wife will never know about. However, if you end up getting a divorce, chances are that a skilled forensic accountant will quickly identify your scheme. Therefore, you might want to consider renting the property under a fictitious name.

You could also use your corporate account to get extra cash to buy presents for your mistress or even establish a separate bank account without your wife's knowledge. Take the case of Mr. X. In order to get extra cash out of his business without anyone knowing, Mr. X routinely withdrew $300 from his corporate account. He had his secretary enter the $300 ATM charges into the corporate ledger as checks and classify the charges as meals. By the end of the year, Mr. X had managed to withdraw over $40,000 from the corporate account by classifying the ATM charges as meals. The forensic accountant became suspicious of the "meal" charges because he thought them excessive for a man who rarely traveled.

Finally, if you operate a cash business and are inclined to skim money from your business (which is illegal and could result in tax fraud charges), you can use the "extra" cash to finance your extramarital affair. You can also use this cash to play the stock market or to gamble without your wife knowing about your activities.

BRINGING TRUST INTO THE EQUATION

If you want to purchase a condo for your mistress in Beverly Hills without using your own name, you should consider setting up a trust. A trust is an entity created for the purpose of protecting and conserving assets for the benefit of a third party, the beneficiary. In this instance, you can set up a trust in some name other than your own, and then you have the trust purchase the property.

As leading forensic accountant Donald Gursey explains, "It's tough to find hidden money when it's stored in a trust. If you set up a trust and have the trust buy some property, you wouldn't even be on the title. The trust could then hold title to the property. So, if you set up a trust and had the trust give something to somebody, like a condo in Beverly Hills, it would be difficult to trace. The thing is that anybody can set up a trust and transfer property into it, irrespective of the gift rules. It would be the Mr. X trust set up for the benefit of some beneficiary who is unrelated to the person setting up the trust."[3]

Moreover, if you set up a trust that is non–income producing, it will not show up on your tax return. And even if the trust is income producing, you can set up the trust so that it—not you—pays the taxes.

You could also set up the trust in one name and have your mistress be the "beneficiary." In that scenario, your mistress receives weekly or monthly payments from the trust and nobody is the wiser. Some men who were behaving badly chose to have their accountant or lawyer be a party to the trust. The trust was set up with the accountant as trustee and the mistress was designated as the trust's beneficiary. The accountant then just sent the money to the mistress on a regular basis, or she was able to withdraw money herself from the trust.

Summing up, the advantages to using a trust to buy property or support a mistress are:

1. There will be no record of your name on anything.
2. If your trust is a non–income producing trust, there will be no record of it with the IRS.
3. If your wife (or anybody else, for that matter) does find out about the trust, it will be difficult to get any information about it.

Judges are reluctant to order a trustee to divulge information about a trust because of privacy matters. This is especially true when an attorney is a party to the trust. The courts are always reluctant to order any breach of the attorney-client confidentiality agreement.

USING YOUR HOME FOR FUN AND PLEASURE

While a business offers the man behaving badly a variety of ways to get money, taking "tax-free" dollars from one's business can be extremely risky. In essence, you trade your wife's wrath for the wrath of the government. In other words, the man behaving badly who needs some cash to finance his bad habits can be forced to choose between the dog house and the big house.

There are ways to finance your bad habits without risking a hefty jail sentence for tax fraud. If you own your own home, you might want to consider refinancing. When you refinance, you might be able to pull some money out of the house and put it in a separate bank accountant for your own private use. (For example, if a home with a $100,000 mortgage increased in value so that the mortgage could be refinanced for $125,000, the spouse who refinanced would get $25,000 as a result of the refinancing.)[4] In many marriages, the man is in charge of paying the bills and making the financial investments, so a simple refinancing on the house to ostensibly obtain a better interest rate will probably not raise any suspicions. But if

While a business offers the man behaving badly a variety of ways to get money, taking "tax-free" dollars from one's business can be extremely risky. In essence, you trade your wife's wrath for the wrath of the government. In other words, the man behaving badly who needs some cash to finance his bad habits can be forced to choose between the doghouse and the big house.

you decide to take this route, be advised that in the event of a divorce, you will be required to return any and all money taken from the community. That would specifically include money taken by you during the refinancing of the community home.

WHEN THREE'S NOT A CROWD

Surprisingly enough, there is a way to use your joint checking account to pay for your secret apartment. Donald Gursey, renowned Los Angeles forensic accountant, recalls one divorce case in which he was asked by the court to go through the husband's canceled checks to help the court determine the amount of temporary support. After reviewing some of the husband's canceled checks, Gursey realized that several checks were missing. The missing checks were provided by the husband only after repeated requests from Gursey. However, the husband only provided the face of the checks. Gursey, sensing that something was amiss, demanded that copies of the backs of the checks also be turned over to him.

After an order from the court, the husband finally turned over the copies of the backs of the requested checks. It only took a moment for Gursey to realize why the husband had been so adamant in his refusal to relinquish the checks. The checks, which were made out to the husband on their face, had been endorsed by a real estate company on the back. The husband had been paying for a swanky, two-bedroom, beach-front apartment by writing checks out to himself and then endorsing them over to a real estate company. It turned out that this husband had leased the apartment months ago for his girlfriend. When he separated from his wife, he'd told her that he was living at a nearby hotel, but in fact he was living at the apartment with his girlfriend.[5]

Having checks made out to yourself endorsed by a third party is particularly effective in today's no-paper society. Most banks don't provide checking account holders with the actual copies of their checks and they generally only keep copies of the original checks for five to seven years.

GAMBLING AND OTHER BAD HABITS: YOU'VE GOT TO KNOW WHERE TO HIDE

Most men have at least one bad habit that they'd prefer their wife not know about. For some, it's gambling.

Now, any good gambler knows that you never let anyone know how much you've won or how much you've lost. But keeping gambling losses and wins a secret from your wife requires almost as much planning as keeping a mistress. You've got to have a plan for taking your money to Vegas without your wife knowing about it. And then, you've got to have a secret place to put your winnings, if you're lucky enough to have any.

The biggest problem you face when gambling is how to get money out of your account without your wife knowing. So, you decide that you need to open up a separate bank account from which you can withdraw money. You start your plan rolling by withdrawing money from your joint checking account in small sums. You write out checks to cash and then, after cashing the checks at your bank, you store the money in your office safe. After several months, you've managed to take out around $4,000 in cash from your joint account.

Next, you decide to open up a separate bank account. You want to use the account for the money you've siphoned from the joint account and you also want to have a place to store your Vegas winnings. (You could also use funds from this account to finance other bad behavior that you would prefer your wife not discover.)

If you plan on opening up a separate and secret bank account, make sure that you open the account in a city far from where you live. For example, if you live in L.A., consider opening up your bank account in Ventura County. It's close enough for you to travel there by car, but far enough away to make it difficult for anyone to locate.

More important, the account will be registered in a separate database from those accounts located in Los Angeles County. Therefore, if someone decides to try and find any and all of your separate bank accounts, they will have to search for them county by county.[6] If all your community accounts are located at a Los Angeles branch of Bank of America, you might want to consider opening up a non–interest bearing checking account at a Wells Fargo Bank in Ventura County. (If it's non–interest bearing, you won't have to pay any taxes on it.) You can open the new account using the $4,000 in cash you've taken from your joint checking account. Also, make sure that statements from your separate bank account are sent either to a post office box or to your office address. Do not give the bank your home address.

The separate bank account protects you in a number of ways. If you and your wife separate, she'll never know about this account. And even if your wife does suspect that you've opened an account secretly, she'll have a great deal of difficulty finding it in Ventura County. Since you live in L.A., her attorney will probably only think to search the databases in Los Angeles County for the account. With your money safely ensconced in your Ventura County account, you're ready to finance your bad behavior. You can hop a plane for Vegas and no one will be the wiser!

If you truly want to make it difficult for anyone to locate your separate bank account, you might want to consider opening an account at a cyberbank on the

Internet. In recent years, cyberbanks have sprung up all over the Net. Net.B@nk, Inc. (Nasdaq.NTBK) is the first profitable Internet-only bank in the country, having achieved profitability for the past four successive quarters as of this writing. With more than 29,000 accounts and customers in all fifty states and twenty foreign countries, Net. B@nk, Member FDIC (http://www.net-bank.com), is the largest FDIC-insured bank operating solely on the Internet. In addition to checking and money market accounts and certificates of deposits, Net.B@nk offers its customers the ultimate convenience in banking.[7]

Cyberbanks are being regulated like normal banks, although they are often harder to monitor because it's difficult to know where their central processing center is located. The cyberbank allows you to open an account without ever having a face-to-face meeting with anyone. The cyberbank also allows you to open an account in Dallas, even though you happen to live in Florida. If your wife decides to hire someone to try and find the account, it will be extremely difficult as the actual account will be located in a different state. In addition, you can easily transfer money from one account to another merely by plugging in your laptop.

You've Got to Know Exactly How to Spend

In order to catch a flight to and from Las Vegas, you will need to charge that flight without your wife knowing about it. Using your credit card to finance your extracurricular activities is tantamount to giving your wife a road map to follow your every move. She'll be able to know where you've been, whom you've telephoned, where you've shopped, and what you've bought. If you want to be really discreet, you might want to consider charging your expenses offshore.[8] When you decide to obtain your offshore credit card, you'll want to make sure that the offshore issuing bank is in a jurisdiction that has strong banking privacy laws.[9]

As Arnold Cornez, J.D., points out in *The Offshore Money Book,* most offshore credit cards are in reality secured credit cards. "Your credit card is generally between 50 percent and 66.66 percent of the amount on deposit in an interest-bearing savings account with the offshore bank."[10] Cornez also advises that if you're going to get an offshore credit card, you want to make sure that the offshore bank you choose does not have a branch office in the States, in the event that your wife attempts to subpoena your credit card records.

I would also recommend that you make sure that the credit card statements are either mailed to a secure post office box in the States (Mail Boxes, Etc.) or to your office. If you decide to have the statements mailed to your office, you should make sure that none of your employees have access to the statements. This will help you avoid getting into a situation in which you can be blackmailed by a disgruntled employee who is seeking to either keep his job or get an undeserved raise. Once you receive your new credit card, you're free to use the card just as you'd use a

Using your credit card to finance your extracurricular activities is tantamount to giving your wife a road map to follow your every move. She'll be able to know where you've been, whom you've telephoned, where you've shopped, and what you've bought. If you want to be really discreet, you might want to consider charging your expenses offshore.

debit card, only the money won't come from anywhere your spouse knows about. The offshore credit card will allow you make purchases freely without having to explain them to anyone. (See also chapter 7: Victoria's Secrets.)

If you really want to buy some presents for your honey, but you don't want to invest $5,000 in an offshore credit card, you might consider a cheaper alternative— the Macy's gift card. All you need to get a Macy's gift card is $1,000 and a pulse. Once you hand over your $1,000 (no identification required), your Macy's card acts as a debit card. You can take the card out in your mistress's name and then she's free to use the card at any Macy's store. No record of her purchases will be sent to you. But be advised that once you've purchased a Macy's gift card, you will not be able to return the card for a cash refund.

HIDING FOR THE PROFESSIONAL

If you are an attorney, doctor, or accountant, you generally have a greater ability than the average guy to behave badly and not get caught. You can "raise" money for your extracurricular activities relatively easily.

For example, if you're an attorney and you need a little extra cash to spend in Vegas, you can have your client write out a check to you without putting the "Inc." after your name. You can then go to the bank and cash the "personal check" without anyone being the wiser. If you don't keep a separate accounts-receivable master control, you can just give your client a receipt and not enter the transaction into the accounting system. If you're a plastic surgeon, it's also possible for you to arrange with your patient not to bill the insurance company. Your patient pays you in cash following the operation. You then cover your expenses and pocket whatever cash is left. Finally, the attorney with the separate client trust account is probably in the best position to hide money from his wife. The attorney can put his own money into the client's trust account and withdraw it at a later date. Getting access to an attorney's trust account can be extremely difficult. Judges are extremely reluctant to interfere with the attorney-client privilege and thus rarely allow account- ants (or wives seeking an accounting for divorce pur- poses) access to such trust accounts.

IT'S NOT JUST ABOUT THE MONEY: LEAVE NO CLUES

If you do manage to finance your bad behavior without detection, you should realize that you're still not out of the woods. Even though you've made sure to follow a number of my suggestions on how to hide your extracur- ricular spending, you still face the very real possibility of being discovered. The man behaving badly also needs to take the following steps if he hopes to escape detection.

1. Do not create phone records that reveal whom you've called and how often. If you're going to call your mistress or even your out-of-state bank, make sure to use a pay phone. If you decide to use your cellular phone (a favorite choice for men behaving badly), make sure the phone bill goes to the office or to a post office box. The most careful planning can be completely undone by a revealing phone bill. Take the case of Mr. X, chairman of a major entertainment company. Mr. X had the foresight to rent his Wilshire Boulevard apartment in his com- pany's name. He also had the foresight to have his attorney, Arnold Epson, set up a trust account in which his mistress was the named beneficiary and Arnold was the trustee. But all this careful plan- ning was undone by one simple misstep. Mr. X

always called his mistress at their secret Wilshire Boulevard apartment on his car phone. The bill for the car phone went directly to Mr. X's home address. It wasn't long before his wife noticed that on any given day, Mr. X would place over twenty calls to a certain west Los Angeles number. With minimal effort, she discovered the secret apartment, the twenty-something girlfriend, and a hidden bank account in Oregon. Mr. X had also made the mistake of calling his Oregon bank on more than one occasion. The lesson of Mr. X is clear—good hiding is in the details.

2. Do not purchase property in your own name. This is probably one of the easiest things to trace. If you don't get caught by the IRS, you'll probably get caught by your wife once she starts receiving all kinds of solicitations in the mail, asking you to refinance your recently obtained mortgage. Before you apply for a mortgage in your own name, you should know that the information on your application will probably be sold to a marketing firm. And while you might not be opposed to giving your private financial information to your bank, odds are that you don't want every mortgage company in the country to have it. As you're probably aware, few things are more intrusive or intimate than a mortgage application. They generally require information such as how much you've made in the past few years, where you work, how frequently you've changed jobs, how much tax you've paid, your credit card and banking account numbers and balances, and, in some cases, all details about your major assets, including stocks, real estate, and partnerships. Your broker is allowed to store this information and then sell it to anyone who wants it. In fact, no federal statutes currently prevent mortgage brokers or

independent mortgage companies from storing this information electronically and then selling it. So, if you're intent on keeping your latest mortgage private, make sure you don't apply for it in your own name.

3. Unless you've purchased an offshore credit card, don't use credit to finance your bad behavior. Almost nothing is as revealing as a credit card statement. If you feel compelled to use a credit card to pay for your motel room or a small gift for your new honey, make sure the statements don't go to your home address.

4. If you decide to take "unreported cash" out of your business to finance your bad behavior, be prepared to be audited or prosecuted by the IRS. The IRS has a policy of closely examining cash businesses, and every year it targets a particular type of cash business for auditing.

FINAL THOUGHTS

If you're going to behave badly, you shouldn't do so spontaneously. You should take the time to cover your tracks.

Take the case of the cheating husband who managed to withdraw money from the community bank account to buy his mistress a rare painting. When his wife found out that he was cheating on her, she filed for divorce and hired one of the best forensic accountants in the country to trace the community assets. After several months, the forensic accountant managed to discover that a significant sum of money was missing from the couple's joint banking account but couldn't figure out what the husband had used the money for.

It wasn't until the wife's attorney demanded that the husband produce all insurance policies in his name that the lost money was found. After purchasing the rare painting for his mistress, the husband had made the mistake of insuring the artwork for damage and theft. And so, the mystery of the missing assets was solved, demonstrating once and for all that good hiding requires complete and careful planning.

REFERENCES

1. "Mistress Details Relationship with CBS's Kuralt in Court," *Newsday,* February 18, 2000.
2. Keep in mind that non-reporting of income to the IRS is illegal.
3. September 7, 1999, interview with Donald Gursey, CPA, Gursey, Schneider and Co. LLP.
4. Reiss, Stephen, "Reading Between the Lines," *The Matrimonial Strategist,* vol. 16, no. 4 (May 1998).
5. September 7, 1999, Interview with Donald Gursey, CPA, Gursey, Schneider and Co. LLP.
6. According to Stephen Reiss, CPA, finding separate, non–interest bearing checking accounts located in other cities and states is an extremely difficult task for even the best-trained forensic accountant or private investigator.
7. "Intellimedia Security and Net.B@nk to Provide Online Safe-Deposit Boxes," *Business Wire,* June 7, 1999.
8. Offshore banks can provide a wide variety of services including, but not limited to, credit cards. For information on how and where to open a foreign bank account, you should consider reviewing my book *The Complete Guide to Offshore Money Havens,* pp. 243–262.
9. Cornez, Arnold, *The Offshore Money Book,* pp. 109–110.
10. Ibid., p. 110.

CHAPTER 4

THE UNDERCOVER TOURIST: CASH AND THE CAREFUL TRAVELER

At first, I didn't know what to make of Adam Johnson. His jeans were worn, his shirt was dingy, and his loafers were scuffed. Adam Johnson didn't look like a man who had enough money to take a cab, let alone invest offshore.

During my first phone call with Adam, he'd told me that he had over $200,000 that he wanted to invest. For the last four years, he'd worked as a television writer on several successful sitcoms, earning in excess of $250,000 each year. He'd managed to save over $200,000 and now he was ready to let his money work for him. After a few telephone discussions about Adam's resources and his investment needs, I'd arranged for him to fly to Vancouver for a face-to-face meeting.

I spent around an hour with Adam, explaining what offshore investment opportunities might be available to him. We discussed the tax consequences of the different options, as well as how much it would cost for him to eventually invest offshore. At one point, Adam asked, "How much do you need to set up your own bank?"

"It would take at least forty thousand just to set the bank up," I explained.

He nodded and reached for a scruffy brown briefcase, from which he took a stack of airplane tickets. "Forty thousand," he said confidently.

I glanced at the tickets with a puzzled look. "Thank you, but I don't need to go anywhere right now."

He laughed. "You need forty thousand dollars to get this thing going, right? Well, that's forty thousand dollars' worth of airline tickets. Airline tickets are my preferred form of currency—especially when I need to take a large amount of cash out of the country. Nobody in customs ever says anything about a bunch of airline tickets. I got up in Los Angeles this morning, put around $100,000 worth of airline tickets into my old, trusty briefcase, and then just came right across the border. Nobody raised so much as an eyebrow."

I looked through the stack of tickets. They were all first class, for flights originating all over the world. "These are worth forty thousand dollars?" I asked incredulously.

"Yep. I always book first-class trips. I try to stick to the longer leg trips. That way, I don't have to buy as many tickets." He picked out one ticket. "This one's first class from London to India, for example."

"Where did you buy it?"

"Oh, I fly to Hong Kong a couple times a year and I buy all my tickets there. They're totally untraceable. Nobody else can use them but me and I can cash them in anywhere in the world."

"It's kind of like you convert every airline office into a banking kiosk."

"Exactly. The airline offices are like my own personal ATMs."

"Well, I need for you to visit one right now. As much as I admire the whole ticket thing, I still need cash to set up my own bank."

"No problem," he said pleasantly. "I'll be back in about an hour."

True to his word, an hour later Adam returned to my office carrying a $40,000 cashier's check. "Now, are we ready to set up this bank or what?" he said as he placed the check on my desk.

CASH AND CARRY: HOW TO TRAVEL WITH CASH

I can't tell you how many times my clients have been ripped off while traveling. Just last year, a client told me that during a honeymoon trip to Venice, he and his new bride were robbed of over $5,000 in cash. This client has been all over the world, carrying thousands of dollars in his sleek, jet black Gucci briefcase. So when his bride suggested that they take the cash from their wedding and spend it all on a beautiful Venetian chandelier, he quickly agreed. They arrived in Venice early on a Friday morning, checked into their suite at the Danieli, and then walked over to St. Mark's square for some espresso and biscotti. By the time they returned to their hotel for a late afternoon siesta, the Gucci briefcase and its contents were gone. They called the police, who immediately referred them to the American Express office, assuming that the money stolen had been in traveler's checks and could easily be refunded. When my client finally managed to explain that cash had

I can't tell you how many times my clients have been ripped off while traveling. Just last year, a client told me that during a honeymoon trip to Venice, he and his new bride were robbed of over $5,000 in cash.

Most hotel room shower rods are retractable and make convenient hiding places for money or important documents.

been stolen, all the police officers could do was shrug their shoulders and sigh sympathetically.

After telling me the sad details of his honeymoon story, my client concluded irritably, "I can tell you one thing. I'm never going to travel with that much cash again. There's just no way you can keep cash safe in a hotel room." He looked at me and smiled, knowing that I was dying to contradict him.

"I just happen to know a thing or too about hiding valuables in a hotel room," I began amiably.

"Fine. Where would you have hidden the cash? Under the bed? In the bathroom somewhere?"

"What size cup does your wife wear?"

His eyes narrowed. "Did you just ask me how big-busted my wife is?"

I smiled. "I'm going somewhere with this."

"You'd better be." He thought for a moment. "She's a 32b." He held up a cautionary finger. "Don't even *think* about saying anything."

"I'm interested for purely business reasons. Now, I gather that she wears a padded bra." He nodded. "Good. That can be very helpful. You could remove one of those pads, and put some cash in there. Then, you could slip the padding back in. Padded bras are a great place to hide things. Now, if you've got a bigger-busted wife, you can't use the bra thing. Not enough extra room in there. So, you've got to look elsewhere in your hotel room. I would recommend that you check the rod that holds the shower curtain up in your room and slip off the end covering to check if it's hollow. If it is, you can stick your cash in there and then slip the end piece back on."

"That would have worked," he agreed. "But traveling with cash is still a risky proposition."

"It doesn't have to be," I told him then.

And I'm telling you, now.

While you might not need to travel with quite as much cash as the unlucky Venetian visitor, chances are that at some time or another you will find yourself on a trip trying to keep your significant cash supply secure from theft. And chances are that if you're traveling with a large amount of cash, you will be a target. So, you need to learn how to protect your cash, not only while you're en route to your destination but also once you arrive.

AROUND THE WORLD WITH CASH AND OTHER ASSETS

If you plan to take a lot of cash on your next trip to Europe, I would highly recommend one thing: Don't "hide" your cash in a flashy Gucci briefcase. Putting your cash in an expensive briefcase is tantamount to putting a sign over your money that reads, "*Steal this . . . and don't forget to take the briefcase, too!*"

Not only is an ostentatious, expensive briefcase an invitation to thieves, it's also a bright red flag for customs agents.[1] They're more likely than not to stop the guy with the fancy Italian briefcase and matching Gucci loafers. Nothing says "search me" more than Italian designer leather.

If you absolutely have to travel with cash, you need to figure out a way to hide it that is effective, comfortable, convenient, and low-key. (Whenever you travel with large amounts of cash, you want to dress down to avoid alerting would-be thieves.)

The best place to keep your cash when traveling is on your person. If you travel with larger bills and don't need too much space, you could hide your cash inside of your clothing. Sewing cash inside the lining of coats, hats, dresses, and other clothing items has always been an effective way to hide smaller amounts of cash. (Don't sew anything metallic into the lining of your clothes; it will most likely set off the metal detector at the airport.)

However, if your coat happens to be an $800 leather bomber jacket, you should probably look for a different hiding place. You never want to hide things in an item that's worth stealing in and of itself. If you do opt to hide something in your coat or hat, be sure to take your valuable clothing items with you wherever you go. If you leave your seat during the flight to go the restroom, be sure not to leave your coat or hat behind! And if you travel in first class, don't give your coat to the flight attendant when you board. I don't care if you have to sit on it for fourteen hours during your flight, just make sure that you never leave it unattended.

When you travel during the warm weather months, it's probably not a good idea to take a large coat or hat along with you, as that will only make you stand out in the airport or train station (not to mention attract the unwelcome attention of those pesky customs officers). In warmer climates, it's best to come up with a hiding place that can be concealed under your shorts or shirts or in your socks.

When I was in college, I took a two-month backpacking trip through Europe. I had around $1,000 in traveler's checks and approximately $300 in cash.[2] I spent most of that summer staying in pensions, youth hostels, and a variety of dirty, cheap hotels. Sometimes, I even rented a hotel room with another student whom I'd met on the train. And occasionally, I slept in my seat on the train, hoping to save a little money on hotel rooms.

But no matter where I slept, or whom I slept with, I always kept one eye on my money. I carried my passport and my wallet in a pouch around my neck, which I wore tucked under my shirt. No matter what time of the day it was, I never took that pouch off. And, by the end of that summer, I was one of the few people I knew who'd managed to avoid being robbed. Even though the pouch wasn't terribly high tech or even particularly original, it got the job done—keeping me close to my money.

Most travel and spy stores offer travel security products such as money belts, travel pouches, and leather leg wallets. The money belt wraps securely around your waist, usually weighs only about two ounces, and contains several zippered compartments where you can store your cash. The travel pouch, which is frequently used by college students backpacking through Europe, is a great place to conceal passports, I.D. cards, money, and documents by carrying them suspended around your neck. The travel pouch hangs down from your neck, hidden by your shirt. Stores like the Spy Store offer travel pouches that are light, neutral in color, and manufactured to blend in behind your shirt.

Since many would-be thieves are familiar with the travel pouch and the money belt, travel and spy stores now offer items such as the leather leg wallet. The leg wallet is a safe and secure place to carry cash, important documents, or your wallet. It attaches to either leg and is designed to fit snugly underneath pants or even socks.

If you don't care to purchase one of the ready-made security travel items, you can create your own with very little effort. Pin a small pouch to the inside of your pant leg and fill the pouch with cash or other valuables. Shoulder pads in your suit or coat also make for a good hiding place. You simply remove the pad and fill the area with cash. (Before you decide to create cash-filled shoulder pads, be sure that your coat or suit jacket doesn't look like it's out of style. Remember that large shoulder pads for women might catch the attention of a fashion-conscious customs agent.)

If you insist on transporting your cash the old-fashioned way, either in checked or carry-on bags, you need to make sure that those bags are securely locked. This means not using the locks that come with most luggage. Travelers who are concerned about securing their luggage should investigate the mail order catalog from Magellan's, which caters to jet-setters and international travelers with security concerns. Magellan's sells an assortment of tamper-resistant locks and seals for suitcases, briefcases, bags, and even purses, including locks for suitcase zippers.

A BETTER WAY TO FLY: TRAVELING RICH, BUT TRAVELING LIGHT

I have a female client who is involved in a matrimonial dispute. She had $100,000 she wanted to hide from her husband and tried to fly up to Vancouver for a consulta-

> I carried my passport and my wallet in a pouch around my neck, which I wore tucked under my shirt. No matter what time of the day it was, I never took that pouch off. And, by the end of that summer, I was one of the few people I knew who'd managed to avoid being robbed.

"She's got over $50,000 sewn into the lining of that coat and another $10,000 inside the hat."

tion with me during the summer. Instead of arriving at my office, she called me from the Vancouver airport, where she'd been detained by customs because the agents had caught her trying to bring the $100,000 in cash into the country.

Apparently, she'd worn a large, multicolored fox fur coat—in summertime, mind you—filling the lining with bills. Of course, customs immediately asked her to remove the coat and searched it. She needed me to call a lawyer to get her out of the mess.

While I understood the woman's desire to get her cash out of the country, I never understood her choice of hiding spots—or her taste in coats. Few things draw more attention than a woman wearing an orange and white fox fur coat on a hot, muggy day. When I finally got a chance to talk to the woman (several months after she'd struck a deal with the police), I asked her why she'd chosen to hide the money in clothing so clearly inappropriate for the season. She explained that there were simply too many bills to tape them to her body. So, she'd needed a large hiding spot—like the lining of her voluminous fur coat.

I didn't have the heart to explain to my unlucky smuggler that if you need to transport a large amount of bills, it's probably better to convert the cash into something smaller. It makes the currency easier to transport and easier to hide. For example, if you want to take $9,000 with you to Switzerland, you might want to consider using the airline tickets ploy, which I told you about earlier and which requires little or no travel.[3] The tickets are thin and can be easily hidden on your person or even inside your carry-on bag. It's unlikely that a bunch of airline tickets will arouse the suspicion of a customs agent.

You could also consider traveling with a cashier's check made out to yourself. If the check is made out to cash, it's considered a negotiable instrument. (A check in the amount of $10,000 or more that is made out to cash is considered a monetary instrument for purposes of Title 31 CFR 103.23 and each person carrying such a check is therefore required to report it.) However, if your $10,000 check is made out to you and you've not yet endorsed it, you are not required to report it because it is not considered a negotiable instrument. Keep in mind that money orders, traveler's checks, and personal checks that are signed and endorsed are all considered negotiable instruments and, as such, must be reported if their cash value reaches or exceeds $10,000.

If you're not comfortable with buying airplane tickets you'll never use or carrying a cashier's check, you might try purchasing a "Mondex smart card." Mondex smart cards are about to revolutionize the way people travel with cash because you can deposit your money onto the smart card and unload the card at your final destination.[4]

These smart cards work very much like phone cards, in that they contain a certain cash value embedded in a microprocessor chip, which is reduced with every purchase that the user makes. Of course, if the money isn't spent, it can be completely converted back into cash.

Several banks have even developed smart cards wherein the card's chip stores the owner's identity and space for five different cash totals (for five different currencies, for example). The owner puts the card into the slot of a gadget beside the telephone, calls the bank, keys the PIN code followed by the amount of cash he or she wants, and the card is loaded with that amount from the person's account. The cards themselves contain encrypted digital signatures that are needed for every transaction and the system changes frequently to beat counterfeiters.[5] When the users run low in electronic cash, they can get a fresh supply merely by phoning the bank from any phone with a smart card reader attached.[6]

Because the smart card is a relatively new phenomenon, you may be more comfortable transporting your cash in another form, such as a few valuable gold or silver coins.[7] The best thing about carrying coins instead of cash is that sometimes one coin can have a market value exceeding $5,000. Concealing one or two coins with an aggregate value of $5,000 is considerably easier than having to conceal $5,000 in cash. (No giant, multicolored fur coats are necessary for transport.)[8]

Even if you're not interested in converting all of your cash into coins, you might still carry a few with you for emergency situations. A friend of mine always carries two South African Krugerrand coins on her travels—thereby ensuring that she has at least $500 in emergency cash.

When traveling with coins, you can either place them in your carry-on luggage or on your person. (Whatever you do, however, don't put them in your checked luggage. As any frequent traveler knows, checking your baggage can be a risky proposition.) If you choose to hide the coins on your person, remember that they will most likely set off the airport metal detectors. This will probably result in your being searched by airport security personnel. I would recommend that you place the coins in your carry-on luggage. They will most likely not be spotted by airport security and if they are, it's unlikely that airport security will think anything of the fact that you have some loose change at the bottom of your carry-on bag.

While the small size of coins can work for you, it can also work against you. Two highly valuable coins sitting at the bottom of your carry-on suitcase can be lost quite easily. So make sure your coins are securely stored before you even begin your trip. I'd also recommend that you make a notation as to where you've stored the coins—it'll help you avoid a frantic search once you arrive at your final destination.

Another great way to protect your assets while traveling is to convert your cash into diamonds before your trip. If your diamonds are purchased with legitimate money, you are legally entitled to travel outside of the United States with those diamonds.[9] Unlike coins, diamonds are easier to hide and will not set off any airport buzzers. Diamonds are also acceptable in trade throughout the world, particularly in the major capitals of Western Europe.[10] So, if you're off to Italy for an extensive shopping spree and you don't want to travel with $5,000 in cash or traveler's checks, you might consider purchasing a diamond worth $5,000. Once you arrive in Italy, you should have no trouble cashing in your diamond. Be aware, however, that the value of your diamond may vary from country to country—which means that it may be worth more at home than abroad. You should also be aware that if you want to get the best price for your diamonds, it will probably take some time. If you're interested in traveling with some form of currency that can be quickly converted back into cash, you should probably stick with something like coins or even stamps, which can be sold relatively quickly for a good price.

If you're not comfortable with buying airplane tickets you'll never use or carrying a cashier's check, you might try purchasing a "Mondex smart card." Mondex smart cards are about to revolutionize the way people travel with cash because you can deposit your money onto the smart card and unload the card at your final destination.

The best way to make sure that your cash or other assets aren't stolen en route to your final destination is to not travel with a lot of cash. If you don't want to travel with cash but still want to be able to access your funds once you arrive at your final destination, you should consider opening an account at an offshore bank.

Many entrepreneurial banks offer an international debit card with a depository account, which provides the customer with withdrawal privileges at any Visa or MasterCard center in the world. (This type of account also offers the user a great deal of privacy, in that it creates no records except at the point of sale and at the host banking company.)[11] With this account and card, you can withdraw money at an ATM once you arrive at your destination, make purchases at a retail store, or access your money in a variety of ways.[12]

If you tend to travel to the same destination all the time, you might want to obtain a credit card issued at that destination. I recently advised a client of mine who frequently travels to Hong Kong that he should get a credit card that is issued there and use his hotel address as his home destination. I explained that if he has an American Express card issued in Hong Kong, he'll be able to pay for things in Hong Kong dollars, thus avoiding currency change charges.

The foreign-issued credit card also has one other advantage—it provides you with an opportunity to make sensitive purchases because the credit card bills go to a foreign hotel address, rather than to your home or business address.

Finally, if you really want to travel light, you should consider wiring your funds to your final destination. Many hotels allow you to wire money ahead to cover both your bill and any other expenses you might incur on your trip. Once you arrive at your hotel, you can use your hotel account much like a bank account—having the bank advance you cash as needed.

If you plan on shopping at one particular store during your trip, you can also attempt to wire funds to that store. For example, if you always drop a bundle of cash at Harrods whenever you go to London, you might want to wire $5,000 to the store before you arrive to cover your purchases.[13]

If you do choose to wire money, you should be aware that in May 1997, the Clinton administration announced new rules on wire transfer reporting. Under the new regulations, all street-corner check-cashing services, as well as large money-transmittal services such as Western Union and American Express, are required to file reports with the Treasury Department for wire transfers of more than $750. So, if you're wiring more than $750 and less than $10,000, you should use a full-service bank.[14]

Wiring funds is a safe and effective way for the careful traveler to ensure that his money is waiting for him when he arrives at his final destination. I once had a client who made it a policy to never travel with cash—he always moved his money by EFT (electronic funds transfer). Before every trip, he'd withdraw cash from his bank and convert it either to Western Union money orders or wire transfers from another licensed transmitter. At Western Union, a money order can be obtained that can be cashed anywhere on the system by using a code phrase. So, wire transfers provide security and anonymity to the user.[15] Major electronic funds transfer systems include Fedwire, CHIPS (The Clearing House Interbank Payments System), and SWIFT (Society for Worldwide Interbank Financial Telecommunications).

These are the largest and most complex of all the systems, and they move the most money. Whereas CHIPS and SWIFT are international in scope, the main domestic electronic transfer system is Fedwire. In addition to the aforementioned systems, Telex can also be used as a means of initiating international financial transfers. By wiring your funds via any of the previously mentioned systems, you no longer have to be concerned about how to hide cash from your unscrupulous fellow travelers.

HIDING IN YOUR HOTEL

Only a few years ago, a friend and I took a trip to London to do some research for a book of mine on offshore banking. We checked into a very pricey hotel close to Buckingham Palace. As we were checking in, the clerk asked us if we wanted to store any valuables in the hotel safe. Although I was traveling with quite a bit of cash, I declined the offer. Ever since my wife's gold necklace was stolen from a safe at a fancy Barcelona hotel, I've not been a big fan of hotel safes.

After I was shown to my room, I dumped my stuff on the bed and immediately headed for the bathroom to take a quick shower. By the time I emerged from my shower ten minutes later, my wallet and my Rolex watch were both missing. Even though I was still wet and only wrapped in a towel, I went running out of my room in a desperate attempt to find the thief, but the hallway was empty. I returned to my room, frustrated, depressed, and angry at myself for forgetting to bolt the door before my

The hotel room is filled with great hiding spots if you know where to look.

shower. As I contemplated what to do next, I berated myself for being so stupid as to leave my money and my watch out in plain sight. I, of all people, should have known better.

As I learned the hard way, hotel rooms remain one of the least secure places in the world. Despite code keys, bonded housekeepers, hallway cameras, and other hotel security precautions, patrons of hotels truly are sitting ducks for burglars. Everyone, from housekeepers to maintenance men, can access your room while you're out. (Some burglars become hotel guests for the express purpose of gaining access to other guest's rooms.) Therefore, whenever you travel with cash or other valuables, you need to take precautions.

If you plan on hiding anything in your hotel room, you should always travel with a small tube of glue, a roll of tape, a box of push-pins, a small pocket-clip screwdriver, and a Swiss army knife.[16] As soon as your bellman leaves, start looking for a good place to hide your cash and other valuables.

Like your house, the hotel room provides a wide variety of hiding places for the educated and prepared hider. When you first arrive in your room, take a good look at the walls for anything mounted. Wall-mounted radio speakers make great hiding places and are relatively easy to get inside. Even though the pictures hanging on most hotel room walls aren't much to look at, they can make for good hiding places. Provided your "stash" is relatively flat, you can simply tape it to the back of the picture and then hang the picture back on the wall.

As with your home, air-conditioning ducts also make for an excellent hiding place and are easily removed. However, if you do opt to use the air-conditioning duct, make sure that you don't disrupt the paint around the duct when you remove it. In addition, if you use the air-conditioning duct as a hiding place, you should be aware that a maintenance man might have an occasion to open the duct if some other guest reports trouble with the heating or air-conditioning in the building.

If you've remembered to bring a small screwdriver, you can easily remove the outlet covers in your hotel room and stash valuables behind them—provided the valuables aren't likely to catch fire in the event of a loose hot wire. If your hotel room has a large utility box on the wall, this makes for an excellent hiding spot.

Ceiling light fixtures also often provide space for hiding.[17] And if your hotel room ceiling is made up of acoustic tiles, you can use that space to hide things as well. Just push up a tile and then place your objects inside the ceiling. Once you replace the tile, nobody will ever be the wiser even if you happen to dent one of the tiles. The beauty of acoustic tiles is that they always look broken, moved, and dirty.

One of the best hiding places in your hotel room is the bathroom. You only need to remember one thing if you plan on using your hotel bathroom to hide things: bring rubber gloves! Chances are that if you stay at an older hotel, you'll probably have a toilet with a tank attached. (If it's a European hotel, the tank may be above the toilet, but that still makes for a good hiding place.) All you have to do is lift the toilet tank lid off and place your items in the tank. Naturally, you'll want to place your valuables in a waterproof bag before dropping them into your toilet tank. If you're concerned about your valuables interfering with the flow of water in your toilet tank, tape the plastic bag to the inside of the tank lid—above the water.

If you'd rather not fish around inside your toilet tank, your hotel bathroom has other good hiding places. You can always tape your valuables within the curves and contours of your room's bath fixtures. And with very little effort you can remove the mirror in your hotel bathroom. All you need to do is lever off any plastic screw head covers and then release the mirror from its mount. Usually, there will be a small space behind the mirror where you can hide some valuables. You can also carve out a small space, provided you have the proper tool with you. Once you've hidden your valuables, just remount the mirror and go on your way. Chances are, even if a thief suspects you've hidden something behind the bathroom mirror, he will not take the time to remove it from the wall—he needs to get in and out quickly.

Your hotel room furniture also provides a multitude of clever hiding spots. Beds, chairs, sofas, and so on, usually have an easily detachable layer of material glued or stapled across the bottom. This material can be lifted and then resealed by glue or those trusty push-pins you remembered to bring along. (If you're really in a bind, you can try to hammer the old staples back in with a book or some other hard object in your hotel room.)

You can use the cushions on your hotel room furniture to hide things. It's easy to slip something inside a chair cushion. If the furniture in your room is older and somewhat damaged, you might consider detaching the furniture moldings and use that space to hide smaller

> As I learned the hard way, hotel rooms remain one of the least secure places in the world. Despite code keys, bonded housekeepers, hallway cameras, and other hotel security precautions, patrons of hotels truly are sitting ducks for burglars.

objects. Finally, you can always use the back of dresser drawers to hide items. You merely pull out the drawers and fasten a bag to the back. You then push the drawer back in and your valuables will be hidden from sight. If a thief decides to rummage through the drawers, chances are he won't check the back of the drawer for valuables.

For those who believe the best hiding places are in plain sight, you can use common travel items to stash some of your valuables. If you know that your hotel room has a VCR, you might want to travel with a VCR tape safe. It looks like a normal VHS tape, but is hollow on the inside. You simply place the tape filled with cash or jewelry alongside some tapes rented from the hotel and your hotel burglar will never be the wiser. Many companies sell travel safes that look like other common travel items.[18] And, of course, if your hotel room has a safe, you might want to use it. I prefer not to use hotel safes, as they generally have only a four-letter or number combination lock that most amateur thieves can easily decipher.

RIDING AROUND WITH YOUR CASH

While I've always had a sense that my hotel room could be made relatively secure, I've never been foolish enough

Wheel wells make great hiding places.

to believe that anything in my rent-a-car or even my own car was safe. Let's face it—breaking into a car isn't rocket science. The trick, then, is to hide things in unusual places inside and outside of your automobile.

Anyone who saw the movie *The Big Chill* probably remembers when the character played by William Hurt is stopped by the police for speeding and his car is searched. Although he is carrying a lot of drugs, the police come up empty. That's because Hurt had carefully taped the drugs to an area just above his right front tire in the fender well. (I recommend using fender wells for hiding only legal valuables. If you follow Hurt's example, you're on your own.) Keep in mind, however, that although a fender well can be a good hiding place, you have to make sure that whatever you hide there is attached securely. One good bump and your valuables could be sitting somewhere by the side of the road.

When you're traveling, the inside of your car can often provide better hiding spots than anything available in your hotel room—with a little careful planning. The ashtray can be a good place to hide things, for example, particularly if you place a false bottom in the tray. The visor can also serve as a good hiding spot. All you need to do is open the visor covering at the seam and remove some of the padding. You can then put your cash or other flat valuables inside the visor, replace a little of the stuffing, and smooth the seam back down.

The dashboard makes for a roomy hiding place, provided you're handy with tools. Once it's removed, you'll find a lot of hollow spaces behind the dash where you can store valuables. You can remove one or two gauges to make even more space—just make sure you don't remove anything important! Keep in mind that removing a dashboard is a very difficult process. If you're not handy, you should consider an alternate hiding spot. Finally, the glove compartment in your car can also be a good hiding place if it has a lining. Loosen it, slip a few items inside, and reattach.

FINAL THOUGHTS

While it's always risky to travel with large amounts of cash, a little planning can go a long way. Before you go on your next trip, take a little time to think about how you want to protect your money and other valuables while you're on the road. If you're traveling on business, consider what your financial needs will be. And if you're off for a shopping spree, decide whether you'll even need cash, because credit would suffice.

With a little careful thought, anyone can protect his or her cash and valuables from theft.

Finally, a legal note: Travelers who plan to take more than $10,000 out of the United States should be familiar with Title 31 CFR 103.23, which requires anyone physically transporting currency or any other monetary instruments over $10,000 in or out of the United States to fill out a Currency and Monetary Instruments Form #4790 with U.S. Customs. Monetary instruments could include any type of negotiable check, traveler's checks, or other bearer-type money equivalent. For example, a personal check written to cash would be negotiable.

The good news, for now, at least, is that items such as diamonds, casino chips, tour vouchers, train tickets, airline tickets, Mondex smart cards, and non-endorsed cashier's checks made out to specific people are not considered negotiable instruments for purposes of Title 31 CFR 103.23.[19]

REFERENCES

1. Title 31 CFR 103.23 requires that each person who physically transports, mails, or ships, or causes to be physically transported, mailed, or shipped . . . currency or other monetary instruments in an aggregate amount over $10,000 at one time from the United States to any place outside of the United States, or into the United States from any place outside of the United States must file a CMIR (Currency and Monetary Instruments) form with the Customs Service.
2. Traveler's checks can be a good way to travel with a large amount of cash because there is no limit on how much cash you can convert to traveler's checks. And if the checks are lost or stolen, they will usually be replaced by the issuing company. American Express claims that it honors 98 percent of all claims for theft or loss. My personal experience is that American Express will honor a theft or loss the first time around, but if your checks are stolen a second time, it's a lot more difficult to get them replaced.
3. Moreover, airline tickets do not constitute a monetary instrument according to U.S. Customs.

4. Customs does not yet require people carrying "smart cards" with a cash value in excess of $10,000 to report them. According to a U.S. Customs official, smart cards are still viewed as credit cards and Customs does not require people carrying credit cards with a $10,000 limit to report them.

5. The likelihood of "Smart Cards" catching on is good. Visa conducted a study in which 83 percent of consumers said that they would use a cash (or stored value) card instead of cash itself.

6. Over 850 McDonald's restaurants in Germany now house smart-card load terminals where customers can now download money from their bank accounts into smart cards.

7. If you pay for coins with cash or traveler's checks and the transaction exceeds $10,000, the coin dealer is required to file a Currency Transaction Report with the Treasury Department.

8. Be aware that if you travel with coins valued at $10,000 or more, you have to report that amount to Customs pursuant to 31 CFR 103.23.

9. If you transport over $10,000 in diamonds for commercial purposes, you must declare them. However, if you transport $10,000 in diamonds for noncommercial purposes, you have no legal obligation to report the diamonds to U.S. Customs.

10. Skousen, Mark, *The Complete Guide to Financial Privacy,* Alexandria, VA: Alexandria House Books, 1979, p. 146.

11. Before opening an account in a foreign country, be sure to consult with a financial expert about that country's banking secrecy laws.

12. Pankau, Edmund J., *Hide Your Assets and Disappear,* New York: HarperCollins, 1999, pp. 134–135.

13. If you decide to wire money ahead to a particular store, be sure to find out ahead of time how the store accounts operate and what the store's policy is on account refunds.

14. Under federal law, full-service banks are required to report all international transactions in excess of $10,000.

15. Federal law requires that all transmitters of money by wire also be licensed. Presently, about forty businesses are so licensed. These include, among others, American Express, Deak International, Citicorp, and Bank of America.

16. Connor, Michael, *How to Hide Anything,* Boulder, CO: Paladin Press, 1984, p. 96.

17. If you are intent upon detaching the ceiling fixture in your room for hiding purposes, be careful not to electrocute yourself.
18. To purchase empty videotape shells, screws that can't be unscrewed, and other travel security items, contact Specialty Store Services at (800) 999-0771. At least fifteen online stores carry other travel security safes, including but not limited to, the Spy Store at www.spy-store.com.
19. If you're unclear as to whether a particular item constitutes a "negotiable instrument," you can always contact U.S. Customs at 1-800-232-5378 or access their Web site at www.customs.ustreas.gov.

CHAPTER 5

LIFE IN THE RED LANE: STAYING ONE STEP AHEAD OF CREDITORS

A friend introduced me to Carmen Bracca about five years ago, when I was in Los Angeles promoting one of my books. Carmen represented a number of successful writers, and my friend thought that she might be interested in helping me sell my next book. Although I told my friend that I was perfectly happy with my current agent, he insisted on dragging me over to meet Carmen.

When I finally shook her perfectly manicured hand, all I could think was that Carmen looked more like a movie star than a literary agent. She had long, curly red hair, bright blue eyes, and a devious grin.

The rest of that evening is a blur. All I recall is that by the time the gorgeous and extremely personable Carmen Bracca was finished with me, I'd promised to let her represent me for the rest of my life. It didn't matter to me that I'd never heard of her before. It didn't matter to me that she wasn't affiliated with any established agency. And it certainly didn't matter to me that she'd never represented anyone who wrote books dealing with offshore

investment. In just hours, Carmen had managed to convince me that she was the only person in the world who
could properly represent my books.

After I had a few days to come down from the party,
I began to wonder whether placing my future in Carmen's
hands was the prudent thing to do. After all, I had a great
relationship with my existing agent. I discussed the situation with a few friends and finally phoned Carmen to let
her know that I wasn't interested in signing with her. She
began to pour on the charm again, but she wasn't quite
as convincing over the phone because I couldn't see those
intense blue eyes lighting up every time I uttered anything remotely amusing. We chatted for a while and the
conversation ultimately ended on a good note, with Carmen suggesting that perhaps I might be able to give her
some investment advice in the future. I told her to call
anytime.

Only weeks after I'd rebuffed Carmen's attempts to
sign me, I read some disturbing news about her. She was
being sued by four of her authors for stealing their royal-
ties. Carmen had responded by counter-suing the authors
for back commissions and defamation, claiming that the
lawsuit had seriously and permanently damaged her professional reputation.

Eventually, Carmen called me. She briefly informed
me about the details of the lawsuit and then took a few
minutes to proclaim her innocence. She explained that
while she was certain that justice would prevail, she was
still concerned about how an adverse verdict might affect

**Trying to hide assets after a lawsuit has been
filed is somewhat like closing the barn door
after the horse has already escaped.**

her finances. She had an extensive stock portfolio, as well as other assets that she wanted to protect in the event that the writers won their suit. She asked if I could help her move some of her assets around . . . maybe by transferring some of her investments to her mother's name. . . .

I told Carmen that although I appreciated her difficult situation, I could do nothing at this point to help her protect her assets. She'd simply waited too long. Trying to hide assets after a lawsuit has been filed is somewhat like closing the barn door after the horse has already escaped. I explained that if she transferred her assets now, a court would probably conclude that she'd fraudulently transferred her assets to defraud her creditors.

Under the Uniform Fraudulent Conveyances Act and the Uniform Fraudulent Transfers Act, any transfer of property made with the intent to hinder, delay, or defraud creditors is voidable by those creditors at their option. In other words, if you know you're being sued, and you suddenly transfer your assets into your mother's or wife's name, a creditor can use U.S. law to void that transfer and seize your property. Or, if you sell property and then hide the proceeds of that sale in an offshore bank while your debts go unpaid, you could face creditor charges of fraud.

In order to prove a claim of fraudulent conveyance, the plaintiff/creditor must show "subjective fraudulent intent." This is done by proving the existence of *badges of fraud*—which are conveyances made in secret, conveyances made while creditor litigation is pending, or conveyances made in which the debtor retains possession and use of the property after it's been transferred.[1] And even if a plaintiff or creditor fails to prove subjective fraudulent intent, the court can still find *constructive fraud*—in which a conveyance results in preventing the debtor from paying his debts, forcing him into insolvency, or removing sufficient capital to operate his business as debts come due.[2]

Despite my advice, Carmen Bracca ended up hiding a good portion of her assets. She gave some real estate to her mother, sold other property to friends for less than its market worth, and moved a large amount of cash to an offshore account.

By the time the writers won a $1,000,000 verdict against her, Carmen Bracca was worth only around $150,000—considerably less than the $500,000 she'd made the year before, according to her tax return. The writers immediately filed to void Bracca's transfer of property, arguing that she was trying to shelter the assets from an adverse legal judgment. Bracca argued that she had no fraudulent intent when she transferred property to her mother and to her friends, but the court didn't buy her story. It voided Bracca's transfers and ordered an attachment of the property.

The lessons of the Bracca case are simple. Like most effective financial planning, asset protection plans must be organized and executed well in advance of any potential financial trouble. Sloppy, after-the-judgment attempts to hide money from legitimate creditors will rarely pass muster with U.S. courts. And don't think you can avoid U.S. law simply by doing your asset transfers at the offshore center. Some offshore havens either have laws equivalent to the Uniform Fraudulent Conveyances Act and the Uniform Fraudulent Transfers Act, or they actually recognize the U.S. fraudulent conveyances statutes.[3] If you want to use offshore havens to protect your assets, don't wait until there is a suit filed or an outstanding judgment against you.

THE OFFSHORE ASSET PROTECTION PLAN

If you have cash, savings accounts, and other negotiable liquid assets that you want to protect, you should consider moving these assets offshore *before* you find your-

And don't think you can avoid U.S. law simply by doing your asset transfers at the offshore center. Some offshore havens either have laws equivalent to the Uniform Fraudulent Conveyances Act and the Uniform Fraudulent Transfers Act, or they actually recognize the U.S. fraudulent conveyances statutes.[3]

self in any type of a lawsuit. Offshore havens offer a wide variety of asset protection options, depending on your net worth. I often advise my clients who have estates worth more than $350,000 to consider placing their funds in an *asset protection trust.* If properly executed and intelligently maintained, this single offshore option can provide you with an unparalleled level of financial invisibility. It won't protect you from becoming the target of a lawsuit or claim, but the asset protection trust can make it difficult for any creditor to enforce a judgment entered against you.

One of the keys to a successful foreign trust is selecting an offshore haven country that maintains strict laws against enforcing foreign judgments. For example, the British Virgin Islands (BVI) recognizes a properly structured trust as a separate legal entity—independent of its creators—and will not allow creditors of any of the parties to the trust to obtain the trust's assets. In contrast, some offshore havens recognize the Uniform Fraudulent Conveyances Act and the Uniform Fraudulent Transfers Act or have similar legislation of their own. Therefore, before you set up an asset protection trust in an offshore haven, you need to make sure that you choose a friendly host country that maintains stringent laws against enforcing foreign judgments.

I always tell my clients to seek the advice of an attorney before setting up an asset protection trust or any other type of offshore financial entity. A poorly set up off-shore asset protection trust can easily be ripped up by a U.S. court.[4]

For example, using a trust to sign away marital assets without your spouse's consent is fraud and will get you in legal trouble. (Moreover, if you use the asset protection trust to try and protect ill-gotten gains, you will also run into problems with U.S. courts.) But an asset protection trust can be used to protect that which you legally own or are entitled to.

If you enter into a marriage with almost $500,000 of your own separate property, you can either sign a prenuptial agreement to protect those funds, or you can legally place those funds in an offshore asset protection trust. In light of several recent court decisions rejecting prenuptial agreements, many divorce attorneys now believe that it's safer for the wealthy bride or groom to protect his or her separate property through an asset protection trust. Prenuptial agreements can be subject to interpretation, whereas asset protection trusts, while occasionally vulnerable, tend to be a fairly safe bet in this type of situation. (Again, if you're concerned about how to best protect your separate property in the event of a divorce, you should consult a divorce attorney.)

If you take care to distance yourself sufficiently from the trust, so that the court will not find that the arrangement is a sham for holding assets under your direct control, no judge or jury can legally give your creditors assets that you earlier contributed to that trust. For example, if a husband and wife set up an irrevocable offshore trust for their children, it's likely that neither one would be able to ignore the provisions of that trust and regain the principal at some later time. Therefore, if either the husband or the wife were sued at some later date by a creditor seeking to break the trust, a court would most likely find against the creditor. This is because if the husband and wife could not break the trust, neither could a creditor. For this reason, an irrevocable trust can be a safe place to hide assets from potential creditors—if you're comfortable with giving up control of the trust.[5]

If you don't have the capital necessary to make an asset protection trust worthwhile, you might consider depositing money in an offshore bank in order to protect your assets from potential creditors. (Again, putting your money in an offshore bank is not something that you want to do after you've been sued, or after a judgment has been entered against you.)

The offshore bank allows you to use a layering technique that makes your assets much more difficult for a creditor to find and/or eventually attach. Individuals are not generally associated with the ownership of a bank, and if you stash a great deal of your money in, say, the Cayman Islands, your adversaries will have to contend with the strict banking secrecy laws there. If your adversary wants to sue you in the Cayman Islands, he has to first deposit with the court the full amount of your estimated legal costs. Then, if your adversary loses his case, you get fully compensated from the court out of your adversary's pocket. This can be a wonderful detriment to someone who has a filed a nuisance suit against you or even to a legitimate creditor who may not have the funds to litigate under the Cayman Islands' system of justice.

While offshore banking laws provide ample secrecy to protect assets in most situations, you can further distance yourself from your business affairs by using layers of trusts and blind corporations. Many banks, management firms, and trust companies located in offshore havens specialize in this sort of asset protection. With their assistance, you can develop a solid and effective asset protection strategy.

Offshore banking creates additional obstacles to determined creditors. For example, the creditor would have to either travel to a foreign locale to litigate against you, pay someone to travel there for him, or hire an attor-

> Offshore banking creates additional obstacles to determined creditors. For example, the creditor would have to either travel to a foreign locale to litigate against you, pay someone to travel there for him, or hire an attorney who lives in the offshore haven—all of which would be costly.

ney who lives in the offshore haven—all of which would be costly.

Another good asset protection device is the creation of an offshore company. Any effective asset protection plan involves putting layers between you and your potential creditors—making it difficult for them to find and then follow the money. By establishing a U.S.-based corporation through which you handle your business activities, you put one layer between you and your would-be creditors. You can also build on those layers by setting up an offshore (as opposed to domestic) corporation. Be aware, however, that certain legal formalities must be followed to properly establish an offshore corporation, and specific IRS reporting requirements must be followed in its administration. Therefore, before setting up an offshore corporation, be sure to check with an attorney.

You can also use offshore havens to protect yourself from the most determined "creditor" of all: the United States government. An offshore bank safe deposit box, for example, can protect valuable assets such as gold bars, jewelry, or title to other property from seizure by the U.S. government. Remember, even when you're not involved in any illegal activity, the U.S. government may seize your property under the liberal forfeiture statutes, and it's extremely easy for the U.S. government to open a safe deposit box in any U.S. bank. In order to protect your property, you might have to go to extremes and hide it in some remote offshore haven. (It's even possible to rent a safe deposit box in an offshore haven without giving your name or other personal identification.)

If you're at all concerned about the U.S. government illegally seizing your property, you should take measures before the property is seized. As things stand now, the laws tend to favor the government when it comes to forfeiture.[6]

The biggest problem with trying to protect assets from the U.S. government is that it doesn't have to follow the same legal rules as most creditors. In 1986 Congress passed the money laundering forfeiture statutes, giving the government the power to seize your real and personal property, based on that property's alleged use or involvement in criminal activities. By passing additional tough asset forfeiture laws since 1970, Congress virtually gave the U.S. Drug Enforcement Agency and other authorities a blank check to seize the property of suspected drug law violators even though they might never actually be charged or convicted.

In asset forfeiture cases, the government has only to show probable cause that the seized property was purchased with tainted money. That's the same standard of proof required to conduct a search, far lower than what's needed to win a typical court case. Once the government seizes something, the owner must prove that the property wasn't purchased with illegally obtained money. Basically, the asset forfeiture statutes are based upon the disturbing and clearly unconstitutional premise that people are guilty until proven innocent.

Any money derived from the selling of seized property goes directly to the agency that seizes it. According to the House Judiciary Committee, the money deposited in the Justice Department's Assets Forfeiture Fund increased from $27 million in fiscal 1985 to $338 million in 1996. Yet while the asset forfeiture statutes have an upside for the government, they definitely have a downside for thousands of innocent U.S. citizens. Though the federal government successfully used the forfeiture laws to confiscate hundreds of millions of dollars a year used in criminal activities, it also abused the forfeiture laws, depriving innocent citizens of property without due process.

Abuse of the forfeiture laws by the federal government is all too common. Many of my clients specifically invest offshore so as to avoid the wide and often unfettered power of the federal government to seize both real and personal property. In late 1999, I read a story in the *Washington Times* that seemed to illustrate how easily the current asset forfeiture laws can be and are abused by our own government. The article told the story of Dr. Richard Lowe, a doctor who lived in the small Alabama town of Haleyville. Distrustful of banks, Lowe chose over the years to keep most of his cash at home.[7] In 1990, when Dr. Lowe consolidated his assets into a charitable account for a small private school in his hometown, he also included his at-home cash savings, which totaled $316,911.

Dr. Lowe's account was immediately seized under the asset forfeiture laws. Law enforcement officials automatically inferred criminal behavior on Lowe's part because of the large amount of cash in his possession. The bank president was indicted for accepting the deposit. Dr. Lowe spent the next six years of his life fighting the seizure of his assets before the 11th Circuit Court of Appeals cleared him and ordered the return of his money.[8]

In fact, abuse of the asset forfeiture laws is so common that in June 1999, a bill sponsored by Judiciary Committee chairman Henry Hyde to overhaul the asset-seizure laws overwhelmingly passed in the House of Representatives, 375-48. (At the time of this printing, two companion bills are still pending in the Senate.) "All the government needs to do to seize and confiscate your property is establish that probable cause existed to believe that the property was involved in some crime . . . that it facilitated a crime or represents its proceeds," notes Hyde.[9] The Hyde bill would require the government to prove its case by "clear and convincing evidence." Moreover, the bill would also provide a court-appointed attorney to people whose property is seized and would establish an "innocent owner" defense, so that people aren't harmed if they buy or inherit property from someone who got it improperly.

Although some government representatives agree that asset forfeiture must be monitored to protect citizens from abuse and unwarranted burden, they remain concerned that the Hyde legislation will undo asset forfeiture's longstanding record of accomplishment. James E. Johnson, treasury under secretary, warned senators that the House bill would have a significantly negative impact on the government's current ability to use asset forfeiture against organized criminal activity. Secretary Johnson noted that "if the use of civil forfeiture is curtailed, it will seriously undermine our effectiveness in investigating drug trafficking, money laundering, fraud, and other financial crimes."[10]

So while reform of asset forfeiture laws is gaining some political momentum, don't expect things to change overnight. The best protection against asset forfeiture is

An offshore bank safe deposit box, for example, can protect valuable assets such as gold bars, jewelry, or title to other property from seizure by the U.S. government. Remember, even when you're not involved in any illegal activity, the U.S. government may seize your property under the liberal forfeiture statutes, and it's extremely easy for the U.S. government to open a safe deposit box in any U.S. bank.

to (1) stay away from any sort of illegal activity and (2)
make sure your assets are protected from government
seizure by placing those assets beyond the grasp of the
U.S. government. You need to remember that even if your
involvement in the illegal activity was minimal, your
property can still be subject to forfeiture.

And if you think that you don't have anything worth
seizing, think again. Property can include anything you
own: land, cars, boats, bank accounts, stocks, and bonds.
It can include something in your home or even property
that you carry on your person. One witness told the
House Judiciary Committee that agents seized $9,000 in
cash he was carrying in the Nashville airport merely
because he'd paid cash for his airline ticket and presum-
ably fit the profile of a drug offender.

LEAVING HOME TO PROTECT YOUR ASSETS

While many Americans choose to open offshore accounts
in order to protect their assets from determined creditors
and/or the government, others have taken things a step
further. They've chosen to renounce their U.S. citizenship
and to obtain a new residence, domicile, and/or citizenship in order to protect their assets from the U.S. government and/or determined judgment creditors.[11]

At first blush, this may sound like a good idea, but if
you're considering renouncing your U.S. citizenship to
avoid tax liability, you should think again. If the IRS
determines that you renounced your citizenship for this
reason, you will face all kinds of criminal charges.
Frankly, there are easier and probably more effective
ways to protect your assets from creditors and predators
than renouncing your U.S. citizenship.

You might consider legally "adopting" another country, for instance. An American may legally acquire a second passport or citizenship without the risk of losing U.S.

citizenship. The second passport can even be acquired in a different name. This offers you many economic advantages in your "adopted" country, including protection from determined creditors. "Adopting" another country is probably easier than you think. Many Central and South American countries offer citizenship to individuals who are willing to invest in their nation's economies.

If you were interested in obtaining a passport from Costa Rica, for example, you would make a sizable investment in a Costa Rican bank or business or purchase real estate there. After you've made your investment, you can apply for a passport at the foreign consulate.[12] And do consider applying for this passport in a different name. This will enable you to open bank accounts and make investments in your "new" country without anyone from home being able to easily identify you.

Once your funds are safely invested in your new Costa Rican bank account, you don't have to worry about abuses by the U.S. government concerning the current asset forfeiture laws—unless you're involved in something illegal. If you are involved in organized crime or any drug-related activities, sending your money to your new offshore home won't protect it from seizure by the U.S. government. Your new offshore bank account could still be subject to a search by the U.S. government if your offshore haven is a signatory to the Mutual League Assistance Treaties (MLATs).[13]

In addition to having economic benefits, your second passport might even save your life. As Americans have increasingly become the favored target of international terrorists, it's probably best for frequent flyers to travel as something besides an American citizen.[14]

STAYING HOME AND PROTECTING YOUR ASSETS

If you're interested in merely creating an alternative U.S. identity to protect your assets, you might want to consider changing your name. Simply obtaining the requisite forms and then filing the paperwork with the appropriate court can often complete a name change. The cost varies from state to state, but it generally isn't more than $200, excluding attorney's fees when legal assistance is required. After you've filed the name change form with the appropriate court, you usually must place an announcement in the local paper stating this. The notice allows anyone who might object to the name change to be present at the court hearing— including creditors who will likely spot the announcement. Be aware that if you are changing your name to evade creditors, you could be prosecuted for fraud. As with most asset protection plans, changing your name is something that you need to do before you're facing angry and determined creditors.

You can take other preliminary steps, short of fleeing the country, to protect some of your property from determined creditors. Unfortunately, the first step that often needs to be taken is filing for bankruptcy. While this can be embarrassing and psychologically damaging to some people, it can also be one of the few ways for a judgment debtor to hold on to his house or his retirement funds. Depending on the state in which you live, filing for bankruptcy can allow you to stave off creditors without giving away the entire store.[15]

For instance, if you're concerned about losing your home to determined creditors, you should consider purchasing property in Texas or Florida. Both Texas and Florida offer unlimited homestead exemptions—state bankruptcy laws that protect your residence from confiscation by a judgment creditor or loss in a personal bankruptcy. (Other states have limited homestead exemptions, depending on such factors as marital status, age, health, and income.)[16]

Make sure that you hire a good attorney to advise you on how to best protect your assets before you file for bankruptcy. In some instances, for example, it might be

If you're interested in merely creating an alternative U.S. identity to protect your assets, you might want to consider changing your name. Simply obtaining the requisite forms and then filing the paperwork with the appropriate court can often complete a name change.

prudent for the debtor to transfer all real estate assets in his own name to a Family Limited Partnership (FLP), which offers protection from a personal judgment.[17]

One of the most effective ways a judgment creditor can get money from you is by having your wages garnished. If a judgment is entered against you, it's usually easy for that judgment creditor to get such a court order. In fact, wages can be one of the most difficult assets to protect. Once a court has ordered your wages garnished, there's not much you can do to protect yourself. You can attempt to arrange for your boss to pay you off-the-books, but this will probably result in more legal trouble. The best way to protect your wages from potential creditors is to plan ahead. If you anticipate that some creditor may get your wages garnished, move to a state that doesn't recognize wage garnishment.[18] Other income, such as an inheritance, can be placed in an irrevocable trust for your family's benefit, and partnership income can be protected by transferring the interest in the partnership to a Family Limited Partnership, which makes the interest exempt.[19]

Pension plans, IRAs, and Keoghs are 100 percent protected by state law in Texas and Florida. They are also afforded varying degrees of protection in other states. Retirement funds are protected by federal law in some instances. If you're concerned about these assets, you should again investigate the asset protection laws of your state. The key is to do it *before* you are pursued by determined creditors.

If you'd rather avoid bankruptcy, you can use other methods to protect your assets. You can set up various legal entities such as trusts, living estates, and family partnerships that purport to own your assets. (As I've already discussed, many of these legal entities are available offshore as well.) You can set up an irrevocable trust in this country. Irrevocable trusts have been recognized by the U.S. courts to be separate from the estates of the individuals who established them. Therefore, if you've set up an irrevocable trust for your children, those assets cannot be seized by one of your judgment creditors.

You can also consider setting up a charitable trust—if you have a considerable amount of assets that you want to protect. Finally, one other very effective asset protection technique can be to form a corporation and then place the corporate stock into an irrevocable trust. This type of asset protection is similar to the offshore bank concept, in that you need to set up legal entities that you ostensibly do not control. Moreover, you also need to be able to demonstrate to a court that you did not set up these trusts and/or other legal entities in an attempt to defraud potential creditors and collectors. Again, if you're interested in protecting your assets, you'd better set up these asset protection devices long before you find yourself facing creditors or collectors.

While both Nevada and Wyoming offer great privacy for corporate shareholders and directors, the laws of other states do not always provide the same advantages.

Putting your assets in trust can be an effective method of asset protection. For instance, if your husband is about to open a medical practice, he should consider putting the bulk of the family's assets into a trust in the event that he gets sued for medical malpractice. Your husband might also choose to transfer a substantial amount of his personal assets into your name, just in case a patient succeeds in obtaining a personal judgment against him.

Although transferring your assets into someone else's name can be an effective asset protection device, it can also be a means by which you are permanently separated from your money. If you transfer your assets to someone else, you'd better be sure that you can trust that other person. (If you and your wife divorce at a later date, she could potentially argue that the assets that you transferred to her were a gift and, as such, no longer community property.) You should always consult an attorney before you undertake any asset protection measures—particularly when you transfer assets to a spouse, business partner, or friend.[20]

If you're a married woman who is intent upon hiding assets from creditors, you might consider transferring assets into an account in your maiden name. Often when creditors search for assets, they neglect to look under a married woman's maiden name. Another asset-hiding technique is to use your mother's maiden name and identification to open up a bank or brokerage account in that name.[21] If you do choose to open an account under a different name, make sure that you do so in a city where you don't reside. It's fairly easy for an investigator to find a bank account in a woman's maiden name . . . especially if she's opened the account near her parents' home.

You can also attempt to hide assets by creating corporations that are far removed from your own individual identity. A number of states, such as Delaware, Nevada, and Wyoming, require very little recorded information from their corporate clients. Incorporating in Nevada or

Wyoming also has a number of other privacy benefits, including the fact that stockholders are not public record, making ownership and control of a Wyoming or Nevada corporation very difficult to discover. The Wyoming law specifically states that the right to inspect corporate records (including the stock ledger) is reserved for shareholders who have been on record for at least six months and who have at least 5 percent corporate ownership. Nevada law also provides a statutory barrier to anyone, including creditors, who is not a stockholder from gaining access to information on a corporation's stock ledger.

While both Nevada and Wyoming offer great privacy for corporate shareholders and directors, the laws of other states do not always provide the same advantages. Before you decide to form a corporation or invest in one, make sure to have your lawyer investigate the privacy laws governing incorporation in that state.

FINAL THOUGHTS

If you're concerned about protecting your assets, you need to keep two things in mind: (1) asset protection is not a last-minute enterprise and (2) protecting your assets is something best left to the professionals.

If you want to protect yourself from potential judgment creditors, you need to act now. If any evidence indicates that you hid your assets in an attempt to evade creditors, it's highly likely that a court will find that your conduct was fraudulent. And if you think that your hiding techniques are more crafty than those of the average Joe, keep in mind that the courts have seen just about everything when it comes to evading creditors. Also, before you start moving your assets around, you should probably contact an attorney and/or a seasoned financial adviser regarding which asset protection devices would best suit your financial needs.

What's more, you will need sound advice if you want to make effective use of asset protection devices. Finding and implementing the best strategies are generally best left to professionals.

REFERENCES

1. Starchild, Adam, *Keep What You Own: Protect Your Money, Property, and Family from Courts, Creditors and the IRS,* Boulder, CO: Paladin Press, 1994, p. 20.
2. Ibid.
3. Schneider, Jerome, *The Complete Guide to Offshore Money Havens,* Roseville, CA: Prima Publishing, 2000, p. 163.
4. In the last few years, there have been a number of important court decisions indicating that the U.S. Courts will not hesitate to tear into a poorly constructed U.S. trust on behalf of creditors.
5. For people who are interested in having more access to their funds, I often recommend that they establish an asset protection trust within a welcoming offshore jurisdiction and then set up a domestic limited partnership. For details on this asset protection plan, see Schneider, Jerome, *The Complete Guide to Offshore Money Havens,* p. 171. You might also want to ask your attorney or financial planner about whether this asset protection plan could work for you.
6. If you are involved in illegal activity, it won't help you much to move your assets to an offshore haven. When it comes to allegations of money laundering or drug smuggling, most offshore havens will provide bank account information to the U.S. government.
7. Roberts, Paul Craig, "Laws Becoming a Drug War Casualty," *Washington Times,* December 3, 1999.
8. Ibid.
9. Superville, Darlene, "Reform of Forfeitures Gains Ground," AP Online, June 16, 1999.
10. Industry Group 99, Treasury Under Secretary (Enforcement) James E. Johnson Senate Committee on the Judiciary Subcommittee On Criminal Justice Oversight, Regulatory Intelligence Data, July 21, 1999.

11. If you plan on renouncing your citizenship to avoid tax liability, keep in mind that you still owe the IRS for a period of up to ten years, even after you've renounced your citizenship.
12. Pankau, Edmund, *Hide Your Assets and Disappear: A Step-by-Step Guide to Vanishing Without a Trace*, New York: HarperCollins, 1999, p. 87.
13. Almost all of the traditional offshore banking havens are signatories to the MLATs. If you're involved in illegal activity and your account is in a MLAT signatory country, your records could be handed over to the U.S. government for review.
14. For more information on how to obtain a second or third passport, Edmund Pankau suggests that you read *The Passport Report* by W. G. Hill (Hampshire, England: Scopes International).
15. If your conduct during a bankruptcy is found to violate the Bankruptcy Code or any of the Fraudulent Conveyances statutes, you could be convicted of bankruptcy crimes and end up in jail. Before you declare bankruptcy in an effort to avoid judgment creditors, you should, as always, consult with a knowledgeable attorney regarding asset protection.
16. Legislation may be pending in your state to limit the homestead exemption. Be sure that you investigate the homestead exemption laws in your state before you declare bankruptcy.
17. Pankau, Edmund, *Hide Your Assets and Disappear: A Step-by-Step Guide to Vanishing Without a Trace*, p. xxii.
18. You should check with an attorney regarding those states that do not recognize wage garnishment. You should also be aware that many states immediately garnish the wages of a parent who has been required by the court to pay child support.
19. Pankau, Edmund, *Hide Your Assets and Disappear: A Step-by-Step Guide to Vanishing Without a Trace*, p. xxiii.
20. If you transfer these assets for fraudulent purposes, you could be subject to criminal prosecution.
21. Pankau, Edmund, *Hide Your Assets and Disappear: A Step-by-Step Guide to Vanishing Without a Trace*, p. 14.

CHAPTER 6

HIDING AND THE SINGLE GAL

Ready for a true fairy tale? It's all about a fair lady whose Prince Charming turned out to be a frog. Fortunately, like most fairy tales, this one has a happy ending. . . .

Once upon a time, I took on as a client a highly successful attorney in her late twenties named Sandy. On the fast track to a partnership at a high-profile Los Angeles law firm, Sandy came to me for advice on how she could best invest $300,000. I told her that by investing offshore, she'd be able to get her money to work for her more effectively, and she agreed.

After that initial investment, we continued to do business together. As Sandy's law firm income increased, we invested a good portion of it in a wide variety of offshore investment vehicles. Meanwhile, Sandy concentrated on her career, winning one high-profile case after the next. It came as no great surprise to me when she was made a full-equity partner at the ripe young age of thirty-five.

Unfortunately, only three years after their marriage, Sandy and Gary divorced. Because Gary was still unemployed, Sandy was ordered by the court to pay a substantial amount of alimony. And because she and Gary lived in a community property state, all of their assets obtained during their three-year marriage were split equally between them.

Two months later, when she flew up to Vancouver to discuss her now substantial investment portfolio, she was upbeat and jovial. At first, I chalked up her good humor to her recent promotion to partner, but I quickly realized that something else was responsible.

It turned out she'd met someone. His name was Greg and he was a construction worker. It had been lust at first sight and they'd been an item ever since.

Sandy believed Greg was the best thing that had ever happened to her. He wasn't working right now, but that was fine with her. It gave them more time to spend together. In fact, Sandy was thinking about getting married.

As I listened to her map out her marital plans, I had a foreboding feeling. I didn't want to say anything to put a damper on her great mood, but, not one to beat around the bush, I looked her straight in the eye and asked, "Have you and Gary discussed signing a prenuptial agreement?"

She looked puzzled. "Even if we get married without a pre-nup, he's not entitled to any of my separate property, right?"

"In theory, that's right. But the problem with bringing separate property into a marriage is that it can very easily transform into community property. All you have to do is use some of that separate money to pay a few community debts and presto, you've got some attorney yelling about how you made a gift to the community of that separate money.

"The first thing we must do is get you a good divorce attorney," I continued. "We'll need someone to draft an airtight prenuptial agreement that expressly protects the separate property identity of your offshore investments. It's basically your call about whether or not you want to even tell Gary about the offshore money. It might just complicate things."

She laughed. "You're the ultimate romantic."

"Sandy, this is about money, not romance. One has nothing to do with the other."

Despite her feelings about my unromantic approach to marriage, Sandy did consult an attorney before marrying Gary. After considerable debate, Sandy and her attorney decided to include her offshore accounts in her list of separate property. The attorney felt that since she already had to declare the accounts on her income tax returns, it was in her best interest to declare them in the prenuptial agreement.

Unfortunately, only three years after their marriage, Sandy and Gary divorced. Because Gary was still unemployed, Sandy was ordered by the court to pay a substantial amount of alimony. And because she and Gary lived in a community property state, all of their assets obtained during their three-year marriage were split equally between them. Sandy was forced to sell her house and split the proceeds with Gary. She was also ordered by the court to give Gary almost $70,000—or half of the money that "they" saved during their marriage.

But as promised, there's a happy ending to all this. Because of good legal advice and careful financial planning, Sandy had successfully managed to keep all of the money earned during the marriage in an account separate and distinct from her premarital savings and checking accounts.

Despite Gary's repeated requests, she'd adamantly refused to withdraw even a penny from her offshore accounts. And so, when Gary ultimately claimed that she'd made a gift to him of several of her offshore accounts, the court ruled that all of Sandy's offshore assets were clearly her sole and separate property.

CASH AND MR. WRONG: HOW TO DATE AND NOT LOSE YOUR SHIRT

According to Faith Popcorn, a respected "trend watcher" and an adviser to such corporate giants as American Express and IBM, one of the most important business trends to watch for in the next millennium is the growing power of women in the marketplace. Popcorn has nicknamed this trend EVEolution.[1] As EVEolution unfolds, the personal wealth of women across the country will increase. Unfortunately, one of the most common by-products of increased wealth is increased theft.

Single women are increasingly becoming the target of scam artists and other unsavory characters. And while single, working males have spent generations learning how to protect their hard-earned money, single women still have a ways to go. They need to perfect a series of hiding techniques that will keep their newly earned wealth safe from predators in the new millennium.

One of the most common mistakes that single women make when it comes to their money is trusting Mr. Wrong. They manage to amass a considerable nest egg and then, in the blink of an eye, they're ready to sign it all away in order to achieve romantic happiness. As much as I support the concept of true love, I don't support the notion of "what's mine is yours." There is no reason why a single woman needs to sign over her entire fortune in order to live happily ever after with her one true love. Men don't do it, so why should women?

The fact is, if single women intend to be a force in the new millennium, they need to learn to play by the same rules as men—both professionally and personally. So, if a single woman with considerable assets falls in love with a minimum-wage boyfriend, she needs to avoid implementing a full-disclosure policy. Her new beau is entitled only to her love and affection—not a peek at her checking account balance or her stock portfolio

When you think about it, you'll realize that if a woman is really interested in discerning her new beau's true feelings, she should probably try to keep her financial worth totally out of the equation. After all, that's the way the big boys play. You can be sure that a man of means wouldn't give his new girlfriend information about his business, credit line, or recent stock purchases. If a single man wanted to share his good fortune with his new love, he'd probably stick to elegant dinners, small thoughtful gifts, and the occasional bouquet of flowers.

If you are a wealthy single gal, keeping your net worth a secret from your new love requires careful planning and a healthy dose of paranoia. If you are dating someone on a consistent basis, you have to assume that there will be times when he's alone in your place and might begin to snoop around. If he does so, will he have easy access to most of your personal financial documents? If your answer is yes, then you should take steps to protect your privacy.

According to Faith Popcorn, a respected "trend watcher" and an adviser to such corporate giants as American Express and IBM, one of the most important business trends to watch for in the next millennium is the growing power of women in the marketplace.

The first thing to do is to find good hiding places for any documents that contain revealing information about your assets. Consider placing those papers you don't need to access on a regular basis in a safe deposit box at your bank. Also, if you're truly concerned about your privacy, you might consider having your brokerage statements that currently come to you at home, sent to the office.[2]

The single gal who needs more immediate access to her important documents should consider hiding those documents in a virtual safe deposit box. Virtual safe deposit boxes involve scanning important documents—such as wills, loan documents, adoption papers, and so forth—onto a diskette that can be carried with you. Intellimedia Security has developed an online service called www.safedepositbox.com that provides the protection of valuable and confidential electronic documents and files using secure online storage.[3] The fee-based service provides consumers online safe deposit boxes for the protection of important documents such as tax returns, wills, legal documents, personal files, and other documents saved in an electronic format. Users transfer electronic documents between their PCs and their personal online storage boxes using a secure Internet connection.

Safedepositbox.com guarantees customers that their documents are always safe, secure, and accessible around the clock, from anywhere in the world. In the case of a lost electronic key or password, the stored documents can

> **The single gal who needs more immediate access to her important documents should consider hiding those documents in a virtual safe deposit box. Virtual safe deposit boxes involve scanning important documents—such as wills, loan documents, adoption papers, and so forth—onto a diskette that can be carried with you.**

always be retrieved. Users also have the option of granting shared access to their documents to other users, a feature that is useful for the storage of items such as contracts, by-laws, and family records. In addition, users can choose to store their highly sensitive documents in an encoded format, making them readable only after the correct decoding key is provided.

If you're more of an old-fashioned gal, you might prefer to keep your important documents and/or other valuable assets somewhere a little more tangible—like your home or garden. If you really want to make sure that no one "accidentally" views your checking account statement or "inadvertently" purloins your rare gold coin collection, you might want to invest in a home safe.

Safes are currently available that can be mounted just about anywhere in your home. If you're chiefly concerned about your date accidentally reviewing your savings account statement, you probably just need a small free-standing safe. It really doesn't matter if this safe is hidden from sight. Its only purpose is to prevent the nosy date or casual thief from having easy access to your important documents or valuables.

For those of you who'd rather not invest in a safe, there are other effective ways to hide your documents and/or valuables in your home. The walls of most apartments and homes are hollow and can provide excellent hiding places for items of any size.[4] You should also consider hiding in the great outdoors.

LEARNING TO PROTECT YOUR PRIVACY: CHANGING YOUR MINDSET

Because the dating world is premised upon the concept that the man comes to the woman's home to pick her up for a date, single women constantly expose themselves and their assets to danger. When the man arrives at a woman's home in a dating situation, chances are that he will be invited in and left to wait in the living room while she finishes dressing or putting on her make-up. At that time he has a chance to peruse any documents left out in the open or to go through her purse or look at her calendar, address book, and anything else that happens to be lying around. And while not every suitor is interested in going through your address book, chances are that if you date enough men, you will run into someone who is.

The key to protecting your privacy, then, is changing your mindset. If you're going out to dinner with someone you don't know, consider meeting him at the restaurant. This alleviates your need to hide anything. But if you insist on meeting him at your home or if you think that there's a possibility that he may come over after dinner, you need to make sure that no valuable information is left lying around.

You might think I'm paranoid, but I'm not. I'm just realistic. Even the most mundane items, like your calendar, could lead to a break-in. For example, if you're going away for a long weekend with your best friend, chances are that you've marked out that weekend on your personal home calendar. If your suitor is inclined to return and rob you, all he needs to do is check your calendar to see when you'll be out of town.

My advice is to take a good look at the documents you have in your home and do some serious hiding in some of the locations I've already discussed. Don't leave your credit card receipts in a pile on your living room coffee table. It just takes a second for a casual visitor to your home (which could include any repairman) to grab a receipt with your credit card number on it. Don't leave your checkbook or account statements lying on the kitchen counter. Again, within moments, a thief can have your checking account number without ever having to take a single check. Be safe by hiding your important documents before you open your door to possible trouble.[5]

HIDING CASH FOR MARRIED GALS
WHO ARE READY TO FLY SOLO

I can always tell when one of my clients is getting divorced—he usually shows up begging me for advice on how to hide his assets from his wife. I always tell him the same thing—that once divorce litigation has commenced, it's way too late to start trying to hide assets.

So if you're a woman who's even thinking about getting a divorce, you need to start preparing immediately. Before you start hiding anything, you need to figure out the exact amount of your marital assets. This allows you to (1) have a complete paper trail in case your husband decides to empty all the bank accounts; and (2) know where the cash is located so that you can start putting a little away for that inevitable rainy day.

As almost every lawyer and forensic accountant will tell you, the most important thing any woman can do to protect herself in a divorce is to know and understand all of the family's financial matters. For a variety of reasons, many women make the mistake of leaving financial matters to their husbands. And when their husbands file for divorce, the women have no idea what their husbands earn, who holds the mortgage to their house, and what investments they own.

Stephen Reiss, a forensic accountant with expertise in matrimonial disputes, notes that "Most women who get divorced do not have the education, the business expe-

> If you are a wealthy single gal, keeping your
> net worth a secret from your new love
> requires careful planning and a healthy dose
> of paranoia.

> When the man arrives at a woman's home in a dating situation, chances are that he will be invited in and left to wait in the living room while she finishes dressing or putting on her make-up. At that time he has a chance to peruse any documents left out in the open or to go through her purse or look at her calendar, address book, and anything else that happens to be lying around.

rience, or the background to understand the issues that they need to know about."[6] And he notes that even when a woman is educated enough to understand the family finances, she often doesn't want to take the time to deal with them.[7] Forensic accountant Donald Gursey warns that even if a woman doesn't want to be responsible for paying the bills every week, she should at least "stay awake" about the family finances.[8]

Beyond staying awake, you can take concrete steps to protect your assets before you head into the dangerous waters of divorce. You need to make sure that you have in your possession every document that relates to your marital assets. As Raoul Felder likes to say, "In divorce, he who has the best records wins."[9] Your tax record can often be a good guide as to which documents you should collect. Make sure to collect all documents that support the assets listed on your tax return. (And make certain that you look at your tax records from a time period when your marriage was still in good shape. For all you know, your spouse may have started hiding money before he filed for divorce. So, your more recent tax records may not reveal the full extent of your assets.) You should also do an analysis of the bank statements, investment accounts, and asset acquisitions.[10]

Don't confine your hiding to your home. The great outdoors offers a plethora of hiding spots.

You should start opening and studying all financial documents that come to the house. You can't afford to bury your head in the sand any longer. You need to read the bank statement and carefully examine it—paying close attention to whether your bank has changed in the last few months or whether your bank balance has become significantly lower. (If you keep your old bank statements, compare those to your more recent statements. This will help you identify any major changes in your account.) Look at your mortgage statement, comparing it to your original mortgage documents. Check to see if your mortgage company has changed or whether you've refinanced your home.

This could be a sign that your husband took money out of the house when he refinanced. Review all of your insurance policies—fire, casualty, umbrella. Learn what's covered and what's not. Pay particular attention to any personal article floaters. You may find that there is coverage for an asset that you didn't know about. If your husband purchased jewelry or art without your knowledge, he might have insured the items under your policy.

You should then undertake a cash-flow analysis—that is, figure out what the source of your family income is and how the income is spent. Look at your expenses—mortgage, property taxes, car payments, school bills, and so forth. Then, based on a review of those items, you should be able to get an idea as to how much money you spend on a monthly basis and how much is left over. If you notice that your family income is modest on paper yet you live lavishly, it's a pretty good bet that your spouse is hiding assets that you need to find before you or he takes off.[11] Even if everything seems aboveboard, the cash-flow analysis is useful, because it allows you to inventory your marital assets before your husband gets a chance to hide anything. The key thing to remember here is that before you even utter the word *divorce,* be prepared.

The second thing you want to do if you're considering divorce is to realize that no matter how good a settlement you eventually get, the odds are that your current standard of living will decline.[12] You have to make a preemptive strike if you plan on maintaining the standard of living to which you've become accustomed.[13] That means, if you think a divorce might be in your future, you should immediately open a separate account in another city, county, or even state. (It's probably best to use your maiden name, as that will make it harder for others to search for the account. And make sure that you do not provide the bank with either your social security number or your home address.)

According to Stephen Reiss, the non–interest bearing checking account may be the best place to hide money. "It is extremely difficult to trace a non–interest bearing checking account," says Reiss. "The concept of privacy in the United States is such that people are reluctant to authorize a massive database. So, if you want to know if someone has a bank account in Ventura County just outside of L.A., you can't check for it in Los Angeles."[14]

A separate and private bank account ensures that you're protected. Even if you and your husband ultimately reach a fair and just settlement regarding child support and alimony (which would put you in the minority), it's always a safe bet to have a little money stashed away to see you through the divorce. "Since long-term earning power is one of a marriage's biggest assets, women have difficulty maintaining their pre-divorce standard of living—*even with spousal and child support.*"[15] And if you do manage to beat the odds and get a good settlement, chances are your divorce attorney's fees will leave you in a pretty big hole. Divorces are enormously expensive—even when there is nothing to fight about. The cash in your secret little bank account may come in handy when it's time to pay your legal bills. There's no reason to let a little thing like divorce put you permanently in the poorhouse.

CASH AND THE NEW HUSBAND

While it can be emotionally costly to date Mr. Wrong, it can be financially devastating to marry him. The fact is that more and more financially successful women are

I can always tell when one of my clients is getting divorced—he usually shows up begging me for advice on how to hide his assets from his wife. I always tell him the same thing—that once divorce litigation has commenced, it's way too late to start trying to hide assets.

entering into marriage with substantial assets that they need to protect. And although you can take measures to protect yourself once you're married and realize that you're heading for divorce, it's better to be proactive than reactive. "Never contaminate your separate money with the money acquired after marriage," warns noted divorce attorney Raoul Felder. "Keep good lines between everything you had before, and everything you earn during your marriage."[16]

If you have a substantial amount of assets from an inheritance or a divorce settlement and you're getting married, you should consider putting your separate money in a living trust before you even get engaged.[17] This is one of the best ways to keep your money out of your new husband's hands in the event that the marriage doesn't work out. Well-known forensic accountant Donald Gursey notes that most financially successful women do all the wrong things when it comes to getting married. Despite the fact that it could end up costing them thousands, they often agree to combine all of their assets with their new husband's. Gursey advises that the best way a woman can protect her assets when she's about to get married is to keep them separate—period.[18]

Roseanna Purzycki, a tax partner at the accounting firm of Gursey, Schneider, advises that a woman who is considering marrying can protect her premarital, separate property by "setting up a living trust in which she specifies the extent to which the trust's assets will be used for the support of her children and spousal support."[19] By putting her assets in a living trust, she ensures that her separate property remains separate from the community. And the living trust allows her to specify who will get the money and to what extent the principal of the trust can be invaded.[20]

If you own your own house and are about to get married, make sure that you pay your mortgage from a separate property account. If you pay your mortgage from community funds, then the community will begin to have an interest in your home—even though it was your separate property when you entered into the marriage.[21] You can still claim the mortgage as a joint tax deduction on your return, but the house remains your separate property in the event of a break-up.

Similarly, if you have a separate bank account when you enter into your marriage and you use the money in the separate account for community purposes, a lawyer can credibly argue that you gifted your separate property to the community. The theme here is a simple one—if you have a separate asset, you need to keep everything related to that asset separate as well.

Finally, if you have any assets at all when you remarry, get a prenuptial agreement. If correctly drafted, a prenuptial can protect you and your children from financial disaster in the event of a messy divorce. You shouldn't wait until the last minute to have the prenuptial agreement drawn up. It won't make your new spouse any more amenable to signing a pre-nup if you first mention the idea only days before the wedding. You need to have an open and frank discussion about signing a prenuptial agreement far in advance of your actual wedding date.

And here's a final tip concerning the prenuptial process: You should both be represented by different attorneys. That way, no one can claim that he or she was coerced into signing anything or wasn't adequately represented.

REFERENCES

1. "Faith in the Future," Southwest Airlines *Spirit Magazine,* Robert Deitz, October, 1999.
2. If you have any other sensitive financial information that is currently being mailed to your home, you may want to consider having the information sent to an office or to

your mother's house. You can also purchase a post office box at any Mail Boxes, Etc. store.

3. For more information on virtual safe deposit boxes, contact www.safedepositbox.com.

4. For more home hiding places, see chapter 8: "Please Give Me My Space."

5. If you're thinking of taking in a roommate, you should be careful to check a few of his or her references. Then take the added precaution of hiding all sensitive documents from the new roommate, at least until you're sure that you can trust him or her.

6. September 1, 1999, interview with Stephen Reiss.

7. Ibid.

8. Interview with Donald Gursey, September 7, 1999.

9. Berger, Esther T. "To Love, Honor and Litigate?" *Town & Country Monthly* (January 1, 1998).

10. Interview with Roseanna Purzycki, September 7, 1999.

11. Ibid.

12. "Primary breadwinners (still mostly men) can improve their standard of living as much as 40 percent in the first year following a divorce; during that same period, children and their primary caretakers suffer an average drop of 30 percent." Esther T. Berger, "To Love, Honor and Litigate?" *Town & Country Monthly* (January 1, 1998).

13. Even if you manage to open a separate account without your husband's knowledge, you may have to disclose the existence of that account during divorce proceedings. If you do open a separate account with community assets, you should consult with your divorce attorney regarding disclosure requirements.

14. Interview with Stephen Reiss, September 1, 1999.

15. Ibid.—emphasis added.

16. October 19, 1999, interview with Raoul Felder.

17. It is completely your own personal choice whether to discuss the extent of your assets with your husband-to-be. You might feel that complete financial disclosure is a prerequisite for a happy marriage. However, if you're concerned about divulging your exact worth to your intended, you need to take steps before the marriage to safeguard your financial privacy.

18. Interview with Donald Gursey, September 7, 1999.

19. September 7, 1999, interview with Roseanna Purzycki.

20. Ibid.

21. Ibid.

CHAPTER 7

VICTORIA'S SECRETS

Victoria Porter and her husband, Frank, became clients of mine in the early 1980s. When I first met them, Frank owned and operated two auto repair shops located about thirty miles outside of Los Angeles. Victoria spent most of her time looking after the couple's young children. Whenever we met to talk about their finances, Frank would do all of the talking and Victoria would stare blankly off into space. And when tax time rolled around, Frank would hand her the returns and tell her where to sign. Frank would then turn to me and joke that the only thing Victoria knew about money was how to spend it.

Although I didn't mind Frank as a client, I wasn't crazy about him as a person. He tended to be abrupt, controlling, and condescending. He was easily offended and he often had problems dealing with anyone in a position of authority—particularly females. My office manager complained that whenever she called him, he quickly dismissed her and demanded to speak with me. When a female tax attorney friend of mine cautioned Frank to avoid a particular investment, he became extremely hostile and yelled that he didn't take orders from anyone. The only way to avoid conflict with Frank was to do things his way. If he wasn't in control, he wasn't happy. That's why I wasn't terribly surprised when he announced during our bi-monthly lunch meeting that he and Victoria were thinking about getting a divorce. For most of their marriage, Frank had been able to effectively control Victoria. But in recent years, I'd noticed Victoria becoming resentful over Frank's refusal to give her financial independence. During our last meeting, she'd actually gone so far as to openly question Frank's decision to invest $40,000 of their money in a Mexican leather factory. When Frank ignored her comments, she turned to me and began to voice concerns about the political stability of the region. In the middle of our conversation, Frank abruptly stood up and announced that the meeting was over.

When we met for lunch that spring afternoon, I quietly munched away on my salad as Frank explained how he and Victoria could barely be in the same room without fighting. "I just think that it's time to move on," he explained sadly.

"I didn't realize that things between you were so rocky," I said politely.

"Yeah, well, the fact is that things between us haven't been good for a while," Frank admitted. "We fight all the time and the worst part is that it's always about the same thing. Money. Victoria spends too much damn money. The woman shops night and day. She's relentless."

"She sounds pretty typical," I said matter-of-factly.

"No," he replied, shaking his head. "This is different. She's completely out of control. Every time I turn around, she's got another pair of black shoes. It's ridiculous. How many pairs of black shoes does one woman need?"

"I don't know. Are we talking Imelda Marcos numbers here or what?" I asked with a smile.

> **I've always been of the opinion that just because a woman is married, that doesn't give her husband the right to know everything about her. There's nothing in the marriage vows that says you have to disclose everything you do or say to your spouse for as long as you both shall live. In order to stay sane in any marriage, you usually need to keep a few secrets.**

"She's definitely in the ballpark," Frank said. "And I just can't deal with it anymore. We fight about her spending all the time."

"Maybe you should see a counselor."

"We went about three months ago and for a while, I actually thought things were getting better," Frank replied. "For almost two months, I noticed that she'd stopped charging thousands of dollars on her credit cards. Then I got a huge shock. I was looking through her desk drawer for a pair of scissors and I noticed our savings account book wedged in between some folders."

"I think I know what's coming."

"When I glanced at the account balance it was only $1,000."

"Christ."

"She'd spent over $5,000 from our savings in just the last three months. I guess there's not much need for credit cards when you're paying cash."

"When did you tell her that you'd found the savings book?"

"Last night. And it didn't go well," Frank said. "She got all defensive and started yelling about how I'm always keeping tabs on her. Then she accused me of being extremely controlling about money—that I use money to try and control her. She stormed out and didn't come home until this morning."

I stared at him, struggling to think of something to say. I understood why he was upset about Victoria lying to him, but I also understood why she'd felt the need to lie. She was right about how Frank used money to control her. Frank was a classic *controller:* he needed to control everyone and everything. And unfortunately for Victoria, she was his prime target.

Even though Victoria and Frank were trapped in a desperate battle for control of the finances, Victoria remained committed to staying in the marriage. And while Frank was tired of fighting with Victoria over her runaway spending, he still loved his wife and wasn't ready to divorce her.

A few weeks after my lunch with Frank, Victoria came to see me. She recounted how during a couple of long marriage counseling sessions, she'd agreed to curb her excessive spending and Frank had agreed to give her more financial independence. While she believed that he truly wanted to give her more say in how the family income was spent, she also knew that it probably wouldn't happen. Since she wanted to make her marriage work, she'd come up with a different solution.

She wanted to know how to save and spend money without Frank ever knowing. Could I, she asked, help her learn how to keep a few financial secrets?

During my meeting with Victoria, I explained that the best way for her to stay happily married to Frank was for her to come up with a way to spend what she wanted, when she wanted. If she had to keep asking Frank for permission to spend money, she would end up resenting not only him but also herself. She needed to have some financial independence in order to maintain her own self-esteem. But getting and maintaining financial independence from someone as controlling as Frank wouldn't be easy—particularly for someone who'd never held a job outside the home.

I've always been of the opinion that just because a woman is married, that doesn't give her husband the right to know everything about her. There's nothing in the marriage vows that says you have to disclose everything you do or say to your spouse for as long as you both shall live. In order to stay sane in any marriage, you usually need to keep a few secrets. You have to be able to spend some time doing just what you want without having to account for your actions.

Men do it all the time. In fact, many men are expert at doing things their wives never find out about. Since we're entering the new millennium, I figure that maybe it's time the ladies got in on the act.

While the married woman with her own income can keep some of her purchases a secret from her spouse, the stay-at-home married woman often can't buy a tube of lipstick without her husband knowing about it. In many marriages, the stay-at-home woman has few opportunities to spend money without having to explain or defend herself. So, if she wants to make purchases or investments without her husband's knowledge or just wants to hide a little cash for that inevitable rainy day, the stay-at-home married woman has to exploit each and every opportunity she has to generate and hide cash.

You might think that's impossible, but all it takes is some good planning, the desire, and the ability to keep a few important secrets.

WHAT'S GOOD FOR THE GOOSE IS ESSENTIAL FOR THE GANDER

Before we discuss how to solve Victoria's dilemma, we need to address the issue of how she allowed herself to get into a situation in which she had no financial independence whatsoever. Unfortunately for Victoria, when she

**Learning how to hide will give you the
opportunity to shop without explanations.**

married Frank she gave no thought at all about retaining
her own separate financial identity. Her headlong rush
into the security of matrimony left her little time to con-
template the potential loss of her own identity. From the
moment she said "I do," Victoria became committed to the
idea that there was no such thing as "mine" or "yours";
there was only "ours."

This philosophy resulted in the flagrant misuse of
the "mad money" given to her by her parents on her wed-

ding day. Only hours before her nuptials, Victoria's mother, Ginny, had given Victoria $5,000 in cash, explaining that the money was just for Victoria, just in case she ever needed it. Victoria kept the money a secret from Frank until two years into her marriage, when Frank complained that they had no money with which to celebrate their anniversary. Immediately after that conversation, Victoria took the "mad money" and bought them two first-class, round-trip tickets to Hawaii. When she gave Frank his ticket, she said sweetly, "This is my anniversary present to the both of us."

Although Victoria and Frank had a nice time in Hawaii, her use of the "mad money" was both stupid and shortsighted. Whenever she thought about leaving Frank, she regretted using that "mad money" for the Hawaii trip.

I want to be clear about this. It's Victoria's philosophy of marriage that I'm criticizing—not her generosity in using her mad money for a vacation for the two of them. The idea that "what's mine is yours" is wonderful— if it's shared by both partners. Unfortunately, that's rarely the case. Most men do not enter into a marriage believing that "what's mine is yours." And if they do, you can expect that they will completely reject the concept if they end up in divorce court.

Tax expert and certified public accountant Roseanna Purzycki agrees that women need to be extremely careful that their separate property is not used for community purposes. "When you own your own house, you should pay the mortgage from your own separate account so that the house doesn't become community property," she advises.[2]

That's why a woman needs to understand one thing before she picks out her wedding dress: she must play the way the big boys play if she wants to preserve some modicum of financial independence during her marriage.

For example, when a wealthy man is about to get married, the first thing he does is go straight to his lawyer's office for a prenuptial agreement. Even men who have only a small amount of separate property (like a house or a boat) generally take steps to make sure that there are no misunderstandings about who had what when they entered into the marriage. I hate to say this, but it's usually only women who enter into marriage without taking any steps to protect their own separate property.

Well, ladies, it's time for a big behavioral change. When a woman with significant separate property contemplates marriage, she has to take preliminary steps to make sure that her money stays separate or she'll find herself in the same vulnerable position as poor Victoria Porter. No matter how much you love and trust your husband-to-be, if you've got separate property, take some steps to make sure it stays separate before you say "I do."

Those steps can be as simple as getting a prenuptial agreement, or they can be as complicated as opening an offshore bank account in your maiden name and having the statements sent to a post office box in another state. But no matter where you put your money before the marriage, make sure it stays there during the marriage.

According to famed divorce attorney Raoul Felder, "If you do have a little inheritance or some money in the bank before marriage that you want to hang on to, you must never contaminate that money with money acquired during the marriage."[1]

Tax expert and certified public accountant Roseanna Purzycki agrees that women need to be extremely careful that their separate property is not used for community purposes. "When you own your own house, you should pay the mortgage from your own separate account so that the house doesn't become community property," she advises.[2] And unless you're interested in giving all of your separate property to your husband, don't add his name to any of your savings account books. Because if you do end up in divorce court, your husband will be able to argue that by adding his name to your accounts, you intended to give him a portion of your inheritance.

A LITTLE MONEY OF HER OWN

While the woman with an inheritance faces the problem of keeping her separate property out of her husband's hands, the woman without an inheritance faces an even bigger problem. If she has no inheritance to dip into to buy a few things for herself, how does she (with no independent means of support) get her hands on money without her husband knowing about it? When it comes to spending money, many wives face the same problems as Victoria—their husbands control and closely monitor all family finances. Even in those marriages where both the husband and the wife work, it is often the husband who pays the bills, arranges for the home mortgage loan, or runs the family business. Therefore, it is the husband who usually has the best opportunity to make secret purchases.

He's the one who can pull some money out of the house through a refinance of the home mortgage. He's the one who can skim money from the business to fund an extramarital affair. And because he pays the credit cards and reviews the statements, he's also the one who can fly to Vegas without his wife ever knowing about the trip.

But the news isn't all bad, because even in marriages where the husband manages the finances, the clever wife still has a few ways to "raise" capital to finance her fun.

> But the news isn't all bad, because even in marriages where the husband manages the finances, the clever wife still has a few ways to "raise" capital to finance her fun.

Several years ago, by way of example, a client of mine was being divorced by his wife. The client, like Frank Porter, was a controlling man who'd always closely monitored his wife's spending. And now, the wife wanted a bit of revenge. She had demanded a large amount of alimony and extensive child support. In order to assess how much alimony and support was owed the wife, the court ordered an accountant to perform a lifestyle analysis—to inspect the financial records for a period of time to determine how much the parties spent while they were together. When the accountant reviewed the wife's cashed checks, he noticed a strange pattern. Even though the husband was rarely home for dinner or lunch, the wife went to the grocery store every week and wrote a check for $300. Once the accountant noticed this pattern, he requested to see the checks and found that the wife had spent only $100 per week on groceries. She'd write a check for $300 each week and get $200 back in cash. She'd then use the $200 each week to help pay the rent on a small apartment for herself and her lover.

When the forensic accountant divulged the results of his lifestyle analysis to my client, he was shocked to discover that his wife had been having an affair for over a year. His wife's idea to use the grocery store as a means to get her hands on some cash proved to be an ingenious one.

Even though my client balanced the checkbook every month and saw the grocery checks, he had no reason to question the amount. After all, part of his wife's job was to keep the house stocked with groceries and other supplies. He'd never paid much attention to the household expenses. He had to admit in retrospect that had she not filed for divorce, he probably never would have learned of his wife's affair or the small, one-bedroom apartment she had rented in her lover's name.

While the grocery scheme is a pretty clever one, some husbands might question a consistently hefty grocery bill—especially if the fridge is usually empty. In those situations, the wife can suggest that the husband do the shopping himself, thereby discouraging the husband from any further complaining. Rare is the husband who is willing to actually go grocery shopping himself—even if he thinks the grocery bills are too high. But if, over time, the husband begins to suspect that something is amiss, the wife might want to try spreading the cash-back scheme around a bit—getting cash back at the pharmacy or the bakery or any other store that will honor that type of transaction.

Another method by which the resourceful wife can raise funds for her own private use is to make money selling items at swap meets, flea markets, and garage sales. If your husband has to be out of town for a week on business, you can take the opportunity to sell a lot of the things that have sat around your house for years. By selling off your odds and ends, you can raise a significant amount of money without your husband ever knowing about it.

The first thing you need to do is find out where the best swap meets are located in your particular area. At least four directories list numerous swap meets, including: (1) *Clark's Flea Market, USA,* 2516 Cotton Patch Lane, Milton, FL 32570, (2) *The Official Directory to U.S. Flea Markets,* The House of Collectibles, 201 East 50th Street, New York, NY 10022, (3) *The Great American Flea Market Directory,* Fair Times, Sub Dept., P.O. Box 455, Arnold, MO 63010, and (4) *Swap Meet U.S.A.,* P.O. Box 200, Grover City, CA 93433.[3]

You can also just check your local paper for advertised swap meets, flea markets, and garage sales. Swap meets and flea markets present an opportunity for the married woman to raise cash without having to report the income either to her husband or to the IRS.[4]

If you want to report your income to the IRS, but you want to avoid having your husband find out about your extra cash fund, there are a few preliminary steps to take. First, you need to convince your husband to file separate tax returns. Although he might reject the suggestion at first, you should explain to him that the filing of separate tax returns might allow him to save money in the long run.[5] You can also suggest to your husband that since you hardly earn anything, there's no need for him to review your tax returns. You'll have your dad (or mother) just look them over.

I would also suggest that you tell him that filing separately allows you the small amount of financial independence you need to feel good about yourself. Since it's such a small concession for him and doesn't involve him giving you any money, he might go for it.

If you do succeed in convincing him to file separately, you should try and arrange for all of your tax information to be mailed to your parents' house. This way, your tax returns and accompanying financial information will never even cross your husband's path. Out of sight, out of mind.

Incidentally, this out of sight, out of mind principle should also be applied to any other financial information that you'd rather your husband not be privy to. Many of my female clients insist on having any sensitive mail sent to their mother's home. That way, the mail remains secret from their husbands, and it's easy for them to pick up. All you have to tell your husband is that you're going over to your mother's for a visit. No fuss, no muss. So, I would recommend that if you have a small inheritance from your grandmother that you would prefer to keep to yourself, then have all of the bank information relating to that inheritance sent to your mother's house.

If you're not in the mood to spend your Saturday sitting at a swap meet trying to convince strangers to buy your old junk, there is another, rather old-fashioned, way you could get some money about which your husband will know nothing: Call your mother! In marriages where a woman is completely controlled by her husband, she can usually count on her mother to support her efforts to be independent. If your mother and/or father have a little extra money, you can always hit them up for some cash.

Finally, if you're not comfortable asking your parents for money, you might want to consider raising funds out of your own home. Not too long ago, I was approached by a woman for investment advice. She told me that she was married but that she had some secret income of her own that she wanted to invest. Apparently, she'd taken a part-time job as a call girl and had managed to earn around $60,000 a year, working only afternoons. She'd decided to go into the call girl business because she "just didn't have enough money to spend on clothes and accessories."

While I don't recommend that you spend your afternoons working as a call girl, I am suggesting that a number of "off-the-record" part-time jobs are available to hard-working women looking for a little extra income. Such women can always do a little part-time work as file clerks, receptionists, or, depending on their talents, hair stylists.

These off-the-books jobs allow the married woman to earn some extra cash without disclosing it to her husband. What's more, you'd be surprised how many local business people are willing to pay a part-time employee off-the-books for her services.

Over the years, a number of female clients have sought my advice on ways to invest their "off-the-record" income. Almost three years ago I was approached by a new client, Amanda Harris, regarding how she could best invest the over $100,000 she'd managed to earn over the years. Amanda had set up an "informal" beauty salon in the basement of her home. While her husband was at work and her six-year-old son was at school, she'd perform hair, nail, and other beauty treatments for most of the women in her neighborhood.

Her prices were reasonable, so her customers didn't mind the fact that they always had to pay cash, or that they had to schedule their appointments for times when Amanda's husband and son were not around. Despite the demands of running a household, Amanda was able to make good use of her "free" time. Over a period of around three years, she managed to save in excess of $100,000 without her husband's knowledge. She hid a portion of the money in a post office box at Mail Boxes, Etc. and placed a larger amount in a safe deposit box at Safe Deposit Company of New York.[6]

If you're not comfortable working "off-the-books," you might want to consider getting a legitimate part-time job in order to finance your extracurricular activities. However, if you take a "legitimate" job, you should be prepared for your tax form to arrive sometime after the first of the year. If you want to avoid this, take my earlier advice and convince your husband to file separate returns. Then, have your tax information sent to your parents' house.

Keeping Victoria's Secrets

If, like Amanda, you manage to bring in a substantial amount of cash without your husband's knowledge, you still have to be thoughtful and resourceful about how you spend that money. You must realize that as soon as you start spending your secret income, you run the risk of completely blowing your cover.

Take the case of my client Janet Burns, who, unbeknownst to her husband, made over $10,000 by selling

**A safe deposit box is always a good place
to keep a few secrets.**

various used items at a local swap meet. Once Janet realized that she had some extra money for herself, she completely changed. She took up with an unemployed contractor and began spending most of her new wealth on him. She also made the mistake of buying herself a number of new outfits, which immediately raised her profile around town. It wasn't long before jealous neighbors informed her husband about Janet's new, wild spending habits and her "interesting" friendship with the unemployed contractor. Soon Janet's husband was in divorce court, seeking not only custody of their two children but also his share of Janet's fun money.

As you can see, knowing how to earn income without your husband's knowledge is only part of the equation. You also need to make sure that the income you generate comes to you in the form of cash. If you're paid in checks or by credit card, it's more than likely that your husband will find out about your secret business. When it comes to earning income without your husband's knowledge, cash is king.

After you've managed to hide a substantial amount of secret cash, you still have some serious work to do before you can start spending. In contrast to Janet, my client Amanda succeeded in both earning and spending her salon income without ever alerting her husband. When Amanda approached me about what to do with her secret income, we discussed a wide variety of offshore investment opportunities—and also the fact that Amanda wanted to take some of that hard-earned money and cut loose without her husband ever knowing about it.

I explained to Amanda that with a little careful asset management, she could arrange to spend her earnings without her husband's knowledge. First, I suggested that she set up an offshore bank account and get the bank to issue her a secured offshore credit card.[7] As I told Amanda, one of the first clues to what a wife is spending is her credit card statement. If a husband is interested in discovering what his wife has been up to during the day, he just needs to peruse the latest credit card statements. It will tell him where she lunches, where she shops, how much she spends, and exactly what she buys. And even if he fails to review the statements from time to time, all he has to do is look at the mail to figure out what his wife is spending money on. Credit card companies sell their consumer information to marketing companies all the time. So, if someone buys a lot of clothes at Macy's, that person will probably receive a lot of clothing catalogues in the mail.

> **If, like Amanda, you manage to bring in a substantial amount of cash without your husband's knowledge, you still have to be thoughtful and resourceful about how you spend that money. You must realize that as soon as you start spending your secret income, you run the risk of completely blowing your cover.**

For the interested party, the mail can be a great source of information about who's spending what and where.

For this reason, one of the most effective ways to spend discreetly is to jettison your onshore credit card and go offshore. The offshore credit card allows you to make purchases on credit without the transactions being reported to any credit reporting bureau. Credit reporting bureaus do not have access to the offshore credit system.[8]

But before you go rushing out to get an offshore credit card, you need to realize that not all offshore banks are created equal. Selecting where to open your offshore account or, if you've amassed a sizable sum, which bank to purchase requires thought and expertise.[9] If you are interested in acquiring an offshore credit card, you should make sure that your offshore bank provides that service.

Furthermore, it's probably best not to invest your money in an offshore branch of your present bank. If you bank at Wells Fargo in Los Angeles, you shouldn't open an account at an offshore branch of that same bank. Otherwise, when a potential plaintiff serves a subpoena on your local U.S. bank demanding all of your credit card records, the bank will have to turn over not only your local bank records but also all of your records from its offshore branches.[10]

So in addition to acquiring an offshore credit card, I also suggested that Amanda open a separate, non–interest bearing checking account in another city using her maiden name. By doing this, Amanda could avoid giving her social security number and having to report any earned interest to the IRS (or to her husband, for that matter). The separate account would be difficult, if not impossible, for anyone to locate. Remember, in most cases every county in a state has a separate database in which banking accounts are registered.

If Amanda's husband did go searching for a bank account, he would have to know the precise county in which she'd opened the account. Anyway, since I advised Amanda to have all account statements sent to her mother's house, the chance of her husband finding out about the account was slim.

Although I counseled Amanda that it wouldn't be wise to put too much money into an account that earned no interest, I did tell her that the account would be helpful in two critical ways: (1) she could write checks without her husband's knowledge; and (2) she could get a debit card to use, based on the balance in her checking account. As a result, the checking account would afford her two additional methods by which she could spend money without her husband's knowledge.

After our consultation, Amanda chose to open an off-shore bank account with most of her money. We made sure that all bank statements were sent to a post office box. She also chose to purchase a secured credit card for $5,000.[11] She then took about $5,000 and opened up a non–interest bearing bank account in neighboring New Jersey. The New Jersey bank also issued her a Visa debit card.

FINAL THOUGHTS

If you're married to a controller, you should first think about whether you want to stay in the marriage. If you're interested in getting out and taking some cash with you, take steps to protect yourself before you even meet with an attorney.

If you're committed to staying in the marriage, there are ways that you can create a separate financial identity for yourself that will allow you spend or save money without your husband's knowledge. You just need to decide whether you want to be someone separate and apart from your husband, or whether you're resigned to allowing him to control everything in your life.

REFERENCES

1. October 20, 1999, interview with Raoul Felder.
2. September 7, 1999, interview with Roseanna Purzycki.
3. Cooper, Jordan L., *How to Make Cash Money Selling at Swap Meets, Flea Markets, Etc.,* Port Townsend, WA: Loompanics Unlimited, 1998, pp. 158–159.
4. Failure to report income to the IRS is a crime.
5. Before deciding whether or not to file separately, you should consult with a qualified tax attorney or certified public accountant.
6. Safe Deposit Company of New York, 120 Broadway, New York, NY 10005. This safe deposit box company is not affiliated with any bank.
7. For more information on how to open a foreign bank account, see *The Complete Guide to Offshore Money Havens,* Jerome Schneider, Roseville, CA: Prima Publishing, 2000, pp. 243–262.
8. Cornez, Arnold, *The Offshore Money Book,* Chicago: Contemporary Books, 1998, pp. 109–110. See also chapter 3: "Men Behaving Badly."
9. Before you actually open an offshore account or purchase an offshore bank, you should thoroughly investigate the bank and the country in which the bank is located. Not all foreign banks will provide the services you require. See *The Complete Guide to Offshore Money Havens,* by Jerome Schneider, pp. 250–254.

10. Cornez, Arnold, *The Offshore Money Book,* pp. 109–110. See also the chapter in this volume entitled "Men Behaving Badly."

11. The offshore card line of credit is generally between 50 percent and 66.66 percent of the amount on deposit in an interest-bearing savings account with the offshore bank. *The Offshore Money Book,* Arnold Cornez, p. 110.

Chapter 8

Please Give Me My Space: Finding the Ultimate Personal Hiding Place

When I first met Dr. Arthur Benson, he'd been practicing internal medicine for over ten years. Arthur ostensibly contacted me because he'd read my offshore money havens book and wanted to get advice about which foreign investment opportunities might be available to someone in his income bracket. After our initial phone conversation, he arranged to fly up to Vancouver for a consultation.

During our meeting, I realized why Arthur was truly interested in offshore investment—he and his wife were having marital problems and he wanted to take steps to secure some of his assets before she filed for divorce.

"This is really hard for me." Arthur began, fidgeting nervously in the chair across from my desk. "I just don't know what to do. I'm not sure I'm getting divorced, but things don't look too good right now. You see, last week Helen found some pictures of me and my first wife, Barb."

"So, she's pissed off that you didn't throw away all the pictures of your first wife," I concluded. "Sounds like she's just a little jealous. I'm sure it'll pass."

"Well, there's something else," he added quickly. "Helen didn't know that I'd been married before. I'd been divorced from Barb for over five years when I met Helen. I just didn't think she needed to know about the first marriage—especially since it only lasted four months."

"Four months is more like a long date than a marriage."

"Exactly. I was going to tell her eventually, but then while we were dating she said all this stuff about how she'd never get involved with a divorced guy. I figured that it wouldn't hurt if I never told her about Barb. Only my parents and a few close friends knew about my first marriage. I mean, that's how brief it was."

"But then Helen found the pictures."

"Yeah. I made a big mistake. I only had a few pictures from the wedding. I could have thrown them away, but I just didn't. I hid them in one of those books. You know the kind with the false inside?"

"Some of those fake books look pretty real."

"Well, so did this one. The only problem was the title. When Helen noticed the leather-bound copy of *Sense and Sensibility* in my bookcase, she immediately became suspicious."

"You're definitely not a Jane Austen kind of guy."

"I should have either thrown those pictures away or hid them somewhere better," Arthur sighed sadly. "I just couldn't think of anywhere safe to put them."

"Next time you want to hide something, you really should call me. I know tons of places you could have hidden those pictures."

"For instance?" Arthur eyed me skeptically.

"You could have rented a safe deposit box and then hidden the key behind some molding in your home," I said. "Or, you could hide pictures, documents, and other small, light items in your ceiling. Do you have any acoustical tiles in your house?"

"Yeah."

"Well, those push out and you could place some documents up there. You just have to be sure to tightly fasten them to a beam." I could see he was starting to calm down. "Look, Arthur, it's all going to work out. I'm sure your wife won't leave you over something like this. She'll cool off and everything will go back to normal."

Fortunately for Arthur, my prediction proved accurate. Helen ultimately forgave him. Every once in a while, though, she would search the house for further evidence of his short-lived marriage or other mementos of his past about which he might have neglected to tell her.

But thanks to our productive meeting, she never again found anything that Arthur wanted to keep hidden. You see, Arthur had taken my advice and moved his memories to a more secure location—a place I like to call the "outer sanctum."

Acoustic tiles provide a good hiding place for both large and small valuables. Just be sure that you tightly secure your valuables inside the tiles.

The outer sanctum is a very secure place where you hide your most personal and private possessions. Everyone has at least one secret that he or she needs to keep in the outer sanctum.

What Do You Really Have to Hide?

Many people don't recognize that they need to find or construct an outer sanctum. Over the years, I've noticed that most people tend to hide their most cherished mementos in the most obvious of places. They erroneously conclude that no one will ever find the items because no one is really looking for them.

Well, as Arthur Benton discovered, hidden things have a way of being found when you least expect it. And even if you're lucky enough to keep your private letters and photographs hidden during your lifetime, you always run the risk of those same items being discovered after your death.

If you're not sure whether you have any property worth hiding, you should ask yourself two questions: First, would you be upset if the property was stolen? For those of you who answered yes, you need to consider putting the property in a bank safe deposit box.

Now ask yourself: Would you be upset—or embarrassed—if the property was merely discovered by others? Like Arthur's photographs, for instance?

If the answer to that question is yes, or you want your financially valuable property more easily accessible than it would be in a safe deposit box, you need to start thinking of a good hiding place.

I'm sure a few readers out there still can't imagine the need to hide anything. And they may indeed have nothing to hide. But I would guess that they probably just haven't focused on what valuable possessions they actually keep at home. For instance, if you keep a large amount of cash around the house, you should think about finding a hiding place for it. Burglars have a way of knowing which people keep large amounts of cash in their home.[1] They also have a way of discovering who in the neighborhood has a substantial jewelry collection. So, if you own a lot of expensive jewelry that you'd rather not stash in a bank vault, you might want to purchase or construct a suitable hiding place on your property.

Even if you don't have priceless jewelry or stacks of cash on hand, you still might have items worth hiding, such as gold or silver coins, stock certificates, bonds, wills, valuable family heirlooms, address books, and even keys to your bank safe deposit box. And then there's the personal stuff: photographs, letters, and souvenirs, for example.

My point is that almost everybody has something worth hiding. The problem is that most people don't think about hiding it until it's either stolen or discovered. Don't let this be you. Start searching for your outer sanctum right now.

HOME IS WHERE THE GOODS ARE

After you've identified what you need to hide, your next task is to find a suitable hiding place. As I've mentioned, you can always rent a safe deposit box, but that still

> The outer sanctum is a very secure place where you hide your most personal and private possessions. Everyone has at least one secret that he or she needs to keep in the outer sanctum.

leaves you with little access to your goods. If you want to keep your secret items a little closer at hand, find a place to hide them in your own home. This is easier than you'd think.

Let's say that, like my client Arthur Benson, you've got some pictures you'd rather not share with others in your household. You decide that hiding the items in a hollowed-out book is tantamount to putting them under a flashing neon sign that reads "Look here!" Fortunately, when you begin to survey your house you realize you have a plethora of good hiding places from which to choose.

You glance at the overstuffed chairs and couch in your living room and see that they would be a perfect hiding place for your sensitive documents. Removing the bottom covering of material easily accesses the bases of modern couches and beds. All you need to do is turn over your chair and pull out the staples that are used to secure the upholstery to the underside of the chair's frame. (You

"Most couches have removable skirting that make convenient places to hide money, jewelry, and other valuables."

may need to cut away enough of the internal padding to store your goods inside.) You then place your envelope containing the pictures and the certificate inside the chair's padding and foam. After your package is hidden, secure it with adhesive tape or some other fastener. You might even use Velcro strips. Once your package is hidden and securely fastened, use your staple gun to refasten the upholstery to the underside of the chair.[2] Make sure to do a good job of reattaching the covering on the bottom of the chair. A good searcher will easily spot shoddy work.

If your wife tends to have the furniture reupholstered every few years, you should consider an alternate hiding spot. Michael Connor, author of *How to Hide Anything,* suggests that hi-fi speakers make good hiding places because they can be easily opened and goods can be stashed inside within a matter of minutes.[3] Connor does caution that in the event of a robbery, though, hi-fi speakers will most likely be stolen. So, if you plan to use them to hide things, you should probably just do so in the short-term.

In addition to hiding sensitive documents in common household furniture, you might consider hiding them in the walls, pipes, and other types of infrastructure of your home. The electric light switch on the wall can be removed to provide an excellent, but generally small, hiding area. It's probably best not to use this particular location to hide paper or other flammable objects because of the exposed wires; however, if you want to use the light switch area as a hiding place for sensitive documents or larger items, you could construct dummy outlets. This involves clearing out the socket housing from the wall and using just the face plates. "You do have to remove the plug faces from the guts and glue them into the slots in the face plates. Use plastic cement, super glue, or epoxy. Cut off the screw heads and attach them to the face plate with epoxy and super glue."[4]

If you're not interested in creating your own dummy outlet, you can just buy one from any number of stores.[5] It's easy to install and often comes with a template, key, and installation saw. If you decide to purchase a false outlet or a false light switch with a lock box attached, you merely need to remove the socket housing from the wall and install your "fake light switch" and lock box. When you reassemble, be certain you do a tidy job. Sometimes, it's wise to add an extra coat of paint to the unit, making sure that it covers the screw heads.[6] The paint will also make it more difficult for burglars to unscrew the outlet plate.

If you'd rather not use the wall socket safe, specialty stores offer a wide variety of safes that will be difficult for any intruder to spot. You can choose from a selection of book safes, soda can safes, as well as specialty can safes like Shell Oil, Ajax, peanut butter, STP oil treatment, Desenex, and Pledge. The cans are weighted to give them a realistic feel, while actual product labels and lids are used to ensure an authentic outside appearance. The inner chambers of these fake product safes are usually constructed out of soft, high-density plastic that won't scratch the contents.

In addition to offering soda can safes, wall socket safes, and book safes, Personal Protection Products also sells diversion safe videotapes that look exactly like your real videotapes. They also sell diversion safe stones that can be placed in your garden or bushes. If you need to leave a key for a friend or a few dollars for a delivery person, the hollowed-out, weighted stones make a good hiding place. Be aware, however, that some of the lesser quality stone safes have a "fake rock coating" on the outside that tends to wear off. When it does, the artificiality of the stone can be obvious to even casual observers.

If you're concerned that stones, cans, and socket safes won't protect your valuables, you might consider going a bit deeper into the infrastructure of your house.

**Be sure to mix the storage containers with other
ordinary products around the house.**

Your home's air ducts provide an excellent hiding place
for both large and small items. As Jack Luger points out
in *The Big Book of Secret Hiding Places,* the grills over air
ducts are usually easily removed and provide a large
place in which to store sensitive items.[7] For example, let's
say you have an old 1940s watch from your grandmother
and you're concerned about it being stolen. In order to
protect the watch from theft, you decide to hide it in the
top drawer of your dresser, wrapped in a pair of old socks.
While that may seem like a clever hiding spot, it's probably one of the worst places you could put the watch. When
burglars look for valuable items, they usually check first
in the sock and underwear drawers. They simply turn the
drawer upside down and sift quickly through the contents, looking for valuables.

    If you're really serious about protecting your valuable
watch and other jewelry, you could place everything in a

large box and stick the box just inside the air-conditioning duct. If you do use this spot to hide things, make sure that you've tucked your valuables far enough back in the duct so that they are not easily visible if someone were to shine a flashlight into the duct's grill. Moreover, when concealing material inside a duct, use a horizontal run rather than a vertical one. "You don't want to risk dropping objects down out of reach. If necessary, use magnets to hold light material such as paper, so that it doesn't blow up against and block the grill."[8]

Other hiding places within the home include interior doors. Many have hollow-core construction, which makes them good hiding places. In order to hide things in the doors, often you only have to cut into the top of the door with a utility knife. "This will expose a deep compartment, the hollow core of the door."[9] You can use this space to hide not only the photographs of your secret first marriage, but also money and any other materials you want to conceal.

If you're not skilled at using a utility knife or any other tool, for that matter, you might try hiding things within the walls of your home. Consider the case of Oliver Pierce, model husband and father, and occasional marijuana user.

Oliver believes his marijuana use is harmless but is concerned that his kids might happen upon his stash. After thinking about a wide variety of hiding places,

In addition to offering soda can safes, wall socket safes, and book safes, Personal Protection Products also sells diversion safe videotapes that look exactly like your real videotapes.

Oliver finally decided to hide the stash in a metal curtain rod in his bedroom. While the kids were at a movie one weekend, he carefully drilled a hole in the curtain rod, taking care not to drill out too much of the diameter of the pole.[10] He then inserted a plug made of plastic wood at the end of the pole and covered the end piece with the curtain rod end piece.[11] This hiding place allowed Oliver access to his marijuana without leaving it within reach of his children.

Although a curtain rod is a good hiding place for a relatively small item, you could choose an alternate hiding place if you have something a little larger to conceal. Several years ago, one of my clients converted a large sum of cash into gold coins, which he placed in a safety deposit box at his local bank. When several safety deposit boxes at the bank were robbed, he decided that the coins would be safer at home in a safe. A few weeks later, he read an article about how easy it was to figure out the combinations for many home safes. In that he possessed over $100,000 in gold coins, he decided that he needed to come up with a more secure hiding spot.

After a few days of surveying his property, he noticed that a few floorboards in his living room were loose. He carefully pried up the boards and discovered a small space under the floor where he could store his coins. Once the coins were securely placed under the floorboards, my client nailed the floorboards back into place. He then rubbed the heads of the new nails with sandpaper, so that they would blend in with the other nails in the floor. When he was confident that the floorboards were secure, he placed the oriental rug back over the boards, taking care that the boards were under the center of the rug. This was particularly important because would-be thieves often pick up the edge of carpets to check whether anything is hidden under them. It's a safe bet, however, that the thief will not take the time to completely remove the carpet to look under the center portion.

If you are handy with tools and willing to do a little work, you can create a wide variety of hiding places in your own home. Beams in your house can be hollowed out. Or, with the right tools, you can construct a hollow space behind the wallpaper or the wallboards. (This type of work requires the use of a router or some other tool that will allow you to dig out a trench from the sheet rock plaster covering your wall.[12])

If you plan on stashing important documents or cash within the actual walls of your home, be sure that they are properly protected from the elements. Place the documents in a tightly sealed plastic bag or container. A plastic bag sealed tight with tape will keep out wetness, but if there was moisture inside the bag before you sealed it, it could condense in cold weather and end up wetting your important documents. You should also make sure that the documents are tightly fastened to the wall by nails or some other secure fastening material within your hiding place. If the documents are not secured within the fake bottom of a drawer, for example, a hearty shake by some burglar could easily rattle the contents.

Another good-sized hiding place for important documents, photographs, or cash is behind your medicine chest. Take the case of Hannah, who had $10,000 in "mad money" she wanted to hide from her husband. She needed a place where the money would be secure and out of sight, but where she could get to it quickly.

At first, she considered hiding the money in a sofa . . . but what if her husband suddenly decided to surprise her by throwing the old couch out and buying a new one?

She then ventured into the kitchen and briefly considered hiding the cash under some broken tiles. She discarded that idea when she realized that the tiles could easily come loose and expose the cash.

She tried fastening the money to the back of a bedroom mirror, but the package of cash pushed the mirror

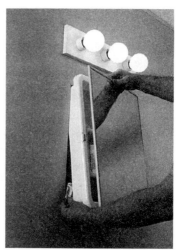

**The simple removal of your medicine cabinet
can open up a great hiding place with a
minimal amount of effort.**

out from the wall. Her husband would surely notice that
the mirror wasn't hanging right and would try to fix it.

Hannah's next stop was the bathroom. That's when
she spotted the medicine chest. It's an especially great
hiding spot if it's sunk into the wall, because an opening
has already been cut into the wall where you can store
things. You merely remove the chest by unfastening a few
screws.[13]

If your medicine chest is hung flush with the wall, you
can still use it as a hiding place. You just need to do a little
work first, by cutting a hole in the wall behind the medicine chest. As Jack Luger explains, "A masonry bit will drill
a hole in the sheet rock to give you a start cutting with a
keyhole saw. If you don't have a keyhole saw or a masonry
bit, cut a rectangular section out with a utility knife. You'll
have to make several passes to cut deeply enough."[14]

When Hannah removed her medicine cabinet, there
was an opening already cut in the wall and a space under

In order to protect the watch from theft, you decide to hide it in the top drawer of your dresser, wrapped in a pair of old socks. While that may seem like a clever hiding spot, it's probably one of the worst places you could put the watch. When burglars look for valuable items, they usually check first in the sock and underwear drawers.

the medicine cabinet that went all the way down to the floor. She placed the cash in a plastic bag and attached a string securely to the bag. She then tacked the string inside the wall before dropping the bag down into the wall space. Confident that her "mad money" was safe from discovery, she screwed the medicine chest back into the wall. She then washed out the sink and used her handy dust-buster to clean up the little pieces of plaster that had dropped onto the bathroom floor.

The whole procedure was so easy that Hannah even had time to cook her hubby his favorite dinner—minus the "greens," of course.

If you're really handy with tools and need to hide more than just documents, you could make a secret compartment in your home to store larger objects such as jewelry, art, or even weapons. Wood paneling in a home can provide the perfect cover for a hiding space. You can remove a piece of the paneling and create a hidden compartment in the wall. You can also cut a hole in the wall to store items and then cover the hole with a mirror. "A full-length mirror gives you convenient access to a large compartment at least sixteen inches wide."[15] Finally, you might want to use a coat or hat rack to stash a bunch of medium-sized goods. This involves cutting a hole in the wall and then selecting the appropriate-sized coat or hat rack to affix over the hole. Even the worst handyman or handywoman could probably handle the hat rack scheme.

You could also construct an excellent hiding place by building a false bottom under one of your dresser drawers. The experts contend that this is an easy and relatively effective way to store items, as long as you don't block off 90 percent of the drawer's total area. (If you need a great deal of hiding space, you should construct false bottoms for several drawers.)

Constructing a false bottom isn't terribly difficult if you follow these simple instructions.

1. Measure the drawer and then go to your local Home Depot and have its employees cut you a piece of wood the same type as the bottom of your drawers. (You might even want to take in your drawer bottom so they can match it perfectly. If it's not such a great match, you can line the drawers with paper.)

2. Hold the false bottom in place with Velcro or plastic strip magnets, which you can buy in hardware stores.[16]

That's all there is to it. Remember, however, that false bottoms in drawers are useful only for hiding flat or small documents.

As you have undoubtedly realized by now, your home is filled with good hiding places. But before you start to use any of them, you still need to consider the various scenarios under which your hiding place could be discovered. Everyone has different habits and you need to be aware of those habits if you hope to successfully conceal objects in your home.

Does your wife like to move the artwork in your home around every few months? Then forget about hiding anything behind your paintings. Or, if your husband likes to send the rugs out for a cleaning at least once a year, you should not create any secret compartments in your floor.

And if you've had trouble with your air-conditioning, don't put anything in the air ducts for the repairman to discover.

Remember, to effectively hide items in the home requires knowledge of all the residents' routines, as well as a cleverly concealed hiding place.

HIDING AND THE GREAT OUTDOORS

If your spouse is a good searcher and also has a suspicious nature, you might want to consider moving your hiding place to the great outdoors. The yard is an excellent hiding place for items that you need to store for a long period—maybe forever.

If you really want to make sure that your hiding place isn't discovered, you should consider going underground—deep underground. By burying your "mad money" in the backyard, you can be fairly confident that it will never be discovered. Or, if you're worried about your wife finding some love letters your girlfriend sent you, bury them in the backyard as well.

The fact is, you can bury just about anything underground, including documents, stocks, bonds, photographs, valuable jewelry, and any other items that can easily be stolen. With the right guidance and information, burying items can be easy, inexpensive, and very effective.

The great outdoors provides the creative hider with still more opportunities.

Finding the perfect spot to bury something requires some thought. You need to be sure that it's not visible from the road so that you can hide your objects there in relative anonymity. Second, you must be confident that the spot will not be exposed by inclement weather—for example, that wind, rain, or snow will not erode the soil above your hiding place.

Select your hiding spot on high ground behind your house. (It's best to pick a place where water won't collect.) Next, make certain that no wires, junction boxes, telephone lines, or any other kind of underlying structure might be disrupted by your buried container. (You should also avoid burying anything *near* an underlying structure, in the event that the structure needs to be repaired—such as a broken cable connection.)

Make sure that you can easily find the location of your buried treasure. Though it sounds unlikely, it's all too possible to bury your goods underground and then be unable to locate the exact spot of your stash. So, remember the location of your buried treasure by some landmark or landscaping. If nothing is nearby, you might want to plant or build a landmark. For instance, if you bury your items near the driveway, you could plant a rosebush nearby to help point you to your hidden goods.

Another good buried hiding place might be under the flagstones of your patio or walkway, if you have them. Just pick a flagstone and dig a hole beneath it sufficient to house whatever you're hiding. Then place your goods in the hole, cover it with dirt, and replace the flagstone.

If you'd rather leave your patio intact, you might consider hiding your valuables in a lawn ornament of some sort. Lawn ornaments provide excellent hiding spots and are easily available from novelty stores and mail order catalogs. The catalogs often feature lawn ornaments like frogs and turtles with secret hiding spots inside of them.[17]

But if you're looking for a bigger hiding place, you'll need to go with a large ornament. "[A] big hollow donkey might be more ostentatious than you'd like, but it also provides a larger hiding spot than the little metal frog," writes Dennis Fiery in *How to Hide Things in Public Places*.[18] Fiery also notes that if you're opposed to lawn ornaments, you can hide things in fountains, pots, vases, and other sculptures that often have hiding spaces built into them.[19]

Once you've decided where to bury your goods, you need to purchase the appropriate container. Burial containers generally need to have three features: (1) imperviousness to water pressure/moisture; (2) resistance to crushing earth; and (3) the ability to be resealed.[20]

Number 3 is particularly important if you plan on regularly accessing your items. One of the best burial containers is called "Hide-a-Vault," made by Monsanto and marketed by a variety of firms.[21] While the dimensions of the Hide-a-Vault are small, the container is still useful for hiding things such as paper, gold, or jewelry. (For a complete listing of places where you can purchase manufactured burial containers, read the appendix to *How to Bury Your Goods*.)

The great outdoors provides the creative hider with still more opportunities. If you have a woodpile outside your home, you might consider hollowing out one of the logs to use as a hiding place. This process is relatively simple. You remove a strip of bark, gouge out a hole underneath where the bark was, and then insert your valuables.[22] Next, merely glue the bark back on and place the log somewhere deep within the pile.

The compartment inside the log can be as big as necessary. However, if you plan on storing documents, they should be packaged in a leak-proof container or bag.

All you have to do, then, is remember where you put your hollow log, and always be the guy or gal who goes out for the firewood. Otherwise, you might find your valuables going up in smoke in the middle of winter.

As you have undoubtedly realized by now, your home is filled with good hiding places. But before you start to use any of them, you still need to consider the various scenarios under which your hiding place could be discovered. Everyone has different habits and you need to be aware of those habits if you hope to successfully conceal objects in your home.

FINAL THOUGHTS

If you just don't feel comfortable keeping your most valuable or personal items at home, you can always fall back on renting a safe deposit box at a local bank. Most financial institutions offer safe deposit boxes as a service with annual renting fees starting as low as $15. Moreover, if you choose to hide unreported cash in your safe deposit box, it is extremely difficult to trace and seize since there is no paper trail to follow. It takes a great deal of time and money to locate another individual's funds stored in a safe deposit box.

If you do hide your valuables/cash in a safe deposit box, you might want to pick a non-chartered institution, because it's not subject to state or federal banking regulations. In addition, in the event of your death, only assigned individuals are allowed the right of entry. So, if you have some love letters that you want your children never to see, make sure they have no access to your safe deposit box in the event of your death.

Put that personal letter in one box. Put those documents you do want your children to have in another. That's the way to keep your secrets safe, sealed, and secure.

REFERENCES

1. Many home invasion robberies target people who are known to have large amounts of cash on the premises.
2. Connor, Michael, *How to Hide Anything,* Boulder, CO: Paladin Press, 1984, pp. 1–2.
3. Ibid., p. 4.
4. Luger, Jack, *The Big Book of Secret Hiding Places,* Port Townsend, WA: Breakout Productions, Inc., 1999, pp. 36–37.
5. Several companies sell home diversion safes on the Internet. You can also contact the Spy Store at www.spystore.com or Personal Protection Products at www.protectionproducts.com. In addition to these two stores, at least ten other stores sell personal protection products on the Internet.
6. Luger, Jack, *The Big Book of Secret Hiding Places,* p. 6.
7. Ibid., p. 39.
8. Ibid., p. 40.
9. Ibid., p. 45.
10. Connor, Michael, *How to Hide Anything,* p. 9.
11. In his book *How to Hide Anything,* Michael Connor suggests that for added security, the end piece of the curtain rod should be glued into place. While this does provide additional security, it doesn't allow the hider easy access to whatever he's stashed in the pole. So, if you need to be able to get into the curtain pole easily, you should consider not gluing the end piece onto the curtain rod.
12. Ibid., p. 10.
13. Luger, Jack, *The Big Book of Secret Hiding Places,* p. 51.
14. Ibid.
15. Ibid., p. 55.
16. Ibid., p. 31.
17. Fiery, Dennis, *How to Hide Things in Public Places,* Port Townsend, WA: Breakout Productions, Inc., 1996, p. 48.
18. Ibid.
19. Ibid.
20. Eddie the Wire, *How to Bury Your Goods,* Port Townsend, WA: Breakout Productions, Inc., 1999, p. 53.
21. Ibid.
22. Ibid., pp. 50–51.

CHAPTER 9

TAKE THE MONEY AND RUN: KEEPING THE IRS OUT OF YOUR BUSINESS

Before people think about hiding money from robbers or even from their spouse, chances are that they've already thought about how to hide money from the IRS. It's been my experience that most money-hiding schemes are designed to hide money from the most aggressive creditor of them all: the Internal Revenue Service. Many Americans spend their entire lives trying to figure out a way to outsmart the IRS. Some stay within the law, exploring and implementing a wide variety of investment plans to minimize their tax exposure. But others choose to become part of the growing underground economy. The tax evasion schemes run the gamut from failing to report income, to cashing paychecks to bogus employees. The only thing the schemes have in common is that they're illegal and increasingly popular. The American businessman is waging a war against the IRS and his tactics are becoming increasingly more desperate.

As I did research for this book, I came across a news-
paper story about a man who'd just been indicted for
felony tax evasion. Burt Myers, who owned ten hair
salons in the Southern California region, had managed to
funnel over $500,000 in unreported income to Switzer-
land over a five-year period. His tax evasion scheme was
simple but effective. Every week, he paid out salaries of
around $2,000 to a number of nonexistent employees. He
then cashed the endorsed paychecks for those employees
at his local bank, where he provided the teller with a
small weekly bonus for "helping" him out.

For over five years, Burt continued to cash checks for
his phantom employees and to quietly invest the money
in offshore bank accounts. It's likely that the scheme
would have gone undetected if not for Burt's own vanity.
Because he was trying to avoid detection by the IRS, the
salon owner tended to live a fairly understated lifestyle.
While his family, friends, and employees appreciated that
he was doing well, they had no idea how enormously
wealthy he'd become over the last five years. And as the
balance in Burt's offshore account grew, he became
increasingly obsessed about showing everyone that he
wasn't some small-time salon owner anymore.

After years of saving, Burt finally decided that it was
time to spend. He withdrew over $200,000 from his off-
shore account and bought himself a flashy new $1.6 mil-
lion home in glamorous Hollywood Hills. The walls of the
house were almost entirely made of glass—providing
Burt with views of the city stretching all the way to the
Pacific Ocean. Burt filled the house with the best that
money could buy in an effort to further impress everyone
with his newfound wealth. And he succeeded. Within
months of moving into the new house, everyone who
knew Burt was talking about how wealthy he was and
how he spent money like it was water.

He'd only lived in the house three months when most
of his salon employees decided to ask for a raise. After all,

It's been my experience that most money-hiding schemes are designed to hide money from the most aggressive predator of them all: the Internal Revenue Service.

if the business was doing well enough for Burt to move to the Hills, they reasoned that it was also doing well enough for all of them to receive large raises. Among those demanding a large 10 percent raise was Susan Parks, the accountant for the Studio City beauty salon. During her two years at the salon, Susan had noticed that there were a number of employees on the payroll whom she'd never met. When Burt rejected Susan's raise request, she casually mentioned the employees and asked Burt when she'd get a chance to meet them. Realizing that Susan was on to his tax-evasion scheme, Burt quickly agreed to give Susan a raise to keep her from talking. But the cat was out of the bag. Susan had already mentioned her suspicions to other employees at the salon and someone had talked.

A month later, IRS investigators came knocking on Burt's door. They wanted to know about all the new employees whom Burt had hired in the past few years. They also wanted to know how Burt had come up with enough cash to buy his $1.6 million home in the Hollywood Hills. They had a lot of questions, and they weren't satisfied with Burt's answers. They indicted him for felony tax evasion almost a year to the date after he'd purchased his Hollywood Hills mansion. Burt was ultimately found guilty and ordered to pay the U.S. government over $500,000 in back taxes and penalties.

Although Burt's tax evasion scheme was eventually uncovered by the IRS, the truth is that he probably would have gotten away with everything had it not been for his

excessive spending. It's actually very difficult for the IRS
to trace unreported income that's deposited offshore.
Established forensic accountant Dave Fox agrees that
undeclared offshore bank accounts can be almost impossible to trace. He notes, however, that fortunately for the
IRS, people always end up doing something with the cash
that the government can latch on to. "They often get
caught because they end up using the money," notes Fox.
"They transfer the money back to the States because they
want to buy something."[1]

While Burt Myers's attempts to minimize his tax
exposure ended in disaster, it doesn't have to be that way
for you. If you're a successful businessman who is tired of
paying out the bulk of your earnings to the IRS, you can
use a number of legal ways to avoid the tax collector. With
proper planning and professional guidance, it's possible
for most of you business people to legally minimize your
tax exposure. Hiding your money from the U.S. government can be safe, profitable, and uniquely satisfying if
you decide to follow the rules.

STOP-GAP MEASURES TO KEEP SOME OF YOUR MONEY OUT OF THE IRS'S HANDS

Before you start doing business off-the-books or start paying phantom employees, you might want to look into
some legal ways you can minimize your business's tax
exposure. A number of loopholes exist in the current tax
code—if you know where to look.[2] Unfortunately, most of
the loopholes are only available to people who have substantial earnings and/or investment income. But if you're
fortunate enough to be in this category, there are several
legal means by which you can shelter some money from
the government.

For certain types of businesses, for example, it's possible to hire minority group members and get a 25 percent tax credit on their earnings. A wide variety of restrictions apply to this tax code provision, so before you start hiring large numbers of minorities, make sure you know the rule. Followed correctly, this rule can provide a very useful tax loophole even for the small businessman.

Incorporation is another good solution for small- to medium-sized businesses that are looking for legitimate tax breaks. This is particularly true if you incorporate in a company-friendly state like Delaware or Nevada.[3] Delaware's franchise tax compares favorably with that of most other states, and there is no corporate income tax for companies conducting their business outside of the state. Therefore, if your business is located in California, you can easily incorporate in Delaware, continue to do business in California, and minimize California's corporate taxes. Moreover, you can also run your Delaware corporation from another state. Under Delaware's business-friendly laws, a Delaware corporation may hold its annual meetings, keep its books and records, and have its principal office in another state.

Delaware offers small businesses the ability to conduct corporate affairs with minimal government interference and taxation. The following are among the many other advantages to incorporating in Delaware: (1) Shares of stock owned by persons outside the state are also not subject to taxation; (2) There is no sales, personal property, or intangible property tax for Delaware corporations not doing business in the state; (3) Shares of stock that are part of the estate of a deceased nonresident are exempt from the state inheritance law; (4) The State's courts have established a record of being pro-business; (5) Corporate directors have greater statutory legal protection from personal liability than in many other states; (6) There is no minimum capital requirement necessary to

> **Although Burt's tax evasion scheme was ultimately uncovered by the IRS, the truth is that he probably would have gotten away with everything had it not been for his excessive spending. It's actually very difficult for the IRS to trace unreported income that's deposited offshore.**

form a corporation; and (7) Your identity as the owner of a corporation may remain anonymous, and a single individual may incorporate.[4]

Incorporating in Nevada also provides the business owner with some possible tax relief. If you incorporate your business in Nevada, you will not have to pay any corporate income tax. Nevada is also one of only a few states that has no state personal income tax. Like Delaware, it also has no franchise tax. Many larger corporations choose Nevada for warehousing because there is no inventory tax. However, you don't have to be a large business to realize some tax benefits out of incorporating in Nevada. If you incorporate in a high tax state, such as California, your corporation will pay a minimum of $9,600 on every $100,000 of taxable income.[5] Therefore, even if you're incorporating a smaller company, it still may be financially beneficial for you to form your corporation in Nevada.

While they may not be quite as effective as incorporating in Nevada or Delaware, there are other ways to reduce your tax exposure. If you're a businessman looking to maximize your deductions, you need to focus on keeping all of your receipts. Although most people know that business-related expenses are deductible, they tend to be very lazy about keeping track of their business receipts.

When tax time comes around, they find themselves frantically searching their offices and homes for any potentially helpful business receipts. If you are a businessman whose expenses are not reimbursed by the company, you should be careful to keep each and every receipt. Even if you think that the expense will not be deductible, you should keep the receipt so that a professional can assess the situation. It never hurts to have too many receipts. If you don't need them, you can always throw them away.

Receipts can be anything from canceled checks to a hand-scrawled note from a taxi cab driver with the amount left blank.[6] When the amount is left blank, you have the opportunity to fill in the amount yourself. The best policy is to be honest about this amount. But if you insist on being dishonest, just be generous, not stupid.

IRS auditors are given guidelines and tables of average deductions and expenses. Therefore, if your deductions fall outside of these tables, you will find yourself answering a lot of uncomfortable questions. Any IRS agent will ask you a few questions about a cab receipt over $100—even if you took the cab ride in New York City. Moreover, if you insist on using falsified receipts, you may be prosecuted for fraud. So, if you're thinking of catching a break by using fraudulent receipts, you'd better consider all of the possible repercussions.

Some other IRS provisions offer a small amount of relief to the over-taxed businessman. Next time Christmas comes around and you find yourself giving large cash gifts to at least half of your staff, don't despair. These gifts are deductible. There is a provision in the tax code that allows tax-free gifts to employees of up to $400.[7] If you follow the rules, it's possible for everyone to benefit when you give nice presents to your employees.

For those who are desperate to realize some tax savings, they might want to look into investing in an individual retirement account (IRA, or a Keogh Plan if they are self-employed). These accounts are a great way for

debt-ridden individuals to force themselves to save a little money. What's more, taxes are deferred until an individual's retirement, when he'll theoretically be in a lower
tax bracket and have to pay fewer taxes. The retirement
accounts do have a few drawbacks. There are no withdrawals permitted until age 59½. If you withdraw your
money before that point, you'll have to pay a substantial
penalty that will most likely wipe out all of your earnings.
And, of course, there is no guarantee that the tax rate in
years to come won't be even higher than it is now. With
the way taxes are rising, it's highly likely that you'll be
forced to pay even more taxes when your retirement
account finally vests.

One method that many businessmen use to reduce
their tax exposure is to distribute their income throughout the family. If you're running a small business, you
should consider putting some of your family members on
the payroll—if they are at all able to hold down a job.
Their pay is taxable to them, but it's still family income
that's taxed at a lower rate than if you reported the
income on your own tax return.

While I prefer to use only legal options to help my
clients minimize their tax exposure, millions of Americans feel differently. They view the IRS as the enemy and
believe that they are perfectly within their rights when
they avail themselves of all opportunities—both legal and
illegal—to stick it to the government.

In researching this book, I read a number of stories
about what has been deemed "the underground economy"—Americans who have decided to do business completely off-the-record. Tired of long hours and high taxes,
more and more Americans are choosing to do business
underground—far from the reaches of an increasingly
intrusive and greedy IRS. Some of these IRS combatants
manage to mask their underground businesses with perfectly legal and highly visible above-ground businesses.

For example, one highly motivated businessman that I read about runs a perfectly above-board catering business, delivering lunches to a wide variety of commercial customers. During the day, he keeps scrupulous receipts and makes sure that all sales are carefully entered into the books. But as soon as the sun sets, he goes underground. He still delivers meals to business executives trapped late at the office, but he pockets the income without running it through the books. He makes sure that the expenses for his evening business are buried in with his daytime accounts. While this is a system that works for him, it's also obviously illegal.

My businessman friend isn't the only person in America who has chosen to solve his tax problem by going underground. All kinds of Americans who work in cash-intensive businesses are able to use that to avoid paying taxes. Only a few years ago, my friend Tom confessed that he paid for most of his college expenses by working "off-the-books." When Tom was in college, he took a job at a local nightclub, working as a bartender. He told the owner that he'd work for minimum wage, so long as there were no taxes. The bar owner was happy to get someone as hardworking as Tom, so he agreed to Tom's terms. Tom worked at that establishment for almost two years and did quite well. Between tips and his tax-free salary, he never had to ask his parents for any money.

Although working off-the-books or underground can be quite lucrative, it can also be risky. Before you decide to cross the legal line in your efforts to stick it to the IRS, you should know the possible consequences.

There is always the possibility that you won't get caught. Given the IRS's strained budget and resultant cost-cutting measures, fewer personnel are available to find your money. What's more, in these cost-cutting times, fewer tax-paying (and tax-evading) Americans are being audited by the IRS. However, despite its shrinking budget, the IRS still manages to sink its claws into a substantial number of Americans annually. The IRS tends to target specific tax-paying groups each year, focusing on getting as much money out of these individuals as possible. For example, I've heard that in the last few years they've targeted physicians with home offices for audits. I actually have a doctor friend who has been audited four times in the last six years. So, despite the decreasing number of audits, if you're in one of the IRS target groups, you're still extremely vulnerable.

And if you fail that audit, you will be forced to pay all of your back taxes—plus interest and penalties. (This can also happen if you just make a mistake on your return.)

There is also the very outside possibility that you'll be criminally prosecuted. But the reality is that the government tends to only prosecute tax fraud when the tax evader has committed a number of other serious offenses for which the government cannot obtain a conviction. I call this the Al Capone syndrome. When the government failed to convict Al Capone of murder and other serious crimes, they finally used tax fraud to put him behind bars. Prosecuting someone for tax evasion is often the last resort of a desperate government.

SENDING YOUR MONEY ABROAD TO ESCAPE THE LONG ARM OF THE IRS

Many American businessmen and women have reacted to skyrocketing taxes by renouncing their citizenship and moving to the nearest tropical tax haven. They decided that the benefits of American citizenship are outweighed by the detriments of its increasingly onerous tax laws. Unfortunately, giving up your U.S. citizenship probably won't help you avoid the U.S. tax collector.[8] The Tax Compliance Law of 1995 was specifically designed to make it more difficult to give up U.S. citizenship without triggering some tax difficulties. The law provides that Americans giving up citizenship must pay a 35 percent tax on appreciated assets at the time of relinquishment. The tax only applies to gains greater than $600,000. The new law was aimed at collecting $2.4 billion a year in new taxes over a five-year period. Although the implementation of the law has eased up a bit, it is still in effect.[9]

In addition to the Tax Compliance Law, other procedures are in effect that discourage Americans from giving up their citizenship to avoid taxes. If the IRS determines that your motive for leaving the country is to avoid taxes, the Immigration and Naturalization Service can exile you in the same way it exiles convicted rapists and drug dealers. So, if you leave to avoid taxes, it might be impossible to return. If you want to prove to the IRS that you're not renouncing your citizenship for tax reasons, you might want to move to a country like Canada, which has a higher tax rate than the United States. If you move somewhere that has a higher tax rate than the United States, it will be hard for the IRS to argue that you're attempting to avoid taxes.[10]

Due to the efforts of Congress and the IRS, renouncing your citizenship probably won't provide you with a substantial tax advantage. Fortunately, you can keep your U.S. citizenship and still minimize your tax exposure. You simply need to send your money on a trip to

With proper planning and professional guidance, it's possible for most of you businessmen to legally minimize your tax exposure. Hiding your money from the U.S. government can be safe, profitable, and uniquely satisfying if you decide to follow the rules.

some sunny offshore haven. Despite rumors to the contrary, it is neither illegal nor immoral to move your money outside of the government's sphere of tax authority. As long as you follow all U.S. laws governing foreign investment as well as the laws of the country where you choose to invest, you're free to send your money to the offshore haven of your choice.

Because the laws governing offshore investment are constantly changing, it's difficult for me to give you concrete details on how one legally invests offshore. I can, however, offer you a brief sketch of why offshore investment entities can help you minimize your tax exposure. An offshore corporation or bank is as much a legal entity as you are. Therefore, its assets, liabilities, and income are its own. This means that you can sell investments to a foreign bank (that you own) and immediately make the bank responsible for any tax due on the profits of that investment.[11] Since the bank incurs no tax at the corporate level, your investments operate tax-free. You need to treat this bank as a business and, as it accumulates assets, you'll be able to finance local operations and potentially fund export activities.

In order to make this offshore tax-avoidance formula work, you need to remember three basic characteristics of true tax protection arrangements:

1. They separate assets from their creator by guaranteeing that the income the creator receives from his investments cannot be considered part of his taxable income. (Even though you own the offshore investment, you have to be sure that the income from your investment cannot legally be considered part of your income.)

2. Assets are domiciled in countries where the tax situation is better than in the creator's home country. (Basically, this means that you don't want to set up your offshore bank or offshore cor-

poration in Sweden, where tax levels are in the stratosphere.)

3. The assets cannot be controlled by their creator, but may be invested as the creator may suggest, without tax liability in their home country. (The issue of who actually controls the offshore corporation or offshore bank is one of considerable importance. Before you invest offshore, you need to consult an attorney so that your offshore investment will be structured for maximum tax avoidance.[12])

By creating the proper offshore investment arrangement, you can effectively avoid significant taxation. But you need to recognize that it won't be easy. For example, the Controlled Foreign Corporation tax is a major barrier to tax avoidance. It applies to all foreign corporations closely held by a U.S. corporation or individual. The CFC tax allows the government to take a share of "passive income" from each of the shareholders—all of whom are treated as if the corporation (as a separate legal entity) did not exist. Fortunately, this barrier can be overcome by structuring ownership so that U.S. owners do not control the offshore bank. Again, you will probably need some professional help to clear this taxation hurdle.

The Foreign Personal Holding Company (FPHC) tax presents another significant hurdle to offshore investors looking for tax relief. The FPHC tax was adopted many years ago to attack incorporated pocketbooks that operate in tax havens and receive passive incomes. The tax is imposed only in the case of passive income generated by a foreign corporation that is owned by no more than five U.S. citizens. This barrier to tax avoidance is typically insurmountable, but under its provisions foreign banks receive special exemption from the IRS if they can show the bank was created for some express purpose other than tax avoidance. As you can probably guess, certain

> Incorporation is another good solution for
> small- to medium-sized businesses that are
> looking for legitimate tax breaks. This is
> particularly true if you incorporate in a
> company-friendly state like Delaware or
> Nevada.[3]

experts can help you effectively "demonstrate" to the U.S.
government that your bank was created for some purpose
other than tax avoidance.

In addition to the FPHC tax, the U.S. government
came up with another hefty tax aimed specifically at offshore corporations—the Personal Holding Company (PHC)
tax. The PHC tax, imposed at the rate of 70 percent,
applies to foreign- as well as U.S.-based corporations that
are owned by less than ten Americans. This tax is incurred
by the company, not by its shareholders. In the case of a tax
haven corporation, the tax applies to closely held haven
businesses and is imposed on all relevant U.S.-source passive income. Offshore banks may be able to avoid this tax
if their income is not considered to be "passive."

The Accumulated Earnings (AE) tax applies to both
foreign- and U.S.-based corporations that are owned by
U.S. citizens. It taxes all accumulated earnings that are
considered "unnecessary" for the business of the corporation and can be as high as 38 percent on undistributed
U.S. source accumulated earnings in excess of $150,000
per year. An offshore bank can qualify for exemption from
the Accumulated Earnings (AE) tax because all banks—
in the course of business operation—accumulate earnings. That's the way they make the portfolio investments
that keep them afloat.

An offshore bank may also allow you to avoid two
additional taxes—the Foreign Investment Company

(FIC) tax and the Passive Foreign Investment Company (PFIC) tax. The FIC tax is imposed annually on U.S.-owned foreign corporations that exist primarily to invest in stocks or commodity futures. An offshore bank is exempt from this tax so long as it functions as more than an international brokerage house. The PFIC tax adds a surtax on all distributions to U.S. shareholders from a foreign company unless the company is actively engaged in business and most of its assets are used in the business. The PFIC rules can be avoided or their impact minimized through careful tax planning.

Finally, the Effectively-Connected-With-U.S. tax basically imposes a tax on the U.S.-source income of any foreign-based but U.S.-owned corporation if that income is effectively connected with a U.S. business. A properly set up offshore bank may be exempt from this tax because its activities, to a large extent, are treated as if they were conducted offshore through a resident agent.[13]

If you're committed to minimizing your tax exposure, but you'd prefer to keep your money a little closer to home, you might want to investigate the current status of a little known bank located in the small Western town of Anadarko, Oklahoma. The bank is First Lenape Nation Bank and it's owned by the Delaware tribe of Western Oklahoma, a sovereign Indian nation whose independence from U.S. state and federal authority was recognized in 1934. First Lenape wants to offer Swiss-style banking to tribal members and nonmembers—including numbered accounts, full nondisclosure of account information, no compliance with snooping law enforcement, protection from civil court judgments (wage garnishments and the like), and no reporting of interest to the IRS or of cash deposits over $10,000 to the Treasury Department.

Whether First Lenape will get to offer these offshore benefits in their distinctly onshore locale remains to be seen. First Lenape is going into uncharted territory, as U.S. tribal law does not specifically relate to banking, and no tribe has ever tried to build an offshore bank on its land. Following a warning by Oklahoma's state banking commissioner's office advising the public to use "extreme caution in any transaction involving First Lenape," the bank stopped taking deposits. The bank is now engaging in talks with the Treasury Department and the Department of Tribal Justice over government concerns that the bank will be used for purposes of tax evasion and money laundering. While the bank has declared that it wants only legitimate capital, the government still remains concerned that the bank will become a repository for dirty money.[14] Moreover, First Lenape continues to face considerable challenges from the federal government.

Another Indian tribe, taking advantage of its Indian sovereignty, is setting up operations that might well turn the Montana wilderness into an "offshore" banking center. The Blackfeet Tribe's bank, Glacier International Depository Ltd., will be based on Indian land near Glacier National Park. In 1997, Montana passed a law making it the first state to allow individuals and corporations to set up foreign depositories. But no such depositories yet exist under state law.

Before you rush to invest your hard-earned dollars in an Indian "offshore" banking center, you should be extremely careful and do your research so you don't fall victim to fraud. In April 1999 two California businessmen, Ronald Sparks and Owen Stephenson, were found guilty of defrauding investors of over $8 million. The two men said an "on-shore, offshore" bank that they ran would shield transactions from federal authorities because it was chartered by the sovereign Apache Tribe of Oklahoma.[15] Tribal officials did in fact negotiate with the two men to start a small lending institution, but they contend that the men never had official authority for a thrift or a bank. The money that was supposedly deposited into the bank in Anadarko, Oklahoma, was actually put into accounts controlled by Sparks and

Stephenson at a Lawton bank. Testimony at the trial showed that the men tapped deposits to pay personal expenses, including condominium and mortgage payments, travel, and expensive hotel stays.[16] After the guilty verdict was announced, the Department of Justice stressed that it was important to recognize that the Apache Tribe, as well as the people who lost money in the scheme, were victims of the fraud.[17]

Following the Sparks/Stephenson fraud, federal regulators expressed concern about the increasing number of bogus, unregulated banks popping up onshore. The "onshore/offshore banks" offer the secrecy and security that for years have attracted tax evaders and money launderers to banking havens such as the Cayman Islands and Switzerland.[18] Therefore, while several onshore/offshore banks located in the United States offer some substantial tax and secrecy benefits, it's important to thoroughly investigate these banks before you invest a single penny. The "onshore/offshore" Indian banking industry is new and untested. If you're really concerned about the safety of your money, you might want to wait until the banks are somewhat more established.

You should also consider the fact that many of these so-called "onshore/offshore" banks are not intended for the American customer—rather, they are attempting to attract foreign investors. In an effort to pacify the IRS, Montana's legislature voted to put their "offshore depositories" off-limits to U.S. citizens and residents. Only nonresident aliens need apply, and they must deposit a minimum of $200,000. Moreover, unlike real offshore banks, Montana's depositories offer only limited privacy. The usual reporting requirements of the Bank Secrecy Act apply and there are no tax-escaping treaties. Therefore, if you're looking for financial privacy, it's probably a better and safer bet for you to invest in a foreign tax haven rather than in a bank located in the American heartland.

But before you invest your money in an offshore
haven, you should be aware that such a move may draw
the attention and the wrath of an increasingly frustrated
U.S. government. In fact, Jonathan Talisman, assistant
secretary for tax policy, recently admitted his frustration
in dealing with offshore tax shelters, noting that address-
ing the problem is like attempting to slay the mythologi-
cal Hydra. "You kill off one over here and two or three
more appear over there."[19] Talisman, however, remained
resolute in his goal to go after those attempting to shelter
assets offshore, warning that the U.S. government "will
examine our own laws to determine what changes are
required to prevent the exploitation of tax havens in ways
that reduce U.S. taxes inappropriately. And we will continue to work with the international community to
develop collective responses to tax havens, including
responses that encourage these jurisdictions to cooperate
with us so that their financial systems no longer act as a
barrier to the effective enforcement of our laws."[20]

Therefore, even though you may be able to find some
tax relief by investing offshore, the relief may be short-
lived. Right now, you can use a number of offshore investment entities to shield some of your income from the IRS,
but who knows what the law will be tomorrow? As I just
discussed, the government is always looking for new ways
to tighten the noose around the neck of the American taxpayer. In fact, government officials like Assistant Secretary Jonathan Talisman believe it is their patriotic
obligation to stop international tax competition and to
force tax havens into cooperating with U.S. authorities.

**By creating the proper offshore investment
arrangement, you can effectively avoid
significant taxation.**

Before you invest offshore, be sure that you've selected a haven that remains committed to providing banking privacy, regardless of resulting U.S. government pressure.

FINAL THOUGHTS

My most important rule is that you should talk to an attorney, accountant, or other qualified financial consultant before you decide to implement a tax-avoidance plan. Someone who is familiar with the tax code may be able to give you valuable advice on how to restructure your assets so as to minimize your tax exposure.

Before you rely on a professional's tax advice, however, you must be sure that you and your adviser are of the same mind.

I've come to realize over the years that a great many people, including a large number of accountants and attorneys, believe that tax avoidance is merely another name for tax evasion. I've personally spoken to some very well-established tax attorneys who refuse on a moral basis to counsel their clients on the benefits of offshore investment. While they admit that offshore investment can serve some sensitive investment goals and offer some asset protection from unhappy divorces, they argue that offshore investment rarely offers any concrete tax savings. In fact, a prominent attorney in Washington, D.C., whom I've debated against on occasion, has gone so far as to argue that offshore tax havens only reduce your tax exposure when you don't follow the law.

If you find yourself sitting across the desk from someone like my Washington colleague, you should probably consider getting other professional advice.

A different school of thought among professional financial advisers accepts the legalities of offshore investment but questions the morality of it. These professionals believe that serious tax avoidance is immoral—even if it's not illegal. They counsel their clients to follow the letter of the law and to pay their fair share of taxes because it's the right thing to do.

If you're not particularly devoted to this philosophy, you again need to quickly move on and find a professional who shares your anger over outrageous and onerous taxes. Don't assume that because someone simply has the professional capability to help you further your tax avoidance strategy that this person necessarily shares your economic and political philosophy and will help you to do it.

REFERENCES

1. October 25, 1999, interview with Dave Fox.
2. If you're interested in exploiting the loopholes in the current tax code, you should seek the assistance of an attorney, accountant, and/or financial consultant. You'll need a professional to help you navigate the ever-changing tax code because today's loophole may be tomorrow's brick wall.
3. It's possible to incorporate in one state and do business in another as long as you fill out the proper paperwork and pay the requisite taxes. Be sure that you consult with an attorney about how to incorporate in the state you choose.
4. Starchild, Adam, *Keep What You Own: Protect Your Money, Property, and Family from Courts, Creditors and the IRS,* Boulder, CO: Paladin Press, 1995, pp. 45–46.
5. Ibid., p. 47.
6. If you're in New York City, your cab driver is legally obligated to provide you with a printed receipt. Unfortunately, the New York City cab drivers no longer leave the amount blank.
7. The provision in the IRS code allowing tax-free gifts also has a number of exceptions. So, before you start giving away too many gifts to your employees, make sure that you know everything about this particular section of the code.

8. It may, however, help you avoid persistent creditors. For more on how to avoid creditors, see chapter 5, "Life in the Red Lane."
9. You should check the current status of the law before taking any action to renounce your citizenship.
10. If you're extremely wealthy, the IRS will probably investigate you—even if you choose to move to a country with a higher tax rate.
11. This entire transaction is, of course, subject to certain legal rules. In order to successfully invest offshore, you will need to know those rules or hire someone who does.
12. For more information on how to use offshore investment to minimize tax exposure, see Schneider, Jerome, *The Complete Guide to Offshore Money Havens,* Roseville, CA: Prima Publishing, 2000, p. 132.
13. Ibid., pp. 136–137.
14. Warner, Melanie, "First: Who Needs the Cayman Islands? The Sovereignty Loophole: How to Bypass Banking Law," *Fortune* (June 23, 1997).
15. The Associated Press, April 30, 1999.
16. Ibid.
17. Ibid.
18. Lowry, Tom, "Onshore Offshore Bankers Indicted," *USA TODAY,* November 4, 1998, p. 3B.
19. Treasury Acting Assistant Secretary for Tax Policy Jonathan Talisman Remarks to the GWU/IRS International Institute on Current Trends in International, Regulatory Intelligence Data, December 10, 1999.
20. Ibid.

CHAPTER 10

EXTREME HIDING: PLAYING THE HIDING GAME FOR ALL IT'S WORTH

For those people who need to push everything to the limit, even the hiding of their assets, there is extreme hiding. While it can be difficult and dangerous, extreme hiding can also have tremendous benefits. The more extreme your hiding place, the harder it is for others to locate.

Whenever I think about extreme hiders, the first person who springs to mind is an old client of mine who would go to any lengths to hide money from the IRS. Although he loved his country, he just didn't believe in contributing to the masses. His name was Mark.

By the time Mark became my client, he was already a successful businessman. He and his wife, Susan, owned a trucking business with annual revenues of over $25 million each year. Only months after I'd started working with Mark, Susan filed for divorce. In her divorce petition, she asked for all of the couple's many residences, and for approximately $40,000 a month in spousal support.

It was Mark's intention, however, that Susan would walk away from the marriage with little more than the clothes on her back. He hired one of the meanest divorce attorneys in Beverly Hills. The attorney immediately filed a financial disclosure statement that indicated that Mark only made around $250,000 annually.

When Susan learned that Mark was claiming an annual income of only $250,000, she went ballistic and instructed her attorney to take him for everything he was worth. She told the attorney that she'd worked hard to help Mark build that trucking business, and she was damned if he would take it all away from her.

For almost six months, Susan and Mark engaged in a vicious divorce war, with Mark winning the majority of the battles. Then Susan decided to pull out all the stops in one do-or-die maneuver.

Mark was actually in my office when his attorney called. I watched with surprise as all the color drained from Mark's face. He quietly asked his lawyer if he was sure and then immediately directed his attorney to settle.

After he hung up the phone, he sat back in his chair and sighed. "I guess we'll have a lot less money to invest next month," he quipped weakly.

"What the hell just happened?" I asked. "One minute you're ready to rip this woman's head off and the next, you're just rolling over."

"She was about to go to the IRS," Mark said. "And let's just say she knows a few things about my trucking business that might be of interest to them."

"But you and your wife jointly own your trucking business," I replied. "She'd be liable as well if the IRS came after you."

"Apparently, it's a chance she's willing to take."

"So, what does she know?"

"That I was hiding a little bit of money from the tax man. I had this thing going where I claimed there were a few subcontractor drivers on the payroll who didn't actu-

> When I finally told him that I could no longer act as his financial consultant because of his questionable financial practices, he immediately promised to change his ways. I smiled and then quietly explained that people like him rarely changed. They enjoyed the thrill of playing and working on the edge—of being one step ahead of the competition. No matter what Mark promised, we both knew that he was a man of extremes who wasn't likely to change.

ally exist. I'd have payroll make out a few checks to these fictitious guys and then cash out the checks. It was a pretty great scam, if I do say so myself."

"How did you cash checks made out to someone else?"

"I had a friend at the bank. And when she wasn't there, I'd just tell the teller that I was cashing a few paychecks for the guys who didn't have bank accounts. Most of the checks were made out to guys with Spanish surnames. Generally, the tellers just assumed they were recent immigrants who didn't have bank accounts yet."

"How much did you net with this little scam?"

"Over $500,000 a year. I'd usually cash out around $40,000 each time."

"Well, now I understand why you were so quick to settle with Susan. I don't imagine the IRS would be very happy to hear that you hid that amount of cash from them."

"Well, it was a good thing while it lasted."

Shortly after his divorce, Mark and I parted company. Although I personally liked the guy, his propensity toward illegal money-hiding schemes made me far too nervous to continue representing him. When I finally told him that I could no longer act as his financial consultant because of his questionable financial practices, he immediately promised to change his ways. I smiled and then quietly explained that people like him rarely changed. They enjoyed the thrill of playing and working on the edge—of being one step ahead of the competition. No matter what Mark promised, we both knew that he was a man of extremes who wasn't likely to change.

THE ULTIMATE THRILL: OFFSHORE HIDING

The first thing you need to know about hiding money in an offshore haven is that it's not for the guy who likes routine and iron-clad guarantees. Offshore havens are for risk takers—or what I've termed "inventurers."

Like the adventurers who settled the old West, the inventurers are also bold, confident, and fearless. They enjoy exploring unknown territory and they refuse to be constrained by conventional wisdom. And like all true adventurers, the inventurers have a different way of looking at the world. They have an all-encompassing financial perspective, liberated from territorial boundaries and legislative decrees.[1]

In short, inventurers tend to be absolutely fearless when it comes to exploring investment opportunities. The true inventurer is open to the global reality that there are great international economic opportunities—for anyone willing to take the risk. The inventurer is not afraid to grapple with foreign languages or deal with the uncertainties that often accompany offshore investing.

Bottom line, the true inventurer does not fear the unknown. He embraces it.

And although the inventurer who wants to hide his money in an offshore haven has to be somewhat fearless, he doesn't have to be rich. The offshore club is no longer restricted to the ultra-wealthy. A new group of individuals is now going offshore—hardworking, upper-income Americans, looking for more financial privacy than they can find domestically.

Peter Djinis, associate director for the Financial Crimes Enforcement Network, Division of the Treasury Department (FinCEN), notes that whereas offshore havens were relegated mainly "to the rich, now you may find that your next-door neighbor has an account in the Caymans. Many middle-class and upper-middle-class Americans with disposable income have started to take a serious look at some of these offshore investment opportunities."[2]

But before you start sending all of your money offshore, you should be aware that despite their improving reputation, using offshore havens still can be quite risky. This is especially true if you're intent on using the offshore haven to "hide" your money from the U.S. government. A lot of powerful organizations believe that anyone who uses an offshore haven to eliminate taxes is violating the law.

In fact, many mainstream tax attorneys actually refuse to advise their clients about the tax benefits associated with offshore investment. Like attorney and former IRS commissioner Donald Alexander, for example, who believes that offshore investments rarely provide tax savings unless someone wants to cheat the IRS. "Many of these tax-motivated offshore transactions are just plain scams that basically involve not following the law," claims Alexander. "They work when you don't follow the law."[3]

Alexander also has a moral objection to citizens using offshore havens to avoid tax liability. "I think the provisions of the IRS code should be respected, not ignored. The proper test for whether something violates the code is not whether you can get away with it."[4]

While the U.S. government recognizes all sorts of legitimate reasons why both individuals and companies might want to set up overseas financial operations, they

The first thing you need to know about hiding money in an offshore haven is that it's not for the guy who likes routine and iron-clad guarantees. Offshore havens are for risk takers—or what I've termed "inventurers."

also believe there are abuses. Peter Djinis admits that "The IRS is spending more and more time and attention on whether there is appropriate tax enforcement of offshore investments. Their concern is that people may be moving their funds offshore and not reporting those foreign bank accounts to the IRS."[5]

In their efforts to target those who use offshore banks for illegal purposes, the U.S. government has entered into MLATs (Mutual Legal Assistance Treaties) with over twenty-five well-known offshore havens. (As I've discussed, MLATs provide for the exchange of criminal information between signatory countries but exclude the exchange of information on tax evasion.[6])

Presently, the United States has MLATs either in force or pending with Uruguay, Jamaica, Spain, Thailand, Belgium, Morocco, Columbia, Switzerland, Mexico, the Bahamas, the Netherlands (including Aruba and the Netherlands Antilles), Canada, the United Kingdom (including the Cayman Islands, Anguilla, the British Virgin Islands, the Turks and Caicos Islands, and Montserrat), Italy, Nigeria, and Argentina.[7] Although some pretty big names are still left off of the list, including Panama, Hong Kong, and Vanuatu, the U.S. government is continuing its efforts to expand the number of MLAT countries.

The government has another concern about the use of offshore havens, and that is the offshore financial adviser. In recent years, the government has discovered that unscrupulous promoters (financial advisers) in the

United States and abroad attempt to entice taxpayers into purchasing fraudulent trusts as well as other fraudulent and illegal offshore investment vehicles.

Ed Federico, IRS deputy assistant commissioner for criminal investigations, notes that his agency, along with the Department of Justice and the Treasury, has begun to work with other governments to target these fraudulent promoters. Federico admits, however, that prosecuting and convicting a fraudulent promoter is a difficult proposition.[8]

So the government often has to settle for just going after the promoter's clients. In most investigations, the taxpayer is a great deal easier to identify than the one who promoted the fraudulent trust. And although the government will rarely initiate a criminal prosecution against the clients of the promoter, they will feel free to audit them.

"Because even if the clients did set up an offshore trust in an unwitting fashion, they are responsible to make sure they paid the proper amount of taxes," notes Federico.[9] So even if you're a taxpayer who had no intention of breaking the law, you will be held responsible for the illegal actions of your offshore promoter/financial consultant.

It all boils down to informed risk. Before you decide to hide even a dime offshore, you need to understand the significant risks involved. If you are making legitimate offshore investments, you may become the target of a government investigation. As Peter Djinis notes, "The problem is that although there are legitimate uses for offshore banking, there is also a high-profile history of illegitimate uses. And it is extremely difficult to separate the criminals from the legitimate investors because of the banking secrecy laws present in many of these offshore havens."[10]

But don't decide that offshore hiding is way too risky for you to even consider. If you receive the right advice and properly adhere to all the applicable laws, it can be *perfectly legal* to use offshore banks to either hide assets and/or to minimize your tax exposure. Even the IRS agrees that many legitimate reasons exist why both individuals and companies may want to set up overseas financial operations. They run the gamut from people wanting to have lower tax rates to insulating themselves from liability. These are all perfectly legitimate.[11]

Not only that, going offshore is also one of the few legal ways to level the playing field between the taxpayer and the IRS. The cards are stacked against the U.S. taxpayer and always have been, of course. When the government has the power to seize your bank accounts, your home, and your assets, as well as shut down your business, the system remains patently unfair.

If you choose to go offshore, you're out of the system. In that way you make it more difficult for the IRS to seize your assets. So, while the benefits of offshore investment outweigh the risks, you still need to do some serious homework first. Using an offshore haven to hide your money is not something that you can or should do at the last minute.[12] First, you need to decide which haven to use as your offshore venue. Second, you have to choose which legal structure to hide your money in—such as a trust, a bank account, or an offshore corporation. Third, you need to know how much this offshore investment will cost you and whether the cost will ultimately outweigh the benefits of moving your funds offshore. Fourth, you have to learn which specific offshore location best suits your financial needs. Fifth, you need to find out how to structure your offshore investment so that it will continue to function effectively for as long as you desire.

Before you attempt to address the five specific areas discussed here, I recommend that you hire an attorney or a financial planner who has specific offshore experience. While a number of good books and pamphlets about offshore investment are on the market—including mine—I still recommend that you personally consult an attorney or a financial consultant.

You definitely will require someone who can help you navigate the complex trail of requisite paperwork and who can specifically address your particular financial needs. You will need a professional who is familiar with the applicable U.S. laws as well as the laws of your chosen offshore haven. Each offshore country has its own specific banking laws—and often its own system of justice.

With careful planning and the right legal guidance, you'll find that offshore havens can be a great way to protect your assets and/or valuables. Keep in mind, it's not only taxes that you have to worry about. There is also the matter of nuisance lawsuits that could destroy you financially.

The odds of being sued in the United States are astronomically high. As we all know, you can be sued for just about anything. What you consider to be a small fender-bender accident could instantly turn into high-stakes litigation. All it takes is one ambitious lawyer looking for a big win. And once that judgment has been entered against you, just about everything you own will be up for grabs. Victorious plaintiffs quickly transform into driven judgment creditors—dedicated to bleeding you dry.

Before you even have a chance to absorb the fact that you've lost the lawsuit, your judgment creditor will have slapped a lien on your real estate and your personal business property. A truly driven judgment creditor can destroy in a matter of months what it took you a lifetime to build.

The cards are stacked against the U.S. taxpayer and always have been, of course. When the government has the power to seize your bank accounts, your home, and your assets, as well as shut down your business, the system remains patently unfair.

EXTREME HIDING PLACES FOR
THE TRUE PRIVACY SEEKER

Many people looking to hide their valuables choose to rent safe deposits in the same bank where they have a checking or savings account. Bank safe deposit boxes can be used to store a wide variety of items, including but not limited to jewelry, heirlooms, passports, securities, birth certificates, bonds, rare coins, marriage licenses, savings certificates, rare stamps, trust papers, school records, and computer disks. Some banks even offer limited insurance coverage on box contents for additional fees.[13] And it's fairly easy to rent one: You simply need to fill out a rental agreement and then produce either a driver's license or a state identification card.

But although renting a safe deposit box in a U.S. bank may be easy, there are a number of negatives. While your rental agreement does not require you to list the contents of your safe deposit box, you must represent to the bank that you have not put anything "unlawful, dangerous, explosive, perishable or offensive in the box."[14] And most U.S. banks have an unwritten policy prohibiting customers from storing cash in their safe deposit box.[15] While taxpayers can deduct the cost of the safe deposit box rental if they use the box to store stocks, bonds, or other investments, I wouldn't recommend it. If you are foolish enough to take the minuscule deduction on your federal tax return, it could lead to an audit if your tax return does not show dividend and interest income, or capital gain or loss transactions. And if you're audited, the IRS can ask you to prove what's in the box and where it came from.

There are other drawbacks to keeping your valuables in a safe deposit box located in a U.S. bank. First, the boxes can be accessed with a court order if someone provides a compelling enough reason. For instance, if you're in litigation with your ex-spouse and she claims that you're hiding assets in a safe deposit box, chances are that she will be successful in getting a court order to open up that box. And, if the IRS claims that you're hiding cash from your business in a safe deposit box, it also can get a court order to take a look. Moreover, if a bank official becomes suspicious that something illegal or dangerous is in your box, under the extremely broad language of most safe deposit box rental agreements, he is fairly free to force it open and empty the contents.[16] In fact, some banks even have a clause in their safe deposit box rental agreement that allows them, after giving notice, to open your box when you're late with your rent.

If a bank official suspects that you're storing more than $10,000 in cash in the safe deposit box, he is legally required to fill out a SAR (Suspicious Activity Report). The purpose of the form is to report any suspicious financial transaction(s) or activity. This requirement is mandatory for financial institutions and includes situations like suspected embezzlement or fraud, as well as any money-laundering type of activity.[17] So if a teller in your bank merely suspects that you're using your safe deposit box for some type of criminal activity, he's legally required to squeal on you. And once the government gets interested in what's in your box, you might as well just hand them the key and save your bank the trouble of drilling the box open.

In the unlikely event that the government doesn't have enough information to get a judge to issue a warrant to search your box, they can probably get what they need from the aforementioned friendly local bank teller.

Bank tellers, especially those in your neighborhood bank, are an excellent source of information for anyone interested in finding out what you've been putting in your safe deposit box and how often. In fact, when the police investigate whether a suspect is keeping something illegal in his safe deposit box, they often question bank tellers about how often that customer accessed his safe

> There are other drawbacks to keeping your valuables in a safe deposit box located in a U.S. bank. First, the boxes can be accessed with a court order if someone provides a compelling enough reason.

deposit box. Bank tellers can be one of the best resources for a diligent investigator because they can identify a suspect by name and face, and occasionally, they can even tell whether a particular customer had stashed cash in his safe deposit box.[18] (And even if a bank teller's memory happens to fail him, an investigator can always rely on the bank surveillance camera, which is usually located in the safe deposit box sign-in area.)

Finally, safe deposit boxes in U.S. banks also have another extremely compelling negative—you have to provide a great deal of personal information in order to rent one. Anyone renting a safe deposit bank at a U.S. bank will most likely be required to fill out an application with his social security number as well as his birth date, place of birth, and other highly personal data.[19] (And if you have a savings or checking account in the same bank, the bank will already have all of the information you gave them when you filled out the application for a checking or savings account.)

If you become involved in litigation, it probably won't take an investigator long to locate your safe deposit box. And once that box is discovered by a legal adversary, we all know that it's only a matter of time before some judge gives the okay to open the darn thing up.

If you're only interested in finding a good place to keep Grandma's jewelry, you should probably consider renting a safe deposit box at your local bank. It's relatively cheap, pretty safe, and convenient.[20] But if you're really concerned about privacy and protection from litigious adversaries, you should skip the local bank and rent a safe deposit box in an offshore haven. Renting a safe deposit box offshore can help you keep the contents of your safe deposit box truly private.

Actually, the only real drawback to a foreign safe deposit box is access.[21] You might have to travel quite a distance to either deposit or withdraw something from the box. But if you think about safe deposit boxes like a real inventurer, you'll probably conclude that the advantages of a foreign safe deposit box clearly outweigh the drawbacks.

A safe deposit box in a foreign land truly makes sense if you travel frequently on business. During your business trips to Geneva, let's say, you can open a safe deposit box at a Swiss bank and use it to store everything from jewelry to bonds.

Unlike their U.S. counterparts, many foreign banks have no policy against your storing cash in a safe deposit box. (Remember, however, that if you transport more than $10,000 out of the United States, you are required to report the transfer of funds. See the reporting requirements under 31 CFR 103.23.) In addition, the banking laws of many offshore havens do not require that bankers file anything resembling the Suspicious Activity Report forms. Therefore, even if a foreign banker suspects that you are using your safe deposit box for illegal purposes, he's not required to report that suspicion to any governmental authorities.[22]

By storing your most valuable documents and assets in a foreign safe deposit box, you can better protect the contents from disclosure and/or seizure. If you're sued and your legal adversary hires a private detective or forensic accountant to locate your assets, it's unlikely that they'll find the safe deposit box you've got in Vanuatu. Most forensic accountants and private detectives tend to locate bank accounts and safe deposit boxes by using your social security number. Unlike their U.S. counterparts, foreign banks rarely require that you provide your social security number, driver's license, or other personal information to open a safe deposit box. In fact, many foreign banks expressly offer their customers almost complete anonymity when it comes to opening a safe deposit box.

It will also be difficult for anyone to find out about your foreign safe deposit box because you probably won't have to report it to the U.S. government. The fact of the matter is that banks in Canada, Mexico, Switzerland, and most other countries offer safe deposit boxes that do not constitute a foreign account and, as such, do not have to be reported to the IRS.[23] Treasury Form 90-22.1, known as the Foreign Bank Account Report or FBAR, only requires that each U.S. citizen who has a financial interest in or authority, signatory, or otherwise, *over one or more banks, or securities or other financial accounts in a foreign country* must report such for each calendar year. The form does not require persons renting a safe deposit box in a foreign country to report that fact.[24]

Finally, even if the U.S. government suspects that you have an offshore safe deposit box, it still has a long way to go before it will be able to prove its suspicion. This is especially true if you've chosen to bank in a country with extremely stringent privacy laws. So, if you're particularly concerned about banking privacy, you should consider opening a safe deposit box in such countries as Vanuatu, the Netherlands Antilles, or Nevis.[25]

THE ULTIMATE HIDING SPOT: LAS VEGAS, NEVADA

The first time I met Charles, I immediately concluded that he wasn't the kind of guy who took chances. From the tip of his brown Rockport shoes to the top of his comb-over,

Charles seemed like he was headed for the ordinary guy Hall of Fame. But sometimes appearances can be deceiving.

It turned out that Charles spent his weekends as a wild-spending, fast-living man in America's favorite sin city—Las Vegas, Nevada. During the week, you see, Charles was the mild-mannered, straight-laced business-man who every day diligently visited all five of his hard-ware stores, making sure that business was good and his employees were happy. Then, at the end of the week, he would diligently deposit his stores' receipts at his local bank—except for the unrecorded money he'd managed to

It's often effective to hide your money in plain sight.

skim off the top, that is. He'd take that money and head to Vegas, where he lived a life of total and complete debauchery. He played $60,000 at a time on the craps table; hired the most expensive call girls in town; and when things were good, bought presents for anyone within a one-mile radius.

That's why Charles came to me. He had around $100,000 left of skimmed profits, but he knew that amount would only finance one or two more weekends in Vegas. Accordingly, Charles needed advice on how to raise some serious capital to finance his Vegas jaunts. He also wanted to know how he could keep some of his money in Vegas without his wife knowing about it.

I suggested to Charles that he consider setting up an offshore bank to raise the capital. When we got around to discussing how he could keep money in Las Vegas without anyone knowing about it, I advised that he seek the advice of a lawyer to be certain he was not breaking the law. The lawyer suggested he open a safe deposit box at his favorite Vegas hotel.

The Casino Cash Cage at almost any Las Vegas hotel leases safe deposit boxes. What's more, when you rent a safe deposit box at a Vegas casino, you are generally required to show very little in the way of identification. For example, Caesar's Hotel and Casino requires only that you show a picture I.D. and a hotel identification card.

That's what makes a Las Vegas safe deposit box an excellent hiding place for the extreme hider. It's a secure spot to keep cash or chips while you're in Las Vegas. And even if you're not a gambler, the Vegas safe deposit box can be used to hide large amounts of cash from a determined creditor or a greedy relative. If you aren't crazy about leaving substantial amounts of cash anywhere, you can always convert your cash into chips and then cash in the chips at a later date.[26]

What's more, if you visit Vegas often, the hotel safe deposit box provides you with the privacy of an offshore haven safe deposit box without the added travel expense. Because Las Vegas is in the business of getting people to spend money, hotel employees don't tend to ask a lot of questions. It's in their best business interest for you to have good, safe, convenient access to your money—so you can give it all to them. Remember, the people who rent you the safe deposit box are the same people who have no problem offering you free drinks to get you drunk while you gamble at their tables.

While a Las Vegas hotel will probably rent you a safe deposit box with no questions asked, don't expect it to have the same policy when you actually begin gambling. Under 31 CFR 103.22(a)(2), a casino is required to file a CTR when a person conducts a currency transaction of more than $10,000 within the casino. (According to my source, this provision can technically be interpreted to mean any cash transaction that exceeds $10,000 in any gaming day—and every house has a different schedule as to when a gaming day begins. Therefore, with a little guidance from your favorite casino, you can conduct transactions that exceed $10,000 so long as you conduct them in two different gaming days.)

GOING OVER THE EDGE: HIDING YOURSELF

For those of you who need to make more than your money disappear, there is probably one last extreme option— hiding yourself.

This extreme hiding option is definitely a method of last resort and not one you should consider lightly. It's difficult, expensive, and permanent.

The first thing you need to explore if you're really intent on disappearing is a name change. This can be legally accomplished by filing a court petition requesting the name change. A notice of your name change request is then published in the local paper—giving anyone opposed to the change an opportunity to object.[27] If no one appears in court on the date of your name change hearing, the request is usually granted.

In addition to a simple name change, you can take several other steps in order to disappear. You can buy yourself a citizenship in another country, for instance.

Many countries, such as Belize and Saint Kitts sell citizenship. All you need to do is apply for a passport at the foreign consulate of that country—using your new name, of course. Once you have your new passport, you should open a savings or checking account in the foreign country. In this way, with the right amount of money, some Spanish lessons, and a good attorney, you can effectively become a new person within a matter of a few weeks.

For those who are anxious to establish a new identity but are reluctant to leave the United States, there is a way you can hide yourself and still remain a U.S. resident. (You can legally change your identity while still living in the United States so long as you don't do it for criminal purposes or lie on the government forms about your previous identity.)

The first thing you need to do is establish a new address. The best way to create a new address is simply

That's what makes a Las Vegas safe deposit box an excellent hiding place for the extreme hider. It's a secure spot to keep cash or chips while you're in Las Vegas. And even if you're not a gambler, the Vegas safe deposit box can be used to hide large amounts of cash from a determined creditor or a greedy relative.

to move to another area with another zip code and a different street name.[28] (Moving to another country is still preferable, but if you're intent on staying in the United States, you should at least consider moving to another state.)

In addition to changing your address, you should also change your social security number. This can only be accomplished if you meet certain requirements. (These requirements include, but are not limited to, harassment and/or abuse of the social security number by an ex-spouse or others, death threats against you, or stalking. In addition, a new number may be obtained if someone misuses your social security number to fraudulently obtain credit, public benefits, employment, etc.)[29]

You'll need to produce corroborating evidence to prove how the social security number has disadvantaged you through no fault of your own. In addition, you must complete form SS-5 (available at all Social Security offices), as well as present documentation to the social security officer as to how the issuance of a new social security number would cure the problems that you are complaining about.[30]

Keep in mind that if you seek a name change, you should not seek a new social security number at the same time because that will arouse suspicion on the part of the Social Security administrator. You should also be aware that obtaining a new social security number for fraudulent purposes is illegal and can result in criminal prosecution and conviction.

Of course, effectively disappearing requires more than just the right legal documents. You'll also need to successfully travel to your new home without leaving a trail. This requires you to follow a few basic rules: (1) travel during high traffic times, so that you won't attract too much attention; (2) don't travel directly to your final destination, or it will be far too easy for people to track you; (3) don't charge anything on your credit cards—it's like leaving people a forwarding address; and (4) don't call or write to anyone.

Remember the one rule carved into stone about disappearing, because it's the rule most frequently broken and the one that trips up most would-be phantoms. . . .

If you're going to disappear, you can't stay in contact with old friends and family. One wrong move and it's all over.[31]

LAST-MINUTE HIDING: WHEN YOU DON'T HAVE TIME TO PLAN

As I've discussed repeatedly, the best way to effectively hide your cash and other assets is through careful planning. But for those of you who prefer to live on the edge, you probably will find yourself needing a hiding place at the last minute.

For example, if you're a woman, alone, out late at night, and find yourself being followed by a suspicious-looking man, you might considering dumping your purse into the nearest mailbox. This will prevent the suspicious man from attempting to rob you, protect your purse and its contents from theft, and allow you to retrieve your purse in the morning when the mailman comes to empty the box. (If you avail yourself of this temporary hiding place, be sure to note the mail pick-up time on the box.)

You might also consider using Federal Express or UPS drop boxes. The drop boxes can be found in a wide variety of locations—and have the added benefit of allowing you to avoid any interaction with the U.S. Post Office.

Public restrooms also offer the last-minute hider a wide variety of temporary hiding spots. You can use the handrails, handlebars, pipes, stalls, walls, and toilet paper rolls to stash your smaller objects.

If you are looking to hide something larger, you should examine the bathroom walls. Public restrooms often have boxes adhered to the walls to dispense anything from toilet seat covers to paper towels. (Many paper towel dispensers can be opened with the press of a button. The paper towel dispenser provides you with a large hiding space. However, the empty paper towel dispenser could attract the attention of a washroom attendant at any time.) If you're intent on hiding something in a public restroom, you should also explore using the soap dispensers, ashtrays, and area under the sink as potential hiding spots.[32]

If the idea of hiding something in a public restroom is too distasteful, consider temporarily hiding your goods either in a parking garage or a parked vehicle. The parking garage can make for an excellent temporary hiding spot, as

If you are being pursued by a mugger or purse snatcher, hiding your purse in a Federal Express or UPS drop box can protect you.

it's generally a place where people don't tend to linger. You can use the area under stairwells in a parking garage to temporarily stash something. You can also use the metal poles where parking meters used to be to hide smaller objects.[33] The ceiling of many parking garages makes for a good hiding spot because the fluorescent lights create a shelf where items can be temporarily placed.[34] If you're convinced that a certain car won't be moving anytime soon, you might consider using it as a temporary hiding spot.

For instance, if you've parked next to a broken-down Chevy for almost a month, you could hide something under that car's fender. But remember that even if the car hasn't moved in a month, the garage owner might suddenly decide to have it towed on the same day you've hidden a couple of hundred bucks under the front fender.

Finally, the inside and outside of public buildings also provide the last-minute hider with a few options. Many public buildings have spigots (and other protruding pipes) coming out of their sides, which can be used to hide small items.[35] The area behind shutters can also be used to store a few items for a short period of time. In addition, hallways in public buildings often have utility boxes that have long ceased to function. The last-minute hider can pry one of the boxes open with his trusty screwdriver and then stash a few small items.

Just remember, you never know when someone might come along and decide to fix that particular utility box. Public hiding always comes with a large amount of risk.

FINAL THOUGHTS

Extreme hiding is not for the faint of heart. If you're going to hide your money offshore, keep an offshore safe deposit box, keep a large amount of cash in Vegas, or stash your bucks under the sink of a public restroom, it will take guts.

You have to worry not only about the person or institution that you're hiding the money from, but also about the place where you hide it. While many offshore havens have beautiful beaches, haute cuisine, and wonderfully accommodating governments, others are hotbeds of political unrest just waiting to erupt.

Vegas may be a safe place to keep your money, but it may not be the best place. As any gambler knows, a lot of money comes to Vegas, but very little ever leaves. And although hiding your cash in a public place might temporarily protect it from theft, if you're interested in protecting the money for the long haul, you should probably investigate a more secure hiding place.

While extreme hiding may get your blood pumping and your heart racing, you've got to remember that along with some of the positives, come some very serious negatives.

Ultimately, only you can decide what will work in your situation. Just make sure your decision is a well-informed one.

REFERENCES

1. Schneider, Jerome, *The Complete Guide to Offshore Money Havens,* Roseville, CA: Prima Publishing, 2000, pp. 28–29.
2. December 18, 1998, interview with Peter Djinis, associate director for Financial Crimes Enforcement Network, Division of the Treasury Department.
3. September 15, 1998, telephone interview with Donald Alexander.
4. Ibid.
5. December 18, 1998, interview with Peter Djinis, associate director for Financial Crimes Enforcement Network, Division of the Treasury Department.
6. The United States also has tax treaties with a number of foreign countries in which information about individuals and their tax status can be exchanged. See *Money Laundering: A Guide for Criminal Investigators,* by John

Madinger and Sydney A. Zalopany, Boca Raton, FL: CRC Press, 1999, p. 295.

7. Madinger, John, and Sydney A. Zalopany, *Money Laundering: A Guide for Criminal Investigators,* p. 295.

8. December 17, 1998, interview with Ed Federico, IRS deputy assistant commissioner for criminal investigations.

9. Ibid.

10. December 15, 1998, interview with Peter Djinis.

11. Ibid.

12. Again, for information on how to begin investing offshore, you should first review my book *The Complete Guide to Offshore Money Havens,* pp. 66–67. I also recommend that you read other books on the subject of offshore banking and seek the advice of a financial consultant or attorney who specializes in offshore investment.

13. Through Aetna Casualty and Surety Company, Bank of America offers a $25,000 insurance policy on safe deposit box contents. But, if you decide to make a claim, you'd better have documentation to prove exactly what was in your box.

14. Bank of America's Safe Deposit Box Rental Agreement.

15. While most banks have a policy that forbids the storing of cash in safe deposit boxes, they do not directly inquire as to what a customer puts in his safe deposit box. If a customer says that he is putting cash in his box, then the bank will refuse to rent the box to him. It's basically a "don't ask, don't tell" financial policy.

16. A bank can easily argue in court that it has cause to suspect that you stored something "offensive" in your box and thus it was within the bank's legal rights to force your box open.

17. Madinger, John, and Sydney A. Zalopany, *Money Laundering: A Guide for the Criminal Investigator,* p. 84.

18. Ibid., pp. 202–203.

19. Once you provide the bank with your social security number, the fact that you have some sort of account there will be relatively easy for anyone to discover.

20. For more information on cheap, safe, and convenient hiding places, see also chapter 8, "Please Give Me My Space: Finding the Ultimate Hiding Place."

21. You can potentially circumvent this problem by opening up a safe deposit box in a nearby country such as Canada or Mexico.

22. If you use your safe deposit box for an illegal purpose, you'd better be sure that your offshore haven isn't a signatory to the MLAT. Under the MLAT, your offshore banker may be required to cooperate with U.S. investigation of your finances.
23. *Mark Skousen's Complete Guide to Financial Privacy,* Alexandria, VA: Alexandria House Books, 1979, p. 103.
24. However, if you transfer over $10,000 to a foreign safe deposit box, you (and any bank involved in the transaction) are required to report the transfer of funds.
25. A number of other offshore havens have tough banking privacy laws. For an extensive list, see my book *The Complete Guide to Offshore Havens,* pp. 224–225.
26. Las Vegas casino chips are a good method by which you can hide large amounts of cash. They are small and can be redeemed at any time in the hotel where they were originally purchased. You can travel with them and, because they are small, you can easily hide them in your luggage or clothing.
27. Objections can come from any number of sources, including creditors, ex-spouses, or law enforcement. See *Super Privacy,* by Bob Hammond, Boulder, CO: Paladin Press, 1997, p. 98.
28. Ibid., at 100.
29. Ibid., at 104.
30. Ibid.
31. Pankau, Edmund J., *Hide Your Assets and Disappear, a Step-by-Step Guide to Vanishing Without a Trace,* New York: HarperCollins, 1999.
32. Fiery, Dennis, *How to Hide Things in Public Places,* Port Townsend, WA: Breakout Publications, 1999, pp. 122–123.
33. Ibid., at p. 11.
34. Ibid., at p. 12.
35. Ibid., at p. 117.

CHAPTER 11

TURNING THE TABLES: HOW THE EXPERTS FIND THE HIDDEN MONEY

The one thing that famed divorce attorney Raoul Felder knows better than most people is that when one spouse wants to hide assets from another, finding the money can be extremely difficult. "Hiding is very often related to hiding from the IRS, and when that's the case, finding the money is a much tougher job," points out Felder. "The real problem is that if the husband had a scheme to hide money from the IRS, then it usually started long before the marriage. And the trails are pretty cold by the time the divorce unfolds."[1]

Therefore, in those divorce cases where one spouse appears to be hiding a large amount of assets from the other, Felder recommends hiring a forensic accountant to find the money.

"Finding hidden assets," explains Felder, "is not a do-it-yourself business. You not only need a professional, you need one who is familiar with the type of business that you are attempting to audit."[2]

For example, if you believe that your spouse is hiding the proceeds from his trucking business, you'll want to hire a forensic accountant who's done an analysis of a trucking company before. That way, you'll have someone on your team who knows what specific questions to ask to reveal if and how the assets are being hidden. Felder points out that "there is a formula for everything in life. All businesses work on formulas and you need to hire a forensic accountant who knows the formula of the business you're interested in investigating."[3]

As with lawyers, not all forensic accountants are created equal. Not only should your forensic accountant be familiar with the business in question, he or she should also have the mind of a careful and thorough accountant and the heart of a private investigator.

Long-time forensic accountant Stephen Reiss insists that his specialty is an art, not a science. "The thorough forensic accountant has to literally be able to reconstruct things from the end backward. If you own a restaurant, for instance, and you want to know if your husband is skimming off the business, the books won't tell you anything. You need someone who can work backward to get an idea of how much business that restaurant really does—someone who thinks to check how many napkins are being used and how many tablecloths are being laundered. Someone who investigates the amount of the average check and who adds up the number of times the tables seem to turn over in any given evening. You need someone who can play with numbers in a very problematic way."[4]

Forensic accounting pioneer Marvin Levy also believes that a forensic accountant should possess certain specific personality traits to be good at what he does. "The forensic accountant often deals with complex business and financial data that may be incomplete or misleading," explains Levy, a partner at Deloitte and Touche. "He lives in the world of evasive acts and sometimes the hypo-

> **Therefore, in those divorce cases where one spouse appears to be hiding a large amount of assets from the other, Felder recommends hiring a forensic accountant to find the money.**

thetical. He must be keenly analytical and be capable of getting to point C from point A, absent point B. He must also be creative and able to pick out the loose threads in what may appear to be a seamless web of falsified financial records. A forensic accountant must understand the levels of proof needed to support his findings and have the ability to teach them to a judge or jury in a clear, concise, and credible manner."[5]

Because the tracing of assets is so difficult, hiring a forensic accountant isn't cheap. The expense can be similar to hiring a high-priced divorce attorney, often as much as $375 per hour. (This is in addition to the cost of retaining an attorney.) Therefore, in order to make hiring a forensic accountant worthwhile in a divorce dispute, a great deal of money must be at issue. Forensic accountant Roseanna Purzycki recommends that before you hire a forensic accountant, you need to decide whether it's financially worthwhile to go after those hidden assets. "If your spouse is hiding $500,000 offshore," she posits, "it can often cost you that much to find it."[6]

Notwithstanding the high cost, the Big Five accounting firms have all increased their forensic accounting services to meet the rising demand. "Forensic and investigative accounting is decidedly the hottest area of our practice nationally," notes Gerard David, the Philadelphia-based Deloitte and Touche partner who directs the firm's dispute consulting practice in that region. The demand for forensic accountants is also on the rise internationally. According to Mark Tantum, a forensic accountant with Deloitte and Touche's London office, many of today's international forensic accountants fill a void that law enforcement can't handle. "Clients come to us and say that they need our help because law enforcement simply can't follow the money quickly enough. Deloitte and Touche has developed a fraud team that uses its contacts and offices all over the world to track money and recover it. Unlike law enforcement, we do not have to go through diplomatic channels and international legal jurisdictions to track money. We have an international infrastructure and forensic network that allows us to function in almost every major section of the world."[7]

WHERE THE EXPERTS LOOK FIRST: THE TAX RETURN

According to most experts, one of the best places to begin a search for hidden assets is in the tax returns of your alleged "hider." Stephen Reiss believes that for purposes of property distribution between divorcing spouses, "the tax return provides a check on the accuracy and completeness of the disclosure statement regarding the parties' income, expenses, assets, and debts."[8] In his article on how to use the tax return to find hidden assets in a divorce situation, Reiss recommends that the investigator focus on certain key elements of Form 1040, the Individual Tax Return. (He notes, however, that careful examination of the Form 1040 may lead to examination of other tax forms, such as Form 1065, pertaining to partnerships.)

Reiss suggests that if a spouse is attempting to locate potentially hidden assets, she should review Lines 8a and b of page 1 of Form 1040, which contain information about interest income—both taxable and tax exempt. The key to effectively using the information provided in the interest income section is remembering that interest income is derived from an asset. Reiss explains that "If there is a substantial amount of interest income on the tax return, it naturally follows that there has to be a substantial amount of principal. The tax return not only speaks about income, it really speaks about underlying assets . . . if you know how to listen."[9]

Reiss also suggests that Line 12 of Form 1040, regarding Business Income or Loss, should also be closely examined if there is some question about the accuracy of the business information reported. He points out that often in a divorce, the spouse in control of the business engages in a blatant underreporting of sales. Reiss suggests that "Testing gross margins against industry standards will suggest if there is an underreporting of sales. It is wise to look at some of the expenses in the cost-of-sales accounts to see if they seem appropriate to the kind of business at hand. These accounts are generally big-dollar amounts and are good places to hide improper charges."[10]

If one spouse or the other has always manifested an interest in the stock market, it's probably prudent for any forensic accountant to review the information on Capital Gains or Losses, Line 13 of Form 1040 as detailed in Schedule D. Reiss warns other investigators that "Sched-

According to Mark Tantum, a forensic accountant with Deloitte and Touche's London office, many of today's international forensic accountants fill a void that law enforcement can't handle. "Clients come to us and say that they need our help because law enforcement simply can't follow the money quickly enough."[7]

ule D is the tip of the iceberg in regard to assets held for investment, as it relates only to assets that have been sold and does not reveal anything about assets that are still being held/owned."[11] Because the total amount of investments cannot truly be determined from Schedule D, Reiss advises that divorce attorneys use a subpoena to produce any and all detailed records that are relevant.

Reiss also tells investigators searching for hidden assets to closely review the following sections of Form 1040: personal expenses, payroll inaccuracies, depreciation expenses, supplemental income, royalty income, trusts, mortgage income, and dividend income.[12] He warns, however, that an important element is missing from Form 1040, which often contains hidden assets—the amount invested in IRAs and other retirement accounts. "However, annual contributions to those accounts are recorded on page 1 at lines 23 and 28," he writes. "Inspection of a number of years of tax returns should show a pattern of contributions that should assist you in asking for the specific accounts that have been funded."[13]

While forensic accountant Roseanna Purzycki agrees that the tax return is a good starting place to find hidden money, she also points out that it's not particularly helpful when searching for money that's hidden in a foreign bank account. "You first look to see if any interest from a foreign bank account has been reported. But if the objective is to hide money, you probably won't find it. There are also statements on the tax returns that ask about foreign bank accounts. Now, if you're hiding money overseas, you probably will lie about that."[14] But Purzycki adds that the tax return isn't totally useless when it comes to finding hidden offshore assets. She suggests that a spouse who suspects that there may be hidden offshore assets should examine tax returns from the years when the marriage was good, which may reveal previously disclosed offshore accounts.[15]

All of the experts admit that the tax return will only take you so far when you're dealing with someone who owns a cash-intensive business. Typical cash-intensive businesses include restaurants, jewelry stores, auto repair shops, parking lots, gas stations, and anything in the garment industry. In these cases, business owners have many opportunities to skim cash. Purzycki admits that it's extremely difficult to ascertain the true amount of earnings in these types of businesses. She notes that "the IRS has a task force set up to look for unreported cash in the garment industry and has had a hard time finding it. So, it won't be much easier for a forensic accountant to do so."[16]

After getting an experienced forensic accountant to examine the relevant tax returns, the experts suggest that you hire a good lawyer who will subpoena all relevant financial documents from your spouse. Stephen Reiss argues that in many divorces, subpoena power is not used effectively when it comes to finding hidden assets. He suggests that one of the first things any good family law attorney will do is have the forensic accountant draw up an extensive and detailed list of all relevant financial documents that need to be subpoenaed. Reiss's list generally includes the following: bank statements, check registers, canceled checks (front and back), every account that the spouse has signing power on even if it's not in that spouse's name, all personal and corporate tax returns, brokerage statements for all accounts for every month as well as an annual summary, savings accounts, insurance policies (liability, fire, casualty, umbrella), leases, credit card statements, partnership documents (including K1s, which state the amount of the opening capital balance), tax return for the partnership (Form 1065), and all documents relating to trusts.[17] While this list is extensive, it is not necessarily exhaustive. You should always check with your attorney before attempting to subpoena financial documents.

Once you've managed to get a good portion of the documents detailed herein, the competent forensic accountant can go to work tracing assets through various bank accounts. Donald Gursey notes that bank account tracing can be difficult, time-consuming, and expensive work. He recalls that in one particularly complicated divorce case, he and his partners were required to trace bank account records back thirty years.[18] Bank account tracing is something that is best left to the professionals. First, you have to find all the bank statements and check registers. This can be a complex undertaking because many people don't keep old checks or registers and most banks only keep records going back seven years. Second, once you've found all the bank statements and check registers, you need to then painstakingly figure out whether a transfer of assets occurred and if so, where the assets went. You do an analysis of bank statements, investment accounts, and asset acquisitions. Basically, you need to figure out what the source of the money was and what happened to it.

Investigating the Business to Find Hidden Assets

All experts agree that when a cash-intensive business is involved, there is usually money coming in that goes unreported. One of the most basic ways to prove the presence of unreported cash is to do a lifestyle analysis—compare the lifestyle of the business owner to the "reported" earnings of the business. If a business owner lives in a house that's completely paid off, you decide whether the income he claimed could accommodate that expense. And if the money is not claimed, there will be a shortfall. "The IRS often tries to prove unreported cash by doing a cash-flow analysis—income versus expenses," explains Roseanna Purzycki. "Generally, the IRS looks at the tax

After getting an experienced forensic
accountant to examine the relevant tax
returns, the experts suggest that you hire a
good lawyer who will subpoena all relevant
financial documents from your spouse.
Stephen Reiss argues that in many divorces,
subpoena power is not used effectively when it
comes to finding hidden assets.

return or checking account as far back as possible and
tries to see if the income claimed can logically accommodate the expenses. Even so, it's not an easy task to try
and find the unreported income that way."[19]

If your cash-flow analysis fails to yield any results,
you could try a slightly different approach. Donald
Gursey notes that on occasion he's been able to obtain a
subpoena to conduct a surprise investigation of a business. But he admits that it is extremely difficult to get
judicial approval for this. "You basically have to be able
to prove to a judge that there is a good chance of cash
being unreported," explains Gursey. "That's really hard to
do."[20]

When the cash-flow analysis proves to be a dead end,
most experienced forensic accountants look for evidence of
double payments. Donald Gursey recalls one case in which
he conducted an audit of a major company and saw a payment under the "A" billing file made out to "Arness Paper."
Almost three days later, when he finally got to the "P" section of the billing file, he saw yet another payment made
out to "Arness Paper" for the same amount as the previous
payment.[21] After spotting the second Arness Paper bill,
Gursey immediately realized that something was amiss
and began to review the entire billing file again. "Things
just didn't look right," Gursey remembers with a smile.

"And the one thing I've learned over the years is that if something doesn't look right, it usually isn't."[22]

In addition to double billing, many business owners engage in the practice of paying phantom employees. This method of skimming can be done on a tremendously large scale and can involve hundreds of thousands of dollars. Forensic accountant Dave Fox was involved in a case in which the owner of the business paid nonexistent employees up to $500,000 a year—although the individual "employee" checks never were more than $5,000. The phantom employee scheme can also be done on a small scale—paying $200 a month to a nonexistent cleaning lady. When searching a business for unreported cash, the careful forensic accountant needs to carefully review the payroll by focusing on everyone from the handymen to the top company executives.

Dave Fox believes that if you really want to find out where the unreported cash is in a divorce case, you usually just need to ask the wife.[23] Fox recalls that in one recent divorce case, it was the wife who led him directly to the unreported assets. "I had one case where the husband had at least ten different bank accounts in several different states and countries. He sent over $1.5 million to one account in Switzerland. He would then transfer it back to the States in $100,000 to $200,000 increments. The account was almost impossible to trace and we probably never would have found it if it hadn't been for his wife. She didn't have any written proof, but she knew

> In addition to double billing, many business owners engage in the practice of paying phantom employees. This method of skimming can be done on a tremendously large scale and can involve hundreds of thousands of dollars.

about the account. Once she told us about the account, we
started looking at the husband's business and noted hundreds of thousands of dollars of money coming in through
wire transfers. We did the subpoenas in Switzerland and
ultimately, we got the money."[24]

Stephen Reiss agrees that even when the wife isn't
involved in the family business, she may turn out to be
the forensic accountant's best source of information when
it comes to finding unreported cash. "Lots of times the
wife will say to me that her husband always had a lot of
cash on him. She'll tell me that they had a safe in the
house and that her husband always kept at least $20,000
in the safe. She may not know where the cash came from,
but she'll usually know that it was there."[25] Even when
the wife isn't able to help, Reiss believes that when it
comes to cash-based businesses, the best course of action
is to assume that there is unreported income. "Any business in which cash is involved is immediately suspect," he
states emphatically. "Anywhere there is a lot of cash, the
forensic accountant needs to go back as far as the business's deposit slips to first see whether any cash itself is
being deposited. If all of the deposit slips consist of checks
and credit cards, you know there is something wrong.
You've got to ask, Where is the cash? The cash doesn't get
deposited. The cash gets pocketed."[26]

Even after the forensic accountant determines that
someone has been "pocketing" the cash, his job is only
half over. He still needs to find that magical pocket, which
could be located anywhere in the world.

One choice hiding place for unreported income is the
non–interest bearing checking account. Even for the most
sophisticated forensic accountant, finding the non–interest bearing checking account is extremely difficult.
Because it earns no interest, there is no record of it on a
person's tax return.

Still, finding a non–interest bearing checking account is
not impossible if you hire the "right" people. Certain private

investigators are able to utilize resources that are not available to attorneys and CPAs. A good private investigator can work miracles with a name, a birth date, and a city. (If he has a social security number, he can probably access financial information on a person in only a matter of hours.) Although a good private investigator can be helpful in finding hidden bank accounts, he still needs as much information as possible to get the job done. If you hire one, make sure that you tell him everything you know about your husband's travel and work habits. If your husband tends to spend at least one weekend a month in Vegas, for example, chances are that he has a bank account there. (It's also possible that he has a safe deposit box at his favorite casino.)

You can assist your private investigator in other ways to find hidden bank accounts or other non–interest bearing assets. Give the investigator all of your phone bills. He can review them to see if your spouse has called any banks. (The phone bills may also help you locate other places where your spouse has hidden money.) Give your investigator all insurance policies—including all personal articles riders. If your spouse has a non–income producing asset like an expensive painting, chances are that he's insured it. (If he's purchased diamonds and/or estate jewelry, chances are that he's insured those items, too.) The insurance policy will tell you what the asset is and where it's being stashed. And if you can't think of where to even begin looking for a hidden account or hidden asset, review your calendar (and if possible, your spouse's office calendar) to try and pinpoint your spouse's whereabouts over the last year.

FINDING THE HIDDEN MONEY IN A PROFESSIONAL PRACTICE

According to the experts, one of the most common and effective places to hide money is the attorney's trust account. Donald Gursey recalls a case in which he represented a lawyer's wife in a divorce suit. "I got bank statements from the trust account, but not the individual canceled checks. So, I could see how at the end of the year, the monthly balance in the client's trust account went up. Clearly, the lawyer was deferring fees and leaving the money in the trust account."[27] However, although Gursey recognized that the attorney was hiding money from his wife, he still needed access to the trust account to prove it. But when he went into court and argued for access to the trust account because it was being improperly used, the court held that the trust account could not be broken because of attorney-client privilege. "I even had a judge deny access after I showed him statements proving that for the last three months of the last five years, the client trust account balance had gone up," states Gursey. "I showed that there was no seasonal fluctuation with this business. We all knew that there was only one reason for the balance to go up at the end of the year: the attorney deferred fees. But the judge denied access anyway."[28]

The problems with attorneys hiding money don't end with the client's trust account. Stephen Reiss notes that many professionals, including attorneys, use their practices to hide money from their spouses and/or other creditors. "In the professional practice, the doctor/lawyer/accountant often has his client make out the check without putting the 'Inc.' after the professional's name. The professional then simply cashes the check at a bank. If he just gives the customer a receipt and doesn't enter the transaction into the accounting system, it will probably never be known."[29] Reiss also notes that he's heard of instances in which professionals perform services for their clients on a strictly cash basis. This alleviates a trail of any paperwork pointing to the transaction.

Therefore, when forensic accountants undertake an audit of an attorney and/or physician, they tend to look for evidence of any transactions that may have occurred off-the-books. They also conduct a cash-flow analysis of the practice at issue. But when you're dealing with attorneys and doctors, you need to bring in an investigator who is familiar with how these professional practices operate. As divorce attorney Raoul Felder advises, "If you're getting divorced from a doctor, you need a forensic accountant who's familiar with that field. You need someone who knows the average price of a consultation with a certain type of physician and who can estimate how many appointments this type of doctor generally has each day. You need him to be able to ask specific questions for you. And if he can't, he's less than useful to you."[30]

And even if the forensic accountant does know the specific type of medical practice your husband is in, he or she still may not be able to find your husband's hidden assets. "In one case, the wife and I knew her doctor husband was hiding money, but we couldn't prove it," recalls Beverly Hills matrimonial-law specialist Arlene Schwimmer. "Then I asked her if he carried a briefcase, and she said that he never went anywhere without it, even kept it locked in his trunk when he was out on the golf course."[31] Eventually, the wife got inside the briefcase, to discover bankbooks that disclosed millions in hidden assets.

Although experienced forensic accountants know a wide variety of avenues in which to search for hidden assets, even they sometimes come up empty. Sometimes, the wife doesn't find a briefcase full of hidden assets worth millions of dollars until years after her divorce is final. Sometimes she doesn't learn that her husband has stashed away thousands of dollars each year by paying phantom employees until her husband is no longer required to pay child support. And sometimes, the husband doesn't find out until years after the divorce that his attorney wife hid over $500,000 in an offshore account in the Caribbean. In years past, all a dishonest spouse had to do was make sure that he kept his money hidden until the divorce was over. Once the divorce was final, there wasn't much his ex could do. Occasionally, a judge might slap a dishonest husband on the wrist for hiding assets, but for the most part, if the husband managed to keep money hidden until long enough after those divorce papers were signed, he was home free.

But things are changing. Although family law remains largely a state-by-state matter, a recent California decision has caused a stir in legal circles everywhere. In October 1999, a San Diego businesswoman won the right to take her ex-husband to civil court for allegedly conspiring with his bookkeeper to artificially depress his earnings by withholding insurance billings until after their divorce was final. The woman claimed that as a result of her ex-husband's fraudulent activities, she received approximately $1 million less than she would have, had the assets been properly accounted for. In years past, similar cases have been thrown out on the grounds that the civil court has no jurisdiction over family law matters. However, earlier this year, the California Court of Appeals held that the family court does not have exclusive jurisdiction over cases like these and that an ex-spouse who believes that he or she has been defrauded in a completed divorce case has the right to sue in civil court and to collect punitive damages when warranted.

Although the California decision is not binding on anyone outside of California at the time of this writing,

One choice hiding place for unreported income is the non–interest bearing checking account. Even for the most sophisticated forensic accountant, finding the non–interest bearing checking account is extremely difficult. Because it earns no interest, there is no record of it on a person's tax return.

it's quite possible that other jurisdictions will follow California's lead in this area. Susan Fogel, legal director of the California Women's Law Center in Los Angeles, notes that "Under the current system, spouses who control the family finances and investments could lie, cheat, and steal in the course of divorce. Traditionally, defrauded spouses have had less access to the legal system than defrauded business partners."[32]

The family courts may still continue to look the other way while spouses hide assets, but California's latest legal decision demonstrates a growing intolerance by the civil courts for spouses who lie about their assets.

How the Amateurs Find the Money

Before you consider hiring a professional to look for hidden assets, do a little looking yourself. Try and collect as much evidence as you can before you bring in the big guns. For instance, you don't want to go off and hire a forensic accountant to search for an offshore account unless you're fairly certain that such an account exists. Almost every forensic accountant I interviewed told me that using offshore accounts to hide unreported income is not as common as most people think.

According to Roseanna Purzycki, before you assume someone is hiding money offshore, you need to ask yourself about that person's "level of sophistication."[33] In most cases, unreported income tends to be hidden in more conventional places like bank accounts, safe deposit boxes, and even safes within the home.

So before you start hunting for offshore accounts, ask yourself a few questions as a reality check. Does the person who you think is hiding money offshore actually have any overseas connections? Is he or she foreign born? An international business person? Do you have any phone bills or fax bills indicating that this person has had contact with international banks, attorneys, accountants, or other financial consultants?

If the person works for a company in the United States and never travels outside of the country on business, it's unlikely that he or she would have the opportunity to set up an offshore account. (It's not impossible; just unlikely.)

Once you're convinced that someone is hiding assets from you, you can search a number of places before you bring in assistance. You can look through every document that comes to your home. If you've refinanced your house, pay particular attention to the mortgage application. If someone wanted to prove that he or she had the resources to afford a home, the mortgage application might list all of that person's true assets. Moreover, if the mortgage application was filled out when the marriage was good, it might actually contain an honest accounting of your community assets.

Finally, even if you only have a suspicion that assets are being hidden, you should start making copies of all financial documents to which you have access. This includes copies of your tax returns, all bank statements, all canceled checks (front and back), property taxes forms, and mortgage statements. If you eventually have to bring in the experts to find the hidden assets, these documents will be invaluable when they begin their search.

REFERENCES

1. October 19, 1999, interview with Raoul Felder.
2. Ibid.
3. Ibid.
4. September 1, 1999, interview with Stephen M. Reiss.

5. "Marvin Levy, Pioneer in Forensic Accounting, Joins Deloitte and Touche Dispute Consulting Group," *Business Wire,* April 29, 1999.
6. September 7, 1999, interview with Roseanna Purzycki of Gursey, Schneider.
7. September 8, 1999, interview with Mark Tantam from Deloitte and Touche's Dispute Consulting Group, London Office.
8. Reiss, Stephen M., "Tips for Uncovering Hidden Assets in Tax Returns," *The Matrimonial Strategist,* vol. 16, no. 4 (August 18, 1999): 1.
9. September 1, 1999, interview with Stephen M. Reiss.
10. Reiss, Stephen M., "Tips for Uncovering Hidden Assets in Tax Returns," *The Matrimonial Strategist,* vol. 16, no. 4 (August 18, 1999).
11. Ibid.
12. Ibid.
13. Ibid.
14. September 7, 1999, interview with Roseanna Purzycki of Gursey, Schneider.
15. Ibid.
16. Ibid.
17. September 1, 1999, interview with Stephen M. Reiss.
18. September 7, 1999, interview with Donald Gursey.
19. September 7, 1999, interview with Roseanna Purzycki of Gursey, Schneider.
20. September 7, 1999, interview with Donald Gursey.
21. Ibid.
22. Ibid.
23. October 25, 1999, interview with Dave Fox.
24. Ibid.
25. September 1, 1999, interview with Stephen Reiss.
26. Ibid.
27. September 7, 1999, interview with Donald Gursey.
28. Ibid.
29. September 1, 1999, interview with Stephen Reiss.
30. October 19, 1999, interview with Raoul Felder.
31. Berger, Esther T., "To Love, Honor and Litigate?" *Town & Country Monthly* (January 1, 1998).
32. Kristof, Kathy, "Suspect Your Ex-Spouse of Hiding Assets? Now You can Sue," *Los Angeles Times,* September 26, 1999.
33. September 7, 1999, interview with Roseanna Purzycki of Gursey, Schneider.

CHAPTER 12

THE DIRTY DOZEN: A TWELVE-STEP HIDING PROGRAM

In order to successfully hide your cash or other assets, you need to follow twelve important steps. If you don't learn and understand these twelve steps to successful hiding, chances are your cash and other assets will be discovered. Successful hiding, after all, is not something that just happens—it's the result of careful and thoughtful planning. Before people can effectively hide their assets, they need to change their mindset. Thoroughly understanding, appreciating, and implementing the twelve basic steps will help you to do that.

STEP 1: CHANGE YOUR MINDSET: EVERYONE HAS SOMETHING WORTH HIDING

The first step to becoming a more effective hider requires that you change your mindset from carefree to cautious. You need to appreciate that you have a number of valuable assets that could easily be taken from you. Everyone has something worth stealing. The sooner you realize this, the better you'll be at protecting yourself.

This is particularly true in today's high-tech society. Even if your bank balance is embarrassingly low and you live at home with your parents, you still have something worth stealing—your identity. It can be gone in an instant, and you can spend years trying to reclaim it. An accomplished thief can turn the theft of your driver's license and social security number into $50,000 in credit card debt. He can use your name and credit clout to purchase automobiles, take trips, and buy real estate. For years after the theft of your identity, you may be forced to explain and re-explain your bad credit rating. You may even find yourself explaining to a potential employer why your background check reveals that you spent time in prison.

My friend Angela Howell had always made fun of my preoccupation with hiding and protecting assets. In fact, when I first told her the idea for this book, she laughed at what she called my "paranoia" over being robbed. Angela felt that it was a waste of time and energy to worry about protecting assets and other valuables. It was her philosophy and her mindset that everything could be replaced. She had locks on her doors, insurance, and money in the bank. She didn't want to be bothered with hiding money or anything else, for that matter. "Besides," she always said with a big smile, "it's not like I own the Crown jewels or anything like that. What the hell do I have that's really worth stealing?"

> Everyone has something worth stealing. The sooner you realize this, the better you'll be at protecting yourself.

As it turns out, Angela had more than she thought. About a year ago, her purse was stolen right out of her office. Several hours later, her empty wallet was found in a nearby dumpster. By the close of business that day she'd canceled her credit cards, reported the theft to the police, and applied for a new social security card. She'd also taken two hours off work to go and get a new driver's license. When she drove home that evening, she figured that in a few days, the theft would be a distant memory. But she figured wrong. It was almost a year later before my friend discovered that her identity had been stolen. There was another Angela Howell who had applied for and received three separate credit cards that she'd then proceeded to max out. The "second" Angela Howell also lived in L.A., although she had her mail sent to a post office box. So, while the "second" Angela Howell was busy applying for and receiving credit cards, the real Angela Howell had no idea.

Angela was forced to spend countless hours on the telephone and writing letters, trying to rectify the damage done by the "second" Angela. Even though she managed to repair her credit rating, she still occasionally has problems getting new credit cards. Every once in a while something shows up in a computer somewhere that marks her as the "second" deadbeat Angela.

After her identity was stolen, Angela Howell changed her mindset about hiding. Gone was the carefree attitude of days past. The new Angela was cautious, careful, and extremely methodical so as to protect her identity, her assets, and everything of value to her. The first thing she did was to start putting documents like her bank and credit card statements into a locked drawer in her office desk. She put her social security card and some important financial documents in a safe deposit box at her bank. The only thing she carried in her wallet was her driver's license, two credit cards, and a picture of her cat, Sammy. It was a small step toward protecting herself, but a large step toward effectively holding on to her assets.

STEP 2: KEEP A LOW PROFILE

The next most important step in being an effective hider is learning how to keep a low profile. The best way to keep your assets safe is to make sure that nobody knows you have any. I've always believed that flaunting your wealth is tantamount to wearing a sign that reads: "I've got lots of money. Want some?" The most effective way to hold on to your wealth is to keep it a secret. While this sounds like a fairly simple task, it tends to go against the grand traditions of capitalism, which have invariably included excess and boasting.

A few weeks ago I watched an interview with Ivana Trump that had been conducted in the mid-1980s, when she was still married to millionaire real estate mogul Donald Trump. Ivana answered questions about Donald's recent purchase of the Plaza Hotel and his decision to have Ivana oversee the restoration of that building. She proudly touted "the Donald's" incredible business acumen, pointing to his recent string of high-profile acquisitions. When the reporter suggested that many Americans find the Trumps' flamboyant and unrestricted spending offensive, Ivana made no apologies. She merely defended the unfettered spending by stating that both she and Donald had worked hard for every penny they had and that they should be free to spend the money as they saw fit.

Unfortunately for both Donald and Ivana, their free-spending ways came to an abrupt end in the late 1980s when Donald's business investments went south. Donald was targeted by everyone from angry creditors to the IRS. He was forced to sell off a large portion of his holdings, including his splashy yacht. By the end of the decade, he came close to declaring bankruptcy. While Donald ultimately recovered his financial empire (and then some), he and Ivana remain symbols of the excessive and unfettered spending of the 1980s, which increased the divide between the rich and poor.

To this day, Donald Trump is viewed by many Americans as an arrogant elitist who has more money and women than he deserves. And while some of this reputation is well earned, some of it is just the result of his high-profile spending. His extravagance has bred contempt and jealousy among many who view him as an uncaring, self-absorbed millionaire who will do anything for a little free publicity—including run for president.

The point of all this is that while Trump's high profile has made him a lightning rod for criticism, a plethora of Americans are far richer than Trump and yet their names, addresses, and faces are completely unknown to most of the public. They've deliberately chosen to keep a low profile and, in doing so, have kept attention off their net worth.

Many wealthy people I know believe in the philosophy of "less is more." Some of them adhere to this lifestyle because they think lavish spending is garish and ostentatious. They believe that people with old money don't advertise it; rather, it's only the *nouveau riche* who need to broadcast their net worth. Others choose to keep a low profile because it's part of their strategy for keeping their assets safe from predators. (They also probably believe that by keeping a low profile, they potentially lessen the possibility of an IRS audit or other government investigation.)

Personally, I fervently believe that by broadcasting your net worth (even if it's not in the millions), you draw all kinds of negative attention. Over the years I've also learned that the best way to attract the attention of the IRS is to spend loudly and lavishly. Even if the IRS computer doesn't mark you for an audit, chances are that your neighbors will. Nothing breeds more animosity, jealousy, and contempt in your neighbor than his having to watch you spend large amounts of money when he is not equally blessed. I've seen situations where the mere presence of a Rolls Royce has prompted an anonymous call to the IRS.

If you find yourself with a little extra cash on hand, the best thing to do is to hide it—don't flaunt it. If you're really interested in changing your mindset and learning how to be an effective hider, you must learn how to live quietly. This doesn't mean you can't spend some of your hard-earned money, it just means that you need to spend the money with as little fanfare as possible.

STEP 3: ALWAYS PLAN AHEAD

The one thing I've learned over the years is that successful asset protection requires careful and thoughtful planning. Before you stick your grandmother's antique watch in a couch cushion, you need to think the hiding place through. You need to think about how often that couch is cleaned and whether the watch might be revealed during one of these cleanings. You need to wonder about whether you could put the watch in a safer place—like behind the medicine cabinet or even in a safe deposit box at the bank. You need to consider how often you wear the watch. If you wear it often, you'll probably want to hide it in a place where you have easy access. Finally, if you don't want your spouse to know about the watch, you'll have to decide whether you should even insure it. (If you insure it, your husband will undoubtedly notice the personal articles floater that you've added.)

As you can see, even with something as small as an antique watch, you need to consider a myriad of things before you stash it somewhere.

If you want to hide something more substantial, like a large inheritance, you'll have even more things to consider before choosing an appropriate hiding place. If you're single and thinking about marriage, you'll definitely want to contact an attorney to investigate putting the money in a trust that will maintain the inheritance

> The point of all this is that while Trump's high profile has made him a lightning rod for criticism, a plethora of Americans are far richer than Trump and yet their names, addresses, and faces are completely unknown to most of the public. They've deliberately chosen to keep a low profile and, in doing so, have kept attention off their net worth.

as separate property. You might also want to invest the money offshore. (Again, you should probably contact an attorney or financial adviser to help you decide whether such a major move is right for your situation.)

The one thing that you shouldn't do is wait until someone tries to get his or her hands on your inheritance. You want to have the money safely hidden before there is any sign of trouble. If you wait until you're married to invest the money offshore, a court might interpret your actions as an attempt to deprive the community of assets. If you try to transfer assets after your ex-partner successfully sues you for breach of contract, chances are that not only will you lose some of your inheritance, you'll probably be charged with fraud. Last-minute hiding can cost you money and your freedom.

If you suspect that your assets or other valuables are vulnerable to seizure by determined creditors, thieves, or even the government, you should be proactive and hide those assets immediately.[1] Even if the government has no legitimate basis under which to seize your assets, it can still take years for you to recover them. Therefore, the best policy is to be prepared.

I remember a particularly exciting episode of the hit television series *The Sopranos,* in which Tony Soprano gets a tip that he and his "family" are about to be indicted by the feds. He immediately goes home and cleans out all of his hiding places—including the air vent above the kitchen counter where he stores his guns and cash and other ill-gotten gains. He then drives over to the nursing home where his mother lives and hides the same items in her closet. When the feds search his home a few days later, they find nothing. I guess that one of the first things they teach you in the mob is how to be an effective hider by planning ahead.

STEP 4: COMPLEX HIDING SCHEMES REQUIRE PROFESSIONAL ADVICE

If you're just going to stick some cash behind a loose ceiling tile, you don't really need to hire an attorney. But if you're interested in effectuating a more complicated asset-hiding scheme, you should contact a professional. As I discussed earlier, a lot of hiding scenarios are illegal. Therefore, it's always best to contact an attorney if you're concerned that your hiding scheme might land you in jail. Moreover, if you have a particularly complicated situation in which you're trying to protect your money from potential creditors, a greedy relative, or the government, it's probably best to get some professional help. If you're a medical professional whose practice is about to be sued by an unhappy patient, for instance, you want to be sure that an adverse judgment won't leave your kids without a college education. And if you have $200,000 in the bank and you're about to get married, you want to ensure that your new wife can't argue that you gave her that money as a wedding present. Finally, if you're trying to keep a little of your hard-earned money away from the government, you'll need professional advice on offshore investment opportunities that give you minimal tax exposure.

While I've been able to suggest a number of effective hiding places to you, I haven't been able to tell you which ones are best suited to *your* particular hiding needs. For example, I can suggest that you investigate hiding your money in an offshore safe deposit box, but I can't tell you whether this would be a legal option for you *personally.* You might be better off investing that money in an off-shore bank or placing it in an offshore asset protection trust. It all depends on the specific reasons behind your desire to hide the assets. Once you impart these reasons to an attorney or a financial adviser, this person will probably be able to provide some direction as to which asset protection plan will work best for you.

Although you can read books like this one in order to get some general ideas about where to hide your money, it's always prudent to seek the advice of an attorney or financial consultant before you devise and implement your strategy. In writing this book, I consulted with a wide variety of professionals, including accountants, attorneys, and financial consultants, about the best and most secure hiding places for everything from cash to documents. I also spoke with a number of people who know how to find money that's been hidden. If you need professional assistance in tracking hidden money, you should definitely contact a forensic accountant. The one thing to remember is that sophisticated and complex financial planning and asset protection generally requires specific expertise.

STEP 5: DETERMINE HOW FAR YOU'RE WILLING TO GO

Before you implement any asset protection strategy, you need to answer one very important question: What type of a person are you?

Are you a conservative person who prefers not to take risks with your money? A person who enjoys gambling and playing the stock market? Or are you somewhere in-between?

Whoever you are, you need to acknowledge that fact and make certain that your asset protection plan takes your personality into account. This is because a certain lack of control comes with the offshore territory.

Offshore investment, you see, has a large number of benefits, but it also has some risks. It's possible that the offshore haven will undergo a change in government, for example, thereby creating a different investment environment. It's also possible that U.S. laws will change, rendering your offshore investment less profitable than before.

For these reasons, and a few others, offshore investing is probably not for someone who needs to have complete control over his assets at all times. In fact, many offshore strategies are specifically structured to demonstrate that the original investor has limited rights over the investment. Finally, if you like to go and visit your money on a regular basis, putting it in a faraway offshore haven will probably drive you crazy.

Before you go offshore, you also need to conduct some research about the true benefits and detriments of offshore banking. You don't want to draw conclusions about offshore banking based on its portrayal in the latest mob

If you're just going to stick some cash behind a loose ceiling tile, you don't really need to hire an attorney. But if you're interested in effectuating a more complicated hiding scheme, you should contact a professional. As I discussed earlier, a lot of hiding scenarios are illegal. Therefore, it's always best to contact an attorney if you're concerned that your hiding scheme might land you in jail.

movie. As I mentioned earlier, because of recent films and articles many people have an incorrect perception of off-shore investment. The fact remains that many stable, legitimate investments can be made offshore. With the proper research, guidance, and preparation, a lot of the risk can be removed from offshore investment. In fact, certain investments in the United States are far more risky. So, before you reject offshore investment as illegal, crazy, or far too risky, do your homework. Once you have an accurate perception of offshore investment, you can decide whether it's a good fit with your specific personality type.

If you're a conservative, risk-averse person, for example, and you have some money that you want to protect from potential creditors, you might investigate depositing it in a non–interest bearing checking account in a neighboring county. If you are concerned about your rare coin collection, however, you might opt to deposit your assets in a domestic bank safe deposit box or merely install a fireproof safe somewhere in your home to protect them.

If you select a hiding strategy that is inconsistent with your personality, there's a good chance you'll inadvertently reveal the hiding spot to family, friends, or even the government. Think of a person who decides to carry a gun and then unconsciously advertises that fact to the world by constantly touching and adjusting the weapon through his or her clothing. The bottom line is that you must be absolutely comfortable with your hiding place before you actually put any assets into it.

STEP 6: KNOW THE RULES
BEFORE YOU HIDE

Before you put a dollar into an offshore account or stash a stock certificate in your bank safe deposit box, you need to know what's legal and what's not. If you want to be a successful hider, you've got to learn to follow the rules. The surest way for someone to find your hidden assets is for you to break the law. For example, if you're concerned about someone stealing your cash when you travel, you should know that it's perfectly legal for you to hide $6,000 in the lining of your coat before you travel to Italy. It's not, however, legal for you to hide over $10,000 or more in that lining, unless you tell U.S. Customs about it first. As with most everything, specific rules govern the hiding of assets.

The first thing I would recommend to people interested in hiding some of their assets is that they consult an attorney and/or other professional financial adviser. If you plan to hide assets, you will need someone to advise you about what you can and cannot legally do. You'll want to know about bank and wire transfer reporting requirements, as well as about the status of "know your customer" legislation. If you decide to invest offshore, you should find out what types of investments might draw unwanted attention from the IRS. For example, the IRS is currently focusing a great deal of its efforts on investigating foreign trusts. If you're at all concerned about an IRS audit, you'll want to have the requisite information to try and avoid one.

So don't start transferring all of your assets into your mother's name until you're aware of what constitutes a

And if you use more sophisticated hiding methods, like offshore investment, you should definitely keep that information to yourself. The fact that you've invested offshore could not only bring you unwanted attention from the government, it could also arouse the interest of potential litigants.

fraudulent conveyance. For example, transferring assets to your mother *after* you've been sued is fraudulent. However, if you transfer those assets far in advance of the lawsuit, then it's very possible that the court will find the asset transfers to be valid. Knowing the law in this situation and others could definitely save you money.

STEP 7: TRUST NO ONE

One of the most important steps to effective hiding is learning to keep your mouth shut. This means not telling your neighbor how big a bonus you just got; it also sometimes means not telling your girlfriend or even your wife. If you're skimming money off your business, you probably don't want to tell your wife the specific details of the operation. It's bad enough if she knows about the scheme; it's even worse if she knows how the scheme works. A few years down the line when things aren't going so well between you and the Mrs., you can bet that she will start talking about the creative way you run your business. The best asset protection scheme can be ruined by loose lips.

Before you decide to hide your cash or any other valuables, you also have to determine from whom you're hiding the assets. If you're hiding from the IRS, you will want to keep the entire hiding operation as secret as possible from everyone. (Even if you and your spouse are incredibly close, there's always the possibility that at some later date, he or she will tell where the money is.) If you're hiding a stash of cash somewhere in the house, you should also keep the hiding place a secret. Even the most innocent of admissions can lead to the exposure of your hiding spot. And if you use more sophisticated hiding methods, like offshore investment, you should definitely keep that information to yourself. The fact that you've invested offshore could not only bring you unwanted attention from the government, it could also arouse the interest of potential litigants. Once an adversary finds out you've got money offshore, his lawyer might decide that you're rich enough to sue and he'll label you the proverbial deep pocket.

Because it's often difficult to ascertain whom you're specifically hiding your money from, it's best to imagine that you're hiding it from everyone. I'm not advocating that you turn into some paranoid scrooge who sees a greedy relative or employee lurking behind every corner. But I am advocating that you exercise prudence and discretion when it comes to discussing financial matters around family, friends, or employees who could potentially want to get their hands on your assets.

STEP 8: KNOW YOUR ADVERSARY

Whenever you think of hiding something, you need to look at the situation from a wide variety of perspectives, including those of your potential pursuers. Ask yourself, How easy would it be for a professional to find your assets?

Andy Hanson was a client of mine back in the 1980s. He owned several apartment buildings on the west side of L.A., but he made most of his money buying and selling rare gems. While a good portion of his profits from the gem business went to the government, some of those profits went into a non–interest bearing checking account located in an Orange County bank. When Andy and his wife, Claire, decided to split up after thirteen years of marriage, she demanded over $10,000 a month in alimony, plus a one-half ownership interest in his real estate holdings and his gem business. Andy agreed to pay his wife the $10,000 per month in alimony and to give her one-half ownership interest in his real estate, but he insisted that she had no ownership in his gem business, which he'd owned long before their marriage.

When Andy refused to give Claire an ownership interest in his gem business, she went to court. Her attorneys persuaded the judge that while Claire might not be entitled to an ownership interest, she was certainly entitled to her fair share of the profits generated in the gem business during the period she was married to Andy. The judge agreed and ordered that a forensic accountant audit Andy's business to determine how much profit the business had generated over the last thirteen years.

The audit proved to be a complete disaster for Andy. After an initial review of the books, the forensic accountant quickly determined that Andy had been skimming money off the business. The accountant, who specialized in auditing jewelry businesses, immediately recognized that quite a few "phantom" employees were being paid large salaries. He also noticed a number of blatant inconsistencies between the amount of inventory and the number of sales. Clearly, many sales had occurred off-the-books. By the time the accountant was finished, he'd calculated that at least $500,000 in profits was missing from the books and missing from Andy and Claire's joint accounts. Although he didn't know where the money was, he knew that it existed.

After the audit, Claire decided to pay the forensic accountant to track down the missing profits. The accountant reviewed Andy's telephone records, which revealed a number of calls made to a Wells Fargo bank branch located in Placentia, California. After reviewing stacks of Andy's canceled checks, the accountant also determined that Andy had far more extensive real estate holdings than he'd revealed to the court. It turned out that Andy had set up a trust in a different name and then used the trust to purchase various real estate properties in San Francisco and Sacramento. The forensic accountant had been able to track the purchases because the same trust had made a number of large payments to Andy's mistress. Finally, after reviewing Andy and Claire's insurance policies, the forensic accountant noticed a personal articles floater insuring a five-carat diamond ring. It only took a phone call for him to figure out that the proud owner of the priceless ring was the mistress. Within three months of the audit, a court ruled that Andy had to pay his wife an additional $250,000. The court also passed on the information regarding Andy's business practices to the IRS.[2]

Although Andy had kept his hiding places to himself, consulted with professionals, and planned ahead, he'd neglected to follow one of the most important steps to being a good hider—thinking like a forensic accountant. He hadn't thought about what would happen if someone close to him actually came looking for his hidden assets. Andy should have realized that most experienced forensic accountants would be able to figure out that he was doing business off-the-books. He also should have realized that by paying his mistress out of funds from a trust, someone would eventually connect the trust to him. If Andy had taken a minute to survey his hiding scheme from the other side, he probably would have spotted the holes in the plan and been able to rectify them.

For example, he should have realized that a good forensic accountant or private detective would assume that he was skimming money off his gem business even if he wasn't. Most accountants (and IRS agents) immediately assume that with a cash-heavy business, some of that money will be kept off-the-books. So, as soon as Claire filed for divorce, it was a safe bet that someone would take a close look at Andy's business. He should have planned for this eventuality by taking steps to ensure that his entire asset protection plan couldn't be unraveled in a couple of months by an experienced forensic accountant. He could have possibly averted complete disaster by having his books reflect a more healthy relationship between inventory and sales, understanding

> For that matter, if you have anything from your past that might hurt someone from your present (and most people do), it's probably safest to find a good hiding spot for those items where you can come to occasionally visit your old memories.[3]

how a cash-flow analysis of his business would immediately reveal unrecorded sales. In addition, he should have been careful never to call his Orange County bank from his own phone. He could have also avoided an audit by paying his wife off and by making sure that his "confidential" real estate holdings couldn't be traced back to him. Finally, if Andy had "turned the tables" before hiding funds, he would have realized that insuring his girlfriend's ring would be a dead giveaway.

STEP 9: CHANGE YOUR HABITS

You'd be surprised to learn that many people have never even thought about hiding their assets. They worry about their kids' education, their mortgage, their pension, and their jobs, but they rarely spend time worrying about hiding their money. For most people, it's just not something that they dwell on. They figure that if they put their savings into the bank, store a few important documents in the vault, and install a new lock on the front door of their home, their assets will be safe. They don't worry that the washing machine repairman might get their bank account number from the statements they left out on the counter. They casually throw away their credit card statements without thinking that someone might go through their trash to steal the numbers. They freely give out their social security number to anyone who asks for it. And they don't concern themselves with how significantly their lives could change if someone stole their driver's license and/or social security number. They just don't comprehend that by making certain changes in how they live, they can avoid being victimized.

If you're someone who thinks that an extra lock on your front door will protect your assets, then you definitely need to change your personal hiding habits. Look around your home and recognize how careless you are with your personal financial information. Notice where you keep your credit card statements, realize how quickly a thief could steal one of your blank checks, and pay attention to the whereabouts of your jewelry, watches, and other treasures.

Once you're aware of how casually you treat your personal information, cash, and other valuable assets, you'll be ready to make a significant change in your hiding habits to protect those assets from casual observers. When your next checking account statement comes, you'll put it in the bedroom safe until you're ready to balance the checkbook. When your stock account statement arrives, you'll check it and then file it in a locked drawer at the office. And before you throw away your credit card statements, you'll put them through a shredder to protect yourself from garbage thieves.

By simply changing a few basic habits, you can put yourself beyond the reach of those who would steal your most valuable assets.

STEP 10: KNOW WHAT TO HIDE

One of the key ingredients to becoming a good hider is identifying what you need to hide. Most everyone knows that it's critical to hide your cash in a safe place, but few people understand the importance of hiding personal items from your past. Some people have a tendency to leave certain revealing items just lying around for anyone to discover.

For example, if you're dating an insecure woman who seems to be irrationally jealous of your ex-girlfriend, you probably shouldn't leave pictures of your ex-flame in a big box under your bed. The fact that you kept the pictures tells your new relationship that you still have feelings for the old one. And the fact that you didn't even bother to carefully hide the box of memories is another slap in the face to your current significant other.

For that matter, if you have anything from your past that might hurt someone from your present (and most people do), it's probably safest to find a good hiding spot for those items where you can come to occasionally visit your old memories.[3] It should be a hiding place that even your lover can't find—especially if he or she is the person you're hiding things from.

It doesn't really matter what you're trying to hide; what matters is that you recognize that your failure to hide the item in question could have serious repercussions.

STEP 11: KNOW HOW TO SECRETLY MOVE YOUR CASH

One of the most important steps to becoming an effective hider is learning how to secretly move your assets for business or for pleasure. Whether you're going off on a honeymoon trip to Italy or traveling to London on business, you'll still want to protect your cash and other valuables from theft or loss.

Although many people who are fearful of being robbed simply convert their money into traveler's checks, others prefer to take their chances. If you prefer cash to traveler's checks, you definitely need to figure out where to hide that cash. Fortunately, a number of clever hiding options exist for the cash-carrying traveler.

You can always hide cash in your clothes or in your baggage or even travel with it strapped to your person. Or you can choose to simply convert the cash to some smaller form of currency—diamonds, stamps, coins—and hide them in your clothes, in your baggage, or on your person. The bottom line is that if you insist on carrying cash, you also need to "insist" on knowing a safe way to hide it. The cash-carrying traveler is a target for all kinds of criminals. So, if you're traveling somewhere and plan on carrying a lot of cash and other valuables, have a strategy for hiding those items somewhere secure. (You should also plan on researching the currency reporting requirements for both the country you leave and the one that you enter. This can save you a lot of headaches.)

But before you can hide money, you need to be able to effectively move it. Even if you decide that you will hide $100,000 in an offshore haven, for instance, you still have to figure out how to transport the money there. Odds are that you don't want to get on a plane to the Cayman Islands carrying a suitcase filled with $100,000 in cash, so you'll want to know another way to quietly transport the money.[4] The fact is, you can choose a number of ways to legally move your assets to another location—all you have to do is really give the matter some serious thought and consideration. If you can't come up with a good way to quietly move your assets, contact an attorney and/or financial consultant for a few ideas.

STEP 12: RECOGNIZE YOUR NEED TO MAINTAIN A SEPARATE FINANCIAL IDENTITY

To become a truly effective hider, you also must commit yourself to one very important principle—not everyone has to know or approve of how you spend your money.

Only when you are committed to this principle can you truly learn how to effectively hide assets. For instance, if you really believe that you should be allowed to gamble some of your money away, then you'll try a little harder to move some of your assets to a safe deposit box at the Las Vegas casino of your choice. If you want to indulge in a few bad habits every once in a while, then you have to be committed to hiding a few of your assets to support those habits.

Only a few weeks ago, the wife of one of my clients called me for advice on how to obtain a "secret" credit card. The wife, who had come to her marriage with a substantial fortune, wanted to be able to buy clothes without the items showing up on her credit card bills. Even though the couple could definitely afford her excessive spending habits, her husband complained constantly about her credit card bills. She finally tired of listening to him and decided that she needed a bit more financial privacy. She wanted me to help her get a credit card that her husband wouldn't know about. She would pay for the card from one of her separate bank accounts—but she still needed to ensure that the credit card statement didn't come to the house. I advised her to purchase an offshore credit card and have the bill sent to a post office box near her home. The card wouldn't show up on her credit report and the statements would never cross her threshold. All in all, it was the perfect solution to her problem.

I fervently believe that everyone needs some modicum of financial independence—even if that person is in a truly committed and close relationship. Though it's always wonderful if both spouses can agree to keep their noses out of each other's financial affairs, this type of "New Age" relationship is quite rare. In most marital situations, spouses use financial information to keep track of each other—and to keep track of what will eventually be their fair share of the community's assets. Therefore, married persons who want to use some of their money to finance a few personal bad habits are generally doomed to failure unless they figure out a way to keep a private stash of cash. That's why I believe that anyone who wishes to maintain a private financial identity in marriage needs to know how to effectively hide money.

FINAL THOUGHTS

I believe that one of the most important aspects of writing a book is that it teaches you something and offers a concise wrap-up.

I am often frustrated when I read other books that there is no summary of useful items. Therefore, I felt that it was important to provide you, in David Letterman style, with the Top Ten Ways to Hide Your Money:

10. Keep an emergency cache of money in your car, either in the wheel well, under the dashboard, or inside the visors.

9. Never deposit more than $10,000 in cash with a bank or other financial institution. Never "structure" a cash transaction to avoid reporting requirements, or you will go to jail.

8. If you are being pursued by a mugger or purse-snatcher, throw your wallet, purse, and valuable jewelry into the nearest Federal Express or UPS drop box.

7. Travel with a screwdriver or small toolkit so you can hide money or valuables in your hotel room.

6. Establish an offshore bank account with less than $10,000 in it and have it linked to a secure offshore credit card.

5. Be certain to shred or burn all credit card statements and receipts that you are not filing to ensure that no one steals your identity.

4. Keep a small supply of emergency cash hidden in your home, either behind the medicine chest, above a ceiling tile, somewhere in your garden, or under a floorboard.
3. Check your TRW Trans-Union credit report at least four times a year to be certain your Social Security number isn't being used by someone else.
2. Open an out-of-state, non–interest bearing checking account. (Women should open this in their maiden name, and men should use a pseudonym.)
1. Don't be flamboyant . . . don't boast or brag about your luxurious possessions. You will create envy and animosity.

REFERENCES

1. If the government is about to seize your assets because you've been involved in criminal activity, I don't really have any advice to give you except that you should get a good lawyer.
2. In most instances, a court having knowledge of tax avoidance is required to report this information to the IRS. Therefore, if you're in divorce court and it's determined that you've engaged in tax fraud, you can expect this information to be passed on to the IRS.
3. For more information on good private hiding places, see chapter 8, Please Give Me My Space.
4. If you're a U.S. citizen who is concerned about going to jail, you will also want to know the legal requirements for transporting over $10,000 outside of the United States.

INDEX

A

Accountants, ability to raise cash for bad habits of, 62–63

Accumulated Earnings (AE) tax, 180

Acoustic tiles
in ceiling of home, hiding documents above, 149
in hotel room, hiding money above, 83

Address, establishing new, 206–208

Affair of husband
costs of, 48–56
example of bad attempt to conceal, 43–47
gifts for girlfriend in, avoiding traces of, 48–53, 62
girlfriend to safeguard assets during, 53
home for girlfriend in, avoiding traces of, 53–58
reasons for leaving trail of evidence of, 44, 46–47
trust for hidden money used in, 54–56
ways to secretly fund, 46–54, 135. *See also* Business

Air-conditioning ducts, hiding valuables behind
at home, 156
in hotel room, 83

Air ducts as hiding places, 155

Airplane tickets as currency, 68, 76, 88n

Alexander, Donald, 193

Ashtray, hiding valuables in false bottom of vehicle's, 87

Asset forfeiture laws, planned overhaul of, 100–101

Asset protection plan. *See* Hiding program

Asset protection trust, 95–97, 107

Asset transfers to another person
legal versus illegal, 244–245
risks of, 107
Assets domiciled in countries
having better tax situation
than United States,
178–179
Assets Forfeiture Fund of Justice
Department for proceeds
from seized assets, 99–100
Assets, hiding existence of, 7–8,
18n
before bankruptcy proceedings, 104–105
determining cause for, 245
during divorce, 53, 119–123
during or after lawsuit, 92–93
family court treatment of,
229–230
illegal, 20–24, 37, 93. *See also*
Money laundering
legality of, 14–15, 19–42,
243–245
marital, trust to sign away, 96
offshore. *See* Offshore methods for hiding money
planning for, 238–240
trusting no one in, 245–246
while traveling, 67–90,
251–252
wife revealing husband's
method for, 224–225
Assets separated from creator,
178
Assets, tracing hidden, 215–232
Attorney-client privilege, 56, 63,
227
Attorneys
ability to raise cash for bad
habits of, 62–63
asset protection trust advice
of, 95–96
assistance in bankruptcy
process of, 110n

assistance in hiding assets of,
108, 240–241
consultation about incorporation with, 186n
for divorce cases, 190
financial documents subpoenaed by, 221
hidden assets in practice of,
226–230
with offshore investment
experience, 196, 212n
prenuptial agreement terms
created by, 113–114
representation for prenuptial
agreement by separate,
125
Automobile, leaving valuables
hidden in, 85–87

B

Backyard, buying valuables in,
162–163
Bad habits, avoiding traces of,
58–60, 252–254. *See also*
individual types
Bank account statements
analyzed by forensic accountant, 222
analyzed prior to divorce filing, 120–121
bank retention of records for
seven years for, 222
hidden from view at home,
118, 249–250
sent to P.O. box or office, 59,
61, 134
Bank accounts hidden from
spouse, 10
avoiding traceable calls to
banks holding, 64
to buy gifts for mistress, 49, 54
cyberbanks for, 60
database storage of account
information for, 59

to finance bad habits and
store gambling win-
nings, 56, 58–59
non-interest bearing, 59, 66n,
122–123
opened in city away from
where you live, 59, 66n,
122, 134
opened prior to divorce filing,
122–123, 126n
phone bills examined to
reveal, 226, 247
protection offered by, 59–60
statements sent to P.O. box or
office for, 59, 61, 134
tracing, 222
Bank accounts in foreign country,
103, 202
Bank accounts of separate property in marriage, 124–125
Bank balances hidden from
spouse, 129–130
Bank Secrecy Act (BSA) (1970)
crime of "structuring" under, 35
forfeiture statutes of, 33–34
regulatory control of wire
transfer businesses
under, 40
reporting requirements to
address offshore money
laundering under, 32,
183
Bank surveillance camera, transactions recorded by, 200
Bank tellers questioned about
safe deposit box holders'
activities, 199–200
Bank transactions, structuring to
avoid reporting threshold
for, 35
Bankcard, funding costs of affair
using separate, 49
Banking secrecy laws of offshore
havens

Cayman Islands as having,
27, 31, 97
legal use for hiding assets of,
39
list of countries known for,
202, 213n
Bankruptcy crimes, 110n
Bankruptcy filing to protect property from creditors, 104
Banks
compliance officers at, 16,
18n, 36–37
customer data sold by, 5
customer identification
requirements of, 36–37
government reporting requirements for, 14, 32, 89n
monitoring of account activity
by, 37
offshore investments by top, 24
paper trail of funds started by,
31, 212n
placement of illegal funds
into, 30–31
watches placed on accounts
by, 27–28
Beams in house, hiding place of
hollowed-out, 158
Beneficiary of trust, girlfriend as,
55
Benson, Arthur, 147–149
Benson, Helen, 147–149
Birth certificate, avoiding carrying, 7
Blind corporations, layers of, 97
Bracca, Carmen, 91–94
Briefcase as bad place to hide
cash, 69–71
Burglars
in hotel rooms, 81–85
typical places searched by,
155, 160
Burns, Janet, 140–141
Burying valuables, 162–163

Business
cash-intensive, types of, 221
cash-intensive, unreported
income of, 222–226,
246–249
legal means of tax avoidance
for, 171–174
searching tax returns for true
earnings of, 219
taking cash surreptitiously
out of, 51–53, 56, 65
Business cards, writing notes
about romantic affair on,
50
Business financial documents
revealed during lawsuit's
discovery process, 12–13

C

Calendars examined to reveal
hidden assets, 226
Call girl example of raising
secret money, 139
Capital flight through private
units of banks, 36
Capone, Al, 176
Car, leaving valuables in, 85–87
Cash. *See also* Money
converted into diamonds
before travel, 78
dressing down while traveling
with, 72
hidden by woman prior to
divorce, 119–123
in home, hiding large amounts
of, 151, 158–160, 166n
incidence of robbery while
traveling with, 69–70
needed to finance affair, 46–52
in safe deposit box, 201,
204–206, 212n
secret income in form of, 142
secretly moving, 251–252
stashed in clothing, 70–73

traveling safely with, 69–75
Cash-flow analysis
of income and expenses prior
to divorce filing, 122
of professional practice for off-
the-books transactions,
228
Casinos
CTR reporting requirements
of, 205
safe deposit box at, 204, 226
SAR reporting requirements
of, 36
Cautious attitude, example of
need for, 234–235
Cayman Islands
process of court case in, 97
strict banking secrecy laws of,
27, 31
Ceiling light fixtures in hotel
rooms, hiding money
above, 83
Cellular phone
avoiding traceable calls by not
using, 49
statements containing incrim-
inating numbers sent to
office or P.O. box for,
63–64
Check records, bank retention of,
58
Checkbook and checks
hiding, 118
made out to yourself, traveling with, 76
marital affair finances traced
through, 43–47, 57–58
of professionals used for personal expenditures,
62–63
for wives making secret
income, 142, 144
Checking account
foreign. *See* Offshore accounts

non-interest bearing, hiding money in. *See* Non-interest bearing checking account
withdrawing small sums from joint, 58
Child support, wages garnished to pay, 110n
Chips, casino, hiding cash as, 213n
Citibank, Raul Salinas as laundering money through, 26–29, 41n
Citizenship, acquiring second country's, 102–103, 206
Clearing House Interbank Payments Systems (CHIPS), The, 81
Clothing, cash hidden in, 70–73, 252
Coins
hiding valuable, 151
traveling with valuable, 77–78, 89n, 252
Community
illegally withholding money from, 19
separate money as gift to, 113, 125
Community property
conversion of separate property into, 112
definition of, in divorce case, 113
home ownership kept out of, 124–125, 134–135
mortgage loan application examined for listing of, 231
premarital assets kept uncontaminated by, 113–114, 124–125, 133–135, 238–239
Connor, Michael, 153, 166n

Containers for burying valuables, 164
Controlled Foreign Corporation (CFC) tax, 179
Corporate records, rights of inspection of, 108
Corporation
foreign depositories of, 182
foreign-based but U.S. owned, 181
starting, 107, 108–109, 171–172
Corporation stock placed in irrevocable trust for asset protection from creditors, 106
Credit card, avoiding payment for secret earnings by, 142
Credit card numbers, criminals copying, 2, 7, 118, 249–250
Credit card statements shredded before disposal, 250
Credit cards
carrying few, 7
evidence of marital affair on, 46–47
issued at destination of frequent travel, 79
not used to establish new identity, 207–208
not used to spend secret earnings, 142
offshore, 61–62, 65, 66n, 142, 253
stolen identity to receive and abuse, 235
used to finance bad habits, 60–62, 65
Credit report, 1
checked regularly, 18n
repairing, 235
Creditors
acting in advance to protect assets from, 108, 238–240

Creditors *(continued)*
  changing names to avoid, 104
  hiding money from, 39,
    91–110
  offshore investment to evade,
    25, 97–98
  professionals as hiding assets
    from, 227
  renouncing U.S. citizenship to
    protect assets from U.S.,
    102–103
  wages garnished by, 105
Currency and Foreign Transactions Reporting Act of 1970,
  14
Currency and Monetary Instruments Form (CMIR) (Form
  4790) filed with U.S. Customs Service, 38, 88, 88n
Currency exchange charges,
  avoiding, 79
Currency Transaction Report
  (CTR) of financial activities
  exceeding $10,000, 14, 15,
  32, 34–36, 205
Curtain rod interior as hiding
  place, 157, 166n
Customs agents. *See also* United
  States Customs
  airplane tickets as not attract-
    ing suspicion of, 76
  clothing attracting attention
    of, 74–75
Cyberbanks on Internet, difficulty in monitoring, 60

D

Dashboard of car, hiding valuables in hollow spaces
  behind, 87
Database services, 4, 8
Databases of banking information, searching, 59–60

Dating, protection of assets during, 114–117
David, Gerard, 217
Debit card
  anonymity of Macy's, 62
  international, 79
  obtained for secret earnings of
    wife, 144
Deductions, tables of average,
  173
Delaware, advantages of incorporating in, 171–172, 180
Diamonds
  commercial versus noncom-
    mercial purposes of
    transporting, 89n
  converting assets for use dur-
    ing travel into, 78, 252
Disappearance, arranging your
  own, 205–210
Discovery process in lawsuit,
  12–13
Discretion about wealth, value of
  using, 8–10, 12, 236–238
Diskette, scanning important
  documents onto, 116
Divorce
  alimony to unemployed hus-
    band in, 113
  asset division in cases of, 10
  assets hidden to protect them
    in cases of, 10–11,
    228–229
  changes in standard of living
    following, 122, 123,
    126n
  documents possessed and ana-
    lyzed by wife prior to,
    120–121
  financial disclosure statement
    filed during, 22
  financial matters understood
    by wife prior to, 119

forensic accountant to trace expenses of affair during, 52, 54, 55, 57–58, 65–66

illegal hiding schemes revealed during, 20–23, 54, 189–192, 246–249

lifestyle analysis during, 136–137

prenuptial agreement terms in cases of, 113, 125

return of money taken from community in event of, 57

settlement from, 113, 123

standard of living following, 18n

tax return examination to reveal assets during, 218–221

using girlfriend to safeguard assets during, 53

wife hiding cash prior to, 119–123

Djinis, Peter, 24–25, 193–194, 195

Doctors

ability to raise cash for bad habits of, 62–63

hidden assets in practice of, 226–230

Documents about assets

copied to help discover hidden assets, 231

hiding, 116–117, 126n

for mortgage, 121–122, 231

perused by date, 118

possessed and analyzed by wife prior to starting divorce proceedings, 120–121

subpoenaed to reveal hidden assets, list of, 221

Doors, hollow-core interior, as hiding places, 156

Double payments, revealing hidden assets in, 223–224

Dresser drawers

false bottom in, 158, 161

hiding items behind hotel, 84–85

Drug smugglers

money laundering of profits by, 30

offshore bank information provided to U.S. government in cases of, 109n

E

Effectively-Connected-With-U.S. tax, 181

Electronic account information, 4

Electronic fund transfers, 16

companies providing, 81

for wiring funds for travel expenses, 80

Elliot, Any, 26

EVEolution, 114

Experts, ways of finding hidden money used by, 215–232

Extracurricular activities, hiding money for, 43–66

Extreme hiding of assets, 189–213

F

Family, distributing income throughout, 174

Family limited partnership (FLP) created for real estate assets before bankruptcy filing, 105

Federal Bureau of Investigation (FBI), control of money flow by, 18n

Federal Express drop box for purse during robbery attempt, 208

Federico, Ed, 195

Fedwire, 81
Felder, Raoul, 120, 134, 215–216, 228
Fender wells of vehicles for stashing valuables, 86
Fiery, Dennis, 164
Financial activities
monitored by government agencies, 14
prudence about discussing, 246
Financial adviser
assistance in hiding assets of, 108, 240–241
assistance with offshore investment of, 212n
assistance with tax avoidance of, 185–186
Financial crime statistics of Secret Service, 6
Financial disclosure statement filed during divorce, 22
Financial independence in marriage, 127–146, 252–254
Financial information revealed during lawsuit, 12–13
Financial privacy
activities that jeopardize your, 5–6
difficulty of maintaining, 4–5
during dating, 115–118
from spouse, 43–47, 127–146, 252–254
Financial profile, stealing another person's, 3
FinCEN. See Treasury Department Financial Crimes Enforcement Network (FinCEN)
First Lenape Nation Bank, 181–182
Flagstones of patio or walkway, burying valuables under, 163

Flea market sales to raise secret money, 137–138
Floorboards, hiding valuables under loose, 157
Florida, protection of assets from confiscation by creditors in
for house, 104
for retirement funds, 105
Flowers, avoiding writing card for girlfriend's, 50
Fogel, Susan, 230
Foreign bank accounts, 66n.8
BSA reporting requirements for, 32–33
unreported, 194, 202
Foreign depositories for individuals and corporations, 182
Foreign hotel address for offshore credit card invoices, 79–80
Foreign Investment Company (FIC) tax, 180–181
Foreign Personal Holding Company (FPHC) tax, 179–180
Foreign safe deposit box, 99, 201–202, 210–211, 213n
Forensic accountants
advise to avoid excessive spending of hidden assets by, 170
advise to wives about financial knowledge by, 119–120
in Big Five accounting firms, 217–218
to examine bank statements for hidden assets, 222
to examine business records for unreported income, 222–226, 247
to examine tax returns for hidden assets, 218–221
expense of hiring, 217

matching type of business or practice being investigated to, 216, 228
personality of, 216–217
professional practice investigations by, 226–230
supporting findings of, 217
transactions for romantic affairs traced by, 52, 54, 55, 57–58, 65–66, 136
void filled by, 218, 219
when to hire, 217, 241
Fox, Dave, 224
Fraud
badges of, 93
constructive, 93
creditor charges of, 93
demonstration of establishing trust with no intent of, 106
in divorce cases, 229–230
from falsified receipts, 173
hiding assets in cases of, 108
in Indian "offshore" banking, 182–183
Suspicious Activity Report filed for suspected, 199
suing ex-spouse in civil court for, 22
Fulworth, Eileen, 43–47
Fulworth, Robert, 43–48
Furniture, hiding documents in, 152–153

G
Gambling
avoiding traces of, 54, 58–60
casino reporting requirements for, 205
hiding cash to finance, 202–205
Garage sale to raise secret money, 137–138
Gift cards as debit cards, 62

Gift certificates as anonymous gifts, 50
Gifts
deductible business, 173, 186n
for partner in romantic affair, avoiding paper trail for, 48–53, 65–66
Girlfriend, paying for. See Affair of husband
Glacier International Depository Ltd., "offshore" banking by, 182
Glove compartment, hiding valuables in, 87
Government officials, hiding assets from, 13–14, 23–24, 98–102, 238–240, 254n
Government reporting requirements, 14–15. See also specific forms
Grocery shopping, wife's cash-back scheme to raise funds from, 136–137
Gursey, Donald, 55, 57, 120, 222–224, 227

H
Habits changed as part of asset protection plan, 249–250
Hanson, Andy, 246–250
Hanson, Claire, 246–250
Harris, Amanda, 139–140
Hide-a-Vault as good burial container, 164
Hiding place for yourself
last-minute, 208–210
planning, 205–208
Hiding places, 147–166
for cash, 70–73, 119–123, 151, 158–160
in ceilings, 83, 149, 210
checked by burglars, typical, 155, 160

Hiding places (continued)
  in curtain rods, 157
  for documents, 116–117, 126n,
      152–153, 158
  extreme, 198–202
  false bottoms of drawers as,
      158, 161
  in home's infrastructure,
      154–156
  kept secret, 245–246
  knowing habits and routines
      of residents before
      choosing, 162, 165
  in Las Vegas casinos, 202–205
  last-minute, 208–210
  outside, 121, 162–164
  in public restrooms, 208–209
  secret compartments as,
      160–162
  in walls, 117, 153–154,
      158–162, 209
Hiding program
  of asset protection trust off-
      shore combined with
      domestic limited part-
      nership, 109n
  legality of, 14–15
  planned and executed in
      advance of potential
      financial trouble, 94, 108
  twelve-step, 233–255
Home address
  establishing new, 206–208
  not given to bank, 122
Home ownership kept separate
    after marriage, 124–125,
    134–135
Home, secret financing of
  after divorce, 53
  during affair of husband,
      53–54
  refinancing mortgage for, 57,
      121–122, 135
  trust for, 54–56

Homestead exemptions
  state legislation to limit, 110n
  Texas and Florida as offering
      unlimited, 104
Hotel room furniture, hiding
    valuables in, 84
Hotel room, hiding cash in, 70,
    81–85
Hotel safes, 81
Household expenses, wife hiding
    traces of romantic affair in,
    136–137
Howell, Angela, 234–235
Husband
  hiding traces of romantic
      affair, examples of,
      43–47, 246–249
  secret finances of wife of con-
      trolling, 127–146,
      253–254
Hyde, Henry, 100–101

I
Identity, creating separate,
    102–106
Identity fraud, 1–6, 8
  ways of correcting, 17n
  ways of preventing, 7,
      234–235
Identity information, ways of
    obtaining other people's, 2–4
Immigration and Naturalization
    Service, exiling by, 177
Incorporation
  in one state for doing business
      in another, 186n
  by single individual, 172
Individual retirement account
    (IRA), benefits and draw-
    backs of, 173–174
Information brokers, 5
Insurance policies
  reviewed for hidden assets,
      226, 248

reviewed prior to divorce filing, 122

Internal Revenue Service (IRS), 18n
audits by, 175–176, 198, 244
avoiding record of trust with, 55
court order to open safe deposit box by, 199
Currency Transaction Reports of bank customer activities exceeding $10,000 filed with, 14, 15, 32, 34–36
foreign trust investigation by, 244
guidelines for auditors of, 173
hiding money from, 167–187
joint liability of married people for fraud to, 190
lavish spending as drawing attention from, 237
leveling playing field between taxpayer and, 196
non-reporting of income to, 66n
separate returns for spouse to report secret money to, 138
targets of, 176

Internet
difficulty in monitoring cyberbanks' activities on, 60
personal identity information obtained from, 3–4

Inventurers
disadvantages of, 210–211
fearlessness of, 192–193
tools used by, 201–205

Investment firms, SAR reporting requirements of, 36

IRS Form 1040, Individual Tax Return, examination for hidden assets of, 218–221

IRS Form 1065 examined for hidden assets, 218, 221

IRS Form 4789a, Currency Transaction Report (CTR), 14, 15, 32, 34–36

Italian designer leather as signal to customs agents, 71

J

Jewelry
as gift in romantic affair, avoiding traces of buying, 49
hiding, 151

Jobs, off-the-books
in underground economy, 174–175
women holding, 139–140

Johnson, James E., 101

K

Keogh Plan for self-employed person, benefits and drawbacks of, 173–174

"Know your customer" policy of banks for preparing financial profiles, 27–28

Kuralt, Charles, 50–51

L

Las Vegas, hiding money in, 202–205, 226

Lawn ornaments, hiding valuables in, 163

Layering of funds
for money laundering, 30, 31
for offshore banks, 97
for offshore corporations, 98

Leg wallet, concealing money and valuables in, 74

Legal issues in hiding money, 14–15, 19–42, 243–245

Levy, Marvin, 216–217

Lifestyle analysis
during divorce settlement process, 136–137

Lifestyle analysis *(continued)*
to uncover unreported income
of business, 222–223
Light switch
fake, 154
as hiding place, 153
Limited partnership, combining
offshore asset protection
trust with domestic, 109n
Litigation
hiding information before discovery process in, 12–13
liens on assets during,
197–198
moving assets offshore before,
94–95
Log in woodpile, hiding valuables
in hollowed-out, 164
Low profile, learning to keep,
236–238
Lowe, Richard, 100
Luger, Jack, 155, 159
Luggage locks, 75

M

Macy's gift card, anonymity of,
62
Mail box for purse during rob-
bery attempt, 208
Malpractice suit, protecting
assets from medical, 107
Marijuana, hiding, 156–157
Marital assets inventoried before
divorce filing, 122
Marriage, secrets in, 129,
131–132
Medicine cabinet, hiding cash,
photographs, or documents
behind, 158–160
Medine, David, 3
Mementos, hiding cherished,
147–150, 249, 251
Miller, Peter, 51–52
Mindset, changing

about privacy in dating,
117–118
about valuable assets that
could be taken, 233–235
Mirror in hotel bathroom, hiding
valuables behind, 84
Mistress, paying for. *See* Affair of
husband
Molding, hiding keys behind, 148
Mondex smart card, 76–77
Money belt, 73–74
Money
finding hidden, 215–232
spending hidden, 140–144
Money, hiding
from creditors, 39, 91–110,
204–206
for extramarital affair
expenses, 43–66
hiding places for, 140,
147–166
illegally, 19–20. *See also*
Money laundering *and*
Tax evasion
from IRS, 167–187
legality of, 14–15, 19–42
playing extreme game of,
189–213
reasons for, 1–18
for single women, 11–12, 15,
111–126
for travel safety, 67–90
from U.S. customs, 75–76,
244, 255n
for wives or husbands, 10,
120–123, 127–146
Money laundering
criminalization of, 33, 42n.18, 99
of illicit drug profits, 30
increased use of financial
institutions for, 36
offshore bank information provided to U.S. govern-
ment in cases of, 109n

Raul Salinas as example of, 25–29
role of private banking industry in, 30
stages of, 30–31
Suspicious Activity Report filed for suspected, 199
wire transfers regulated to help prevent, 40
Money Laundering Control Act of 1986 (Title 18 U.S.C. Sections 1956 and 1957), 33
definitions of structuring under, 35
Money, ostentatious displays of, 8, 236–238
Money skimming revealed during divorce, 21–22, 54, 189–192, 246–249
Mortgage loan application examined for accounting of community assets, 231
personal information disclosed on, 6, 64–65
Mortgage payments made from separate property account, 124–125, 134–135
Mortgage statements studied prior to divorce filing, 121–122
Mother's house. *See* Parents' house
Mutual League Assistance Treaties (MLATs)
accounts subject to search in signatory countries of, 103, 213n
offshore banking havens as signatories of, 110n, 194
Myers, Burt, 168

N
Name
changing, 104, 205–207
married woman's accounts using maiden, 107, 122, 144
transferring assets to someone else's, 107
using mother's maiden, 107
Nest egg kept separate from romantic interests, 111–115
Nevada, benefits of incorporating in, 107–108, 172, 180
Nonexistent employees
business income skimming through paying, 224–225, 247
hiding assets during divorce by paying, 228
tax evasion through paying, 168, 190–191
Non-interest bearing checking account
difficulty in tracing, 59, 66n, 122–123, 143–144, 225, 229
as low-risk means of hiding assets, 243
ways forensic accounts trace existence of, 225–226

O
Office, hidden bank account and credit card statements sent to, 59, 61–62, 125n
Offshore accounts
advantages for wives earning secret income of, 144
amateur gathering evidence of, 230–231
bringing money back to United States from, 170
differing laws among tax havens for, 197
prenuptial agreement expressly protecting separate identity of, 113
to protect separate property during marriage, 134
reporting, 26, 34, 38
revealed on older tax returns, 220

Offshore accounts *(continued)*
  for secret earnings of wives,
    142
  subject to search in countries
    part of Mutual League
    Assistance Treaties, 103
  tax evasion using, 168
Offshore asset protection trust,
  95–99
Offshore banks, 24
  access to funds during travel
    from, 79
  control of, 179
  credit cards issued from, 61,
    66n.8, 143
  native Americans creating,
    181–183
  obstacles to creditors of, 97–98
  researching benefits and dis-
    advantages of, 242–243
  selling investments to your
    own, 178
  setting up, 67–69, 97
  taxes avoided by using,
    179–181, 195–196
Offshore branch of present bank,
  avoiding account with, 143
Offshore corporation
  asset protection through cre-
    ation of, 98
  control of, 179
Offshore credit cards, 61, 65, 66n
  not reported to U.S. credit
    reporting bureaus, 143
  for using secret earnings, 142
Offshore financial adviser,
  194–195, 196
Offshore methods for hiding
  money, 16
  decisions to make about, 196
  during divorce, 20–23
  government's response to, 184
  illegal, 25–29, 109n, 110n,
    195–196

  legal, 38–39, 177–178
  lessons about, 94
  morality of, 185–186
  as protection plan, 94–102
  reasons for wanting, 22–23
  risks of, 29–34, 192–197,
    242
  rules of, 34–39, 243–245
Offshore trusts, risks of, 195
Online storage of important documents, 116–117
Onshore/offshore banks, 181–183
Outdoor hiding places, 121,
  162–164
Outer sanctum for hiding valuables, 149–151
Outlet covers in hotel rooms, hiding valuables behind, 83
Outlets, dummy, 153–154

P

Paper trail of assets before
  divorce, 119
Paper trail of marital affair,
  47–48
Paper trail of money deposited in
  banks
  creating, 32–33, 212n
  breaking, 31–32
Parents asked for cash by financially dependent wife, 139
Parents' house
  having all sensitive mail sent
    to, 138–139
  mailing secret financial infor-
    mation to, 126n, 138,
    140, 144
Parked vehicle, hiding places in,
  209–210
Parking garage, hiding places in,
  209–210
Parks, Susan, 169
Part-time jobs for financial independence of wife, 139–140

Passive Foreign Investment Company (PFIC) tax, 181
Passport
avoiding carrying, 7
having second, in second name, 39, 110n
legally acquiring second country's, 102–103, 206
Pay phones or courtesy phones to avoid traceable calls, 49, 63
Payroll, putting mistress on company, 52
Personal article floaters on insurance policies studied
by forensic accountant, 248
prior to divorce filing, 122
Personal Holding Company (PHC) tax, 180
Personal Protection Products, 154, 156, 166n
Personality, suiting asset protection plan to your, 241–243
Phantom employees paid for work, 168, 190–191, 224–225, 228, 247
Phone cards to avoid traceable calls, 49
Photographs, hiding secret, 147–150, 152, 158, 251
Physicians
ability to raise cash for bad habits of, 62–63
hidden assets in practice of, 226–230
Pictures, taping valuables to back of hotel room, 83
Pierce, Oliver, 156–157
Pipes, hiding valuables in, 153, 210
Plan for hiding assets. See Hiding program
Planning ahead for hiding program, considerations in, 238–240

Popcorn, Faith, 114, 115
Porter, Frank, 127–131
Porter, Victoria, 127–131
Post office box
bank and credit card statements sent to, 59, 62, 126n, 144, 253
hiding secret money in, 140
Prenuptial agreement
example of need for, 111–114
need for women to protect separate property by using, 134–135
to protect assets before remarriage, 125
to protect funds acquired before marriage, 96
Pretexting, 4–5
Privacy laws governing incorporation, 108
Privacy protection during dating, 115–117
changing mindset about, 117–118
Privacy Rights Clearinghouse, 17n
Private banking industry, money laundering by, 29–30
Private investigators as able to find hidden bank checking accounts, 225–226
Professionals
finding hidden money in practice of, 226–230
paperless transactions by, 227
raising money to fund bad habits by, 62–63
Property causing embarrassment, preventing discovery of, 150
Property seizures
abuse of forfeiture laws in, 100–103
burden of proof in, 99

in cases of no illegal activity,
33–34, 98
from money laundering defen-
dants, 33, 99
proceeds from, 99–100
types of property seized in,
102
Property transfers, laws used to
void, 39, 94
Purchases of property and
investments
avoiding using your own name
for, 64–65
to integrate laundered money
into economy, 31–32
secret, 48–58, 62, 135
Purzycki, Roseanna, 133–135,
217, 220–223, 230

R

Radio speakers, hiding valuables
behind hotel's wall-
mounted, 83
Reasons for hiding money, 1–18
Receipts kept to maximize tax
deductions, 172–173, 186n
Reiss, Stephen
advise that women learn family finances by, 119–120
difficulty in tracing non-interest bearing checking
accounts noted by,
122–123
forensic accountants' methods
described by, 216,
218–221, 225, 227
Restrooms, temporary hiding
spots in public, 208
Retirement funds, protection
during bankruptcy pro-
ceedings of, 105–106
Roommate, checking references
of, 126n

S

Safe deposit box
court order to open, 199, 212n
disadvantages of using, 198
documents about assets kept
in, 116
as hard for others to locate,
165
hiding key to, 148
inaccessibility of, 150–152
insurance on contents of, 198,
212n
items to store in, 198,
200–201, 243
keeping more than one, 165
in Las Vegas hotel, 204–206, 210
in non-chartered institution, 165
in offshore haven, 99,
201–202, 210–211, 213n
tellers questioned about,
199–200
in United States, ease of government access to, 98
virtual, 116, 126n
wives keeping secrets in,
140–141
Safedepositbox.com for online
document storage, 116–117
Safes
home, 117. See also individual
types
hotel, 81
in product cans, 154–155
risk level of using, 243
travel, 85
VCR tape, 85, 90n
wall socket, 153–154
Salinas, Raul
funds filtered through personal investment com-
panies by, 37
money laundering through offshore havens by, 26–29, 31

Schneider, Jerome, contact information for, 254
Schreiber, Richard
  customer identification requirements of banks described by, 36
  customer patterns of wire transfers described by, 40
Schwimmer, Arlene, 228
Securities and Exchange Commission (SEC), control of securities money by, 18n
Separate assets acquired before marriage protected from community property, 111–114, 124–125, 133–135, 239
Separate tax returns, hiding money from spouse but not IRS by filing, 138, 140
Shannon, Patricia Elizabeth, 50–51
Shell companies to mask ownership of foreign accounts, 26–27, 31
Shower rods, hiding cash in retractable hotel, 70–71
Shutters, hiding valuables behind, 210
Single woman, reasons for hiding money for, 11–12, 15, 111–126
Skirting of furniture, hiding documents in, 152–153
Smart cards, traveling with, 76–77, 88–89n
Social security card, avoiding carrying, 7
Social Security Form SS-5 to change social security number, 207
Social security number (SSN)
  access to financial history using, 7

avoiding giving bank, 122, 144, 212n
changing, 207
stopping dissemination of, 17–18n, 250
used by other people, 1–3, 207, 250
Sparks, Ronald, 182–183
Speakers, hi-fi, as hiding places, 153
Specified Unlawful Activities (SUAs), 33
Spending habits
  avoiding revealing wealth by excessive, 168–170, 236–238
  ways of discovering wife's, 142–143
Spy Store, 74, 166n
Stamps as currency for travel, 78, 252
Stealth is wealth lesson, 8–10, 12, 168–169, 236–238
Stephenson, Owen, 182–183
Stock certificates, hiding, 151
Stolen identity, uses for, 1–2
Structuring of bank deposits as crime, 35
Suspicious Activity Report
  for contents of safe deposit box, 199
  creation of, 18n, 35
  filed by bank, 15–16
Swap meet sales to raise secret money, 137–138, 141
SWIFT (Society for Worldwide Interbank Financial Telecommunications), 81

T
Talisman, Jonathan, 184
Tantum, Mark, 217–219

Targets
　　displays of wealth as making
　　　　people, 8–10, 237–238
　　of IRS, 176
　　single women as, 11, 15, 114
　　travelers with large amounts
　　　　of cash as, 71, 252
Tax avoidance
　　basic characteristics of true,
　　　　178–179
　　court reporting of, 254–255n
　　help from financial consultant
　　　　with, 185, 187n
　　legal means of, 170–187
　　PFHC tax as barrier to, 179
　　tax evasion versus, 23–24
Tax code, loopholes in, 170–171,
　　186n
Tax Compliance Law of 1995,
　　176–177
Tax credit for hiring minority
　　group members, 171
Tax evasion
　　interest and penalties charged
　　　　for, 176
　　by paying nonexistent employ-
　　　　ees, 168–170, 190–191
　　prosecution for, 176
　　role of private banking indus-
　　　　try in, 30
　　taking money out of business
　　　　without risking, 56–57
　　tax avoidance versus, 23–24
Tax records, collecting docu-
　　ments supporting assets
　　shown in, 120
Tax returns
　　beginning search for hidden
　　　　assets by examining,
　　　　218–221
　　comparing recent with previ-
　　　　ous years', 220
　　kept secret from spouse, 138,
　　　　140

Tax treaties of United States,
　　211n
Telephone calls, avoiding trace-
　　able, 49, 63–64
Texas, protection of assets from
　　confiscation by creditors in
　　for house, 104
　　for retirement funds, 105
Thompson, Mark, 53
Thompson, Mozelle W., 4
Title 18 U.S.C. Section 1960(a) to
　　regulate use of wire trans-
　　mitting agencies, 40
Title 26, wire transfer business
　　reporting requirements
　　under, 40
Title 31
　　CFR 103.22(a)(2), filing of
　　　　CTR required under,
　　　　205
　　CFR 103.23, filing of CMIRs
　　　　required under, 38, 76,
　　　　87–88, 88n
　　wire transfer business reporting
　　　　requirements under, 40
Toilet, hiding valuables in hotel
　　room, 83–84
Tourist, safety tips for traveling
　　as, 67–90
Travel, hiding money safely for,
　　67–90
Travel pouch, concealing money
　　and papers in, 74
Travel safes for valuables, 85
Travel security items, resource
　　for, 90n
Traveler's checks, 251–252
　　as anonymous gifts, 50
　　hidden on your body, 72
　　traveling with, advantages of,
　　　　88n
Treasury Department Financial
　　Crimes Enforcement Net-
　　work (FinCEN), 18n

middle class using tax havens
according to, 193
model of money laundering
cycle developed by, 31
view of offshore investments
as suspicious by, 24
Treasury Form 90-22.1, Foreign
Bank Account Report
(FBAR), 202
Trump, Donald, 236–237
Trump, Ivana, 236–237
Trust
asset protection, 95–97, 107, 109n
of attorney's client, hiding
money in, 63
charitable, 106
corporate stock placed in
irrevocable, 106
creditor access to poorly constructed, 109n
defined, 54–55
foreign, IRS investigation of,
244
fraudulent, 195
to fund home and purchases
during romantic affair,
54–56, 63–64, 247–248
illegally financing asset purchases through, 21
income protected during bankruptcy by irrevocable,
105–106
irrevocable, 97
layers of, 97
offshore, taxation of, 195
protection from medical malpractice suit of assets in, 107
separate property protected from
community property desig-
nation by living, 124
Trust account of professionals,
hidden assets in, 226–227
Trustee, accountant or lawyer as,
55–56, 64

U
Underground economy to avoid
taxes, 167, 174–176
Uniform Fraudulent Con-
veyances Act, property
transfers for creditor fraud
under, 39, 93, 94
Uniform Fraudulent Transfers
Act, property transfers for
creditor fraud under, 39,
93, 94
United States citizenship,
renouncing, 102–103, 110n
checking current laws before,
187n
tax consequences of, 176–177
United States Customs
contact information for, 90n
control of import and export
duties by, 18n
Currency and Monetary Instruments Form filed for off-
shore havens with, 38
reporting assets to, 75–76,
244, 255n
Unrecorded sales
of cash-intensive business as
commonplace, 222
double payments to hide,
223–224
examining tax return to
reveal, 219
from garage sales and swap
meets to raise secret
money, 137–138
lifestyle analysis to uncover,
222–223
pocketing cash to finance
affair from, 51–52
pocketing cash to finance
gambling jaunts from,
204
Upholstery, hiding documents in,
152–153

UPS drop box for purse during robbery attempt, 208
Utility box in public buildings, hiding valuables in, 210

V

Valuables
hidden in car, 85–87
hidden in home, 148–162
hidden in hotel room, 81–85, 90n
hidden outdoors, 162–165
understanding that you have, 233–235
VCR tape safe, hiding valuables in hotel inside, 85, 90n, 154

W

Wages, garnishing
by creditors, 105
some states as not recognizing, 110n
Walls, hiding items in, 117, 153–154, 209
Warranty forms, personal information on, 6
Wife hiding traces of romantic affair, example of, 136–137
Will, legal forms of, 51
Winnings, secret place for storing gambling, 58–59

Wire transfers
consistent patterns as preferable for hiding money using, 40–41
legal use of, 39–41
licensing of transmitters of, 89
reporting requirements for businesses handling, 40, 80
to specific store abroad, 80
for traveling light, 80
Wiring funds for offshore investments, 27
Wives hiding money, 10, 122–123, 126n, 127–146
Women's growth in assets to protect in dating and marriage, 123–124
index.sub:example of, 111–114
Women's power in marketplace, growth of, 114, 115
Wyoming, benefits of incorporating in, 107–108

Y

Yourself, hiding, 205–210

Z

Zadari, Asif Ali, 29

Take Control of Your Financial Future

A wonderful starting place for anyone ready to take the most essential
step in profit planning, *The Complete
Guide to Offshore Money Havens,
Revised and Updated 3rd Edition*,
spells out the latest, most comprehensive strategies for investing
offshore to escape nuisance lawsuits,
exorbitant taxes, and increasing
invasions of privacy. In this book,
you'll discover:

- **Why it may be hazardous
  to your wealth to rely on
  the government to protect
  your money and assets**
- **How the offshore process
  works and who's already
  offshore**
- **Where to go, where not
  to go**
- **How to plan for
  maximum profit**
- **Eight steps to
  offshore success**
- **And much more!**

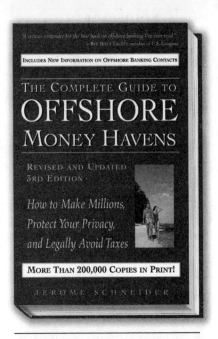

ISBN 0-7615-2010-4 / Hardcover
464 pages / U.S. $30.00 / Can. $43.50

Get $5 Off Using This Order Form on Jerome Schneider's Recommended Reading List

Product Order Form

QTY	PRODUCT	DESCRIPTION	PRODUCT #	S&H* (U.S. ONLY)	PRICE/EACH	NET PRICE
_____	*Offshore Asset Protection Special Report*	A complete how-to book on asset protection trusts.	WPC-002	$6.95	$49.95	$ _____
_____	*Global Investing for Maximum Profit and Safety*	Jerome Schneider's strategies for global investing.	WPC-005	$6.95	$40.00	$ _____
_____	*Complete Guide to Offshore Money Havens, Revised and Updated 3rd Edition*	Jerome Schneider's bestseller revised and updated.	WPC-006	$6.95	$29.95	$ _____
_____	*Hiding Your Money*	How to keep your money and valuables safe.	WPC-008	$6.95	$30.00	$ _____
_____	*How to Start Your Own Offshore Investment Fund*	How to raise capital and start your own fund.	WPC-011	$6.95	$29.95	$ _____
_____	*Finding Your Own Offshore Wealth Haven Set*	Audio and video program.	WPC-014	$12.50	$99.95	$ _____
_____	*How to Own Your Own Private International Bank*	The complete source for starting your own bank.	WPC-020	$6.95	$40.00	$ _____
_____	*How to Own Your Own Private International Bank*	Book and special video hosted by Jerome Schneider.	WPC-021	$6.95	$89.95	$ _____
_____	*Offshore Wealth Summit Catalogue*	Details of Jerome Schneider's semi-annual seminar workshops held around the world.	WPC-022	$0.00	$5.00	$ _____
				Subtotal Before Shipping		$ _____
				Add Shipping & Handling/Rush/Courier***		$ _____
				Less $5.00 Discount		$ _____
				TOTAL ORDER		$ _____

NOTES:
*International standard shipping $12.50
**Shipping prices quoted are for 1 item (Please add $2.00 for each additional item)
***UPS/FedEx extra (Call 800-877-3777 for rates)

Method of Payment
I have enclosed a check for $ _____ made payable to Wilshire Publishing Company Inc.

OR

Mail Payment to: Wilshire Publishing Company, 1219 Morningside Drive, Manhattan Beach, CA 90266

Please charge my (circle one) Visa   MasterCard   Amex   Discover

Credit Card # _____   Expiration Date: _____ / _____

Name of Cardholder: _____

Signature of Cardholder: _____

FOR RUSH ORDERS CALL 800-877-3777 OR FAX 310-640-3121 or visit www.offshorewealth.com

Please Ship to:
Name: _____
Company: _____
Address: _____
City/State/ZIP: _____
Phone: _____
Fax: _____